PRAISE FOR
A DEATH IN CHINA

'Montalbano and Hiaasen have created a Middle Kingdom maelstrom of intrigues, deceits, lusts, and canards. Like China itself, what often seems to be too implausible turns out to be all too real'

Wall Street Journal

'I've been waiting for somebody to use the extraordinary recent history and present character of Peking to place a terrific story . . . Montalbano and Hiaasen have brought it off splendidly'

Time Magazine

'A solid, lively thriller . . . Action that's scenic and varied, and loads of wry, unromanticized China atmosphere'

Kirkus Reviews

'A fascinating look at today's China'

Publishers Weekly

'An insider's glimpse of modern China as well as a suspenseful tale of one narrow escape after another. Tautly written, with a fine flair for character and setting, this rings with authority'

Library Journal

'A novel that offers a rare and authentic look at the Chinese way of life . . . A real page-turner . . . Excellent background and first-rate suspense'

Booklist

Carl Hiaasen is a native of Florida with an outstanding reputation as an investigative journalist exposing local scandals. He now writes a thrice-weekly column for the *Miami Herald* and has been nominated twice for the Pulitzer Prize. Bill Montalbano is one of America's senior foreign correspondents. His reporting from more than seventy countries on five continents has won a dozen national awards. Currently Rome Bureau Chief for the *Los Angeles Times*, Montalbano is at work on his fifth novel.

A DEATH IN CHINA

CARL HIAASEN

AND

BILL MONTALBANO

PAN BOOKS

First published 1984 by Atheneum Publishers, New York

First published in Great Britain 1995 by Pan Books
an imprint of Pan Macmillan Ltd
Pan Macmillan, 20 New Wharf Road, London N1 9RR
Basingstoke and Oxford
Associated companies throughout the world
www.panmacmillan.com

ISBN 0 330 32936 7

5 7 9 8 6 4

A CIP catalogue record for this book is available from
the British Library.

Printed and bound in Great Britain by
Mackays of Chatham PLC, Chatham, Kent

*For Daniel Joseph Montalbano
and Carl Andreas Hiaasen*

In 221 B.C., China came to be ruled by the formidable Emperor Qin Shi Huangdi, whose dynasty was China's shortest, but arguably its most important. It was Qin who unified the feudal country. He built a road system, organized a central government, standardized Chinese language and coinage, and it was he who ordered construction of the Great Wall. Qin's hope for China's future was tied to a belief in his own immortality; to achieve that end, he was both ingenious and brutal, and when he finally died, he was interred in a giant tumulus near his capital of Changan, now the modern city of Xian. In the last decade, no archaeological dig has aroused more world interest than that involving the tomb of Qin Shi Huangdi, the Son of Heaven. . . .

From a lecture by Dr. David Wang
St. Edward's College, Ohio

A DEATH IN CHINA

PROLOGUE

Changan, China, 213 B.C.

"WHERE IS CONFUCIUS?" the emperor demanded.

Princes, nobles, councillors, generals, diplomats, servants and eunuch-ministers mimicked the emperor's angry mien. Square-jawed, flint-eyed, they stared at the cluster of old men whose robes and formal bearing marked them as scholars. Silence wrapped the throne room. It was not a question to be answered. Everybody knew Confucius had been dead nearly three hundred years.

"Is Confucius in heaven? Where is heaven? What do your books tell you? Is he a bush, or a river, or a bird that flies through the forest? Does he live still? Tell me, scholars."

The eldest scholar, gnarled as the cane he clutched with both hands, responded in a voice that held no fear.

"Where the master is we cannot say. But his spirit is among us men."

"You know nothing!" the emperor snapped. "Am I then just a man, like any other?"

"You are foremost among men, and more," answered a councillor named Li Su in prayerlike incantation. "You are Qin Shi Huangdi, August Sovereign, the Son of Heaven. You are the Emperor of the Middle Kingdom."

"Have I lived as other men?"

The ritual required a general to answer: Men Qian, the emperor's best.

"Your feats have surpassed all others."

The emperor allowed himself a smile and cocked an eye; a parody of surprise.

"You have unified the Middle Kingdom," the general continued. "You have given us a great wall, stretching many months' journey, from the great ocean to the desert to protect

1

us from the barbarians. So wide six horsemen may ride abreast. So tall and so strong that it will never be breached."

"So I am not just any man, am I? I am the Son of Heaven, ruler of the mightiest empire. Tell me, scholars, in your wisdom: Is that not right?"

The old man ran a clawed hand through his wispy beard.

" 'Let the prince be prince, minister be minister, father father and son son.' So it is written," he said.

The royal fingers kneaded an elaborate bronze chalice, and a serving boy, unnoticed, carefully poured more wine.

"They are all men. Men die. But I am different; the Son of Heaven. I shall not die. My body may stop, but I shall not die. I shall be *immortal*."

There were none to vouchsafe the emperor a response. The eldest scholar folded his hands around the cane and stared out over the exquisite royal city, where five palaces and fifty temples drowsed in the summer sun.

"I have heard the criticism of the scholars," the emperor said. "They ridicule my dealings with sorcerers and alchemists. They deny immortality because it is not written in their books.

"Scholars! It is not enough for an empire to be strong and orderly. No, they insist as well that the emperor must also be a sage, must also follow the teachings of Confucius, *who is not here*."

The eldest scholar replied softly, as though rebuking a child. " 'To govern is to set things right. If you begin by setting yourself right, who will dare to deviate from the right?' That is what Confucius said."

"I am the Son of Heaven and I have set things right in this world as I will in the next. You have seen my preparations. They have taken more than thirty years." The emperor cocked his head. "Did you not believe what you saw?"

"I believe in the majesty of the work I saw," the old man said evasively.

"Majesty? Yes, my old friend." The emperor nodded. "Majesty indeed. A mountain whose insides have been carved into the shape of the cosmos by hundreds of thousands of workers who have labored a lifetime. I have made a generation of peasants dig through subterranean streams and seal them off with bronze to create a burial chamber where I shall rule for eternity. Palaces, pavilions—with fine vessels, jewels, stones and rarities. With quicksilver I have created the waterways of the empire, the Yangtze and Yellow rivers, and even the great ocean itself, and made them flow mechanically. Perfect models. And above I have depicted the heavenly constellations, and below, the geography of the earth. All this you have seen?"

"Yes," the old scholar answered.

"And the vaults?"

"Yes."

"Majestic, would you say? Large vaults surrounding the mountain, filled with clay soldiers, thousands of them; infantry, archers, charioteers and generals. Each carrying a real weapon." The emperor's eyes flashed.

"Your celestial army," the scholar said.

"It will protect my perpetual reign." The emperor emptied his cup. "And having seen my tomb and my army, scholars, can you still deny my immortality?"

There was a long pause then. Every eye was riveted on the small group of scholars before the throne. After the pause, the eldest replied.

"Ideas, like Confucius, are immortal. Men die."

"Fools!" the emperor screamed.

The next day, four hundred and sixty wise men, gathered from all corners of the empire to assay the emperor's immortality, were made to watch as soldiers burned their books.

Then they were led to a deep pit not far from the emperor's celestial kingdom. From atop the steep sides of the pit jeering peasants shoveled clods of thick red earth. Most of the scholars kept their dignity. A few cursed and one or two of the younger ones cried. Before noon, they were all buried and dead. But then, three years later, so was the emperor, laid to rest under the perpetual vigilance of his fierce clay soldiers.

CHAPTER 1

Peking, August 1983

THE HIGH-CEILINGED LOBBY seemed carved in time, socialist testimony to yesterday's barren promises. A wine-red carpet crawled like a stain toward the horizon. Improvident columns that were neither attractive nor altogether round highlighted bile green walls. The furniture was of blond wood and indeterminate proportion. Waist-high counters cluttered every inch of wall space, each chockablock with white-coated workers. Some were accountants, some receptionists, some managers. Most were watchers.

Tom Stratton threaded through a knot of noisy Americans. He skirted a gaggle of Japanese clustered around a guide waving a flag. He neatly sidestepped a functionary listlessly pursuing a fifty-pound vacuum cleaner. Reaching the stand where an empty-eyed girl protected trays of almost fresh fruit, Stratton bought two apples. She weighed them on a digital scale and made change of his one yuan note with an abacus.

"*Ba lou*," Stratton told the elevator operator in phrase-book Mandarin. He was eventually deposited on the eighth floor.

The room was a monstrous little brother to the lobby, but already, after a week, it seemed like home. Stratton kicked off his shoes and padded into the bathroom. The hot water tap snuffled and growled, barked and hissed. On past experience, the chances that the water would be hot when it finally appeared were exactly one in two.

Stratton ate the apples and fingered leaves of tea into a thin-walled mug. Tenderly, he added water from a thermos on the night table, then threw back the red velvet drapes to let in the last rays of sunshine and sprawled on the bed. It was one hell of a place, Peking. Stratton had not decided whether to love or hate it. The city sprawled in all directions, a flat, dusty, one-

5

story town punctuated by brick chimneys thrusting toward the
smog like phallic exclamation marks. Graceless monuments of
revolutionary architecture dwelt alongside exquisite, gold-
roofed survivors of the city's imperial past. Stratton scissored
off the bed to watch the evening rush hour flow past a hundred
feet below. He had just calculated the bicycle flow at nearly
five hundred per minute when the room door flew open.

"Comrade! The chairman wants to see you right away."

"Hello, Alice." Stratton stifled a grin behind the tea mug.
She had become a China groupie, a parody in blue cotton. The
pants Chinese women wear with shapeless abandon strained
across Alice's ample rump. The jacket was buttoned to the
neck and fashionably wrinkled. The flat-brimmed hat bulged in
a frustrated attempt to contain a mass of bottle-blond hair.
Clinging precariously to the cap was a sheet metal button, red
on white. AAAH, it said.

"You could pass for a native," Stratton mocked. Alice
Dempsey was not his favorite woman.

"Bought it all at the Friendship Store. Why didn't you come
with us?"

"I felt queasy."

"Baloney!" she snorted. "Every chance you get you slip
away from us. What have you got against art historians
anyway? I'll bet you don't even wear your badge, do you?"
She rolled her eyes up toward her own AAAH. American
Association of Art Historians.

"It's a fine group, very nice folks," Stratton said with forced
politeness. Alice Dempsey was ugly as sin and as annoying as
a rash, but she did have wit and will enough to be a prized
member of an excellent faculty in California.

"Fact is, I'd rather walk around than ride on a bus."

"Well, it's rude to our Chinese friends. The guide, little
Miss Sun, is always asking about you: 'Where is Professor
Stratton?' At least don't forget about the acrobatic show
tonight."

"Sure, Alice."

Stratton's heart had not been with the tour since he had
bumped into David Wang outside the Summer Palace, just as if
they had been on Adams Street in Pittsville, Ohio, or at one of
those *ad hoc* seminars Wang had loved to lead at St. Edward's,
stockinged feet curled to the fire in the old library.

It was Stratton's first time in Asia in more than a decade, and he had still not worked out to his own satisfaction why he had come. Asia was a dead letter. Had he come because a two-week package tour of the People's Republic was cheap and exotic? Or because it would spare him dull hours of summer research at the small New England college where he taught? Not that, either. The research would have to be done, sooner or later, one way or the other; long nights followed by a slim volume only initiates would read. The job was waiting when he got back. Say he had come to escape the shards of a divorce that still hurt, a year later. Was that the real reason? Part of it, maybe, but only a lesser part, if Stratton was in the mood to be honest with himself. Carol was gone and he did not really miss her, although sometimes he ached to be with the boy.

Boredom. That was closer to the truth, wasn't it? His friends would know it intuitively. Stratton had worked hard to become a scholar. He was a legitimate historian, an able professor of emerging reputation. And . . . so what? Passing years that dulled the senses, blank-faced students in vacuous procession. What next, Stratton? Mid-life crisis. Male menopause. Maybe there was no next.

So he had come to China. To throttle the boredom. No, there was something deeper. He was also testing the scar tissue, the way an athlete will gingerly measure the recovery of an injured limb. Something else, too. Thomas Stratton, as he alone knew, had come to weigh the man he had become against the one he had once been.

At Peking Airport, standing before the immigration officer in white jacket and red-starred cap, visions of yesterday had come flooding in with a gush he had battled to control. The man had fingered his passport without interest.

"Is this your first time in China?" the inspector had asked in slow, careful English.

"Yes," Stratton had lied. "Yes, it is."

"You are perspiring. Are you ill?"

"No. It is hot."

The man had stamped his passport and Stratton had sought the refuge of protective coloration in the gaggle of art historians.

Stratton shook his head at the memory and sipped his tea.

That night he skipped the acrobatic performance. Too bad about little Miss Sun. Once Stratton was sure his tour mates had left in the green-and-white Toyota minibus in which all tourists in China seemed to live, he went looking for dinner. On the way, he conducted prolonged negotiations with the white-jacketed floor attendants. If there was a telephone call for Professor Stratton, could they transfer it to the restaurant? It might work. Even if it didn't, it was not crucial. If punctilious David Wang called once unsuccessfully, he would either leave his number or call again.

The restaurant—foreigners only—was a purely functional place of round tables, soiled tablecloths, spotted silverware and spicy food in the inevitable blue-and white crockery. The tour group ate three meals a day there, Western for breakfast and Chinese for the other two—a procession of savory dishes that appeared unordered.

Stratton settled into a small table and began leafing through a purple-covered issue of the *Peking Review*. About two paragraphs into the cover story, a gob of wet white rice caromed off the red plastic sign that proclaimed his table 37. From two tables away, Stratton's assailant grinned evilly, gap-toothed and green-eyed. He was about seven years old and his chopstick catapult was poised for another round. A second child carefully probed the innards of the sugar bowl with a spoon. There were two, no three, others in tenuous custody of a pretty woman in her thirties and a great bear of a man with a bushy red beard. Stratton intercepted the next gob with his menu.

"Kevin!" the woman jerked the missile commander around to face his dinner.

"I'm sorry," she told Stratton. It was something she had said before.

The bearded man looked up from a dam of napkins that encircled a lake of spilled soy sauce.

"Somehow it was easier at McDonald's. Sorry," he said.

"No problem. Actually, he's a pretty good shot."

From the waitress, Stratton ordered Sichuan chicken with peanuts, noodles, vegetables and a beer.

"Qingdao beer."

"Qingdao *mei you*." She pronounced it "may-o."

"What kind do you have?"

"Peking."

"Okay."

"Hey, baby, that's a bad mistake," the bearded man called from his chaos. "Peking beer tastes like it was passed through a horse. Tell her you want Wu Xing." He wiggled a green bottle in front of him.

"Wu Xing," Stratton told the waitress.

Stratton abandoned the last hope of a quiet meal when something began gnawing his leg. He carried it, squirming and squealing, back to its tribe.

"An escapee, I think," Stratton said, handing it to the woman.

"Oh, Tracey! Again, I'm sorry."

"That's okay. I'm used to kids. My sister has four."

"Spend a lot of time with them?" the bearded man asked.

"Never go near the little bastards."

"Can't imagine why. Why don't you join us, since we've ruined your dinner anyway? I'm Jim McCarthy. This is my wife, Sheila. I've never seen the kids before."

McCarthy, it turned out, was one of about twenty American reporters resident in Peking, a correspondent for a big East Coast newspaper. He had an office in a hotel and an apartment in a compound on the eastern side of the city where foreigners lived in Western-style buildings behind high brick walls erected and patrolled by the Chinese government to keep Chinese out.

"You here for long?" McCarthy asked.

"Another couple of days."

McCarthy rolled his eyes.

"Jim is not a great China fan," his wife explained.

"Yeah, one day I'll write a book. 'Hold the May-o' it'll be called. It's the national sport. If you want something, they haven't got it—beer to interviews. *Mei you.*"

After dinner, Stratton marveled at the texture of the city as he walked along a broad tree-lined avenue that ran past the Temple of Heaven. The dark summer streets bustled with life. Where puny street lamps cast wan patches of light, people gathered in loose, friendly groups to escape the heat. Almost all were men, in old-fashioned underskirts. They squatted to gossip or play cards. The few cars rode with parking lights only, wary of the swirling stream of hard-to-see bicyclists, who used no lights at all. A young couple conducted public courtship on the stone steps of a government office building. From one alleyway, Stratton heard the muffled click of mah jongg tiles, and from a window, the beat of Western rock music from a cheap tape deck. Like headlights, mah jongg and rock music were forbidden in Peking that summer; the headlights so that bicyclists would not be blinded, the ancient game and the music because they were decadent. It pleased Stratton to realize that people still pursued their own muses on summer nights, and to hell with the Party and its rules.

The aim of Stratton's walk was a downtown park built on an artificial hill. The park itself was nothing special, but the circumstances of its construction were testimony to the siege mentality of Chinese communism. Perhaps forty feet high and a quarter mile around, the hill had been built entirely by hand, one bucket at a time, by volunteer workers who had scooped it from underneath the foundations of the city. In every shop, every factory, every school, Stratton had read, a well-oiled door led down to a network of tunnels. It was the most elaborate bomb shelter in the world, and it had taken more than thirty years to finish.

Bombshelter Park, as Stratton had silently dubbed it, was closed. As he strolled back toward the hotel, he thought of David Wang.

He owed much to the old professor. Wang had sensed the disillusion, no, the despair, that Stratton had brought with him to the tiny college in rural Ohio. Stratton had been running from Asia when he arrived at St. Edward's for graduate studies. Despite Wang's considerable reputation, Stratton had avoided his courses. Still, he had found himself attracted to the gentle and patient teacher. They had become friends, then confidants, and on the bright morning when a changed Stratton had strode forward to receive his Ph.D., no one could have missed the fatherly gleam in David Wang's eyes.

They had drifted apart, more by circumstance than design. With Stratton teaching in New England, rural Ohio had seemed increasingly remote. It had been two years since they had seen one another. Until Peking. Stratton, avoiding his brethren art historians for the first time and feeling particularly exultant at being alone, had stood, back arched, head up, to study the magnificent lakeside arcade of the Summer Palace.

The voice had come from behind him.

"They say she was a fool—profligate—the empress dowager, squandering national riches on a marble boat when she should have spent the money to build a modern navy."

Stratton would have known the voice anywhere, and the professorial restatement of conventional wisdom that was meant to be challenged. He had replied without turning around.

"Perhaps she knew more than most people give her credit for."

"How so?" asked the voice.

"'She may have understood that, even with modernization, the Imperial Navy would have been no match for the barbarian fleets. She foresaw the end of dynastic China and, instead of sending more young men needlessly to their deaths, decided to create that which would give her pleasure in the realization that the end was coming for her kind." It was, Stratton thought, an inspired improvisation.

"Mmmm, an interesting theory," the voice had conceded, "but in the end, I would think history correct in judging her a foolish spendthrift."

"Me, too," said Stratton, turning around to embrace David Wang.

Together, they had strolled the lake, finding amid the crush of Chinese visitors a seat aboard the ludicrous and beautiful boat the Empress Ci Xi had ordered built a century before.

Wang seemed immune to time, Stratton thought. He had looked fit and every bit the elegant, prosperous tourist in tattersall shirt, gabardine trousers, polished loafers and Japanese camera. As always, Wang looked a trifle owlish behind his thick glasses with gold frames.

"I keep hoping that if I put off everything long enough, the publisher will forget about the book contract," Stratton had joked to explain his presence. "But how about you, David? Aren't you the man who once told me never to look back, who persuaded me at a tough time in my life to lay the past aside and get on with life?"

"I would be distressed if I thought you were really as dogmatic as you sound, Thomas," Wang had chided. "But of course you are teasing, and, yes, I was the one who always said that the United States was my country, China just the place I happened to be born. But then I changed my mind. It is an old man's right, you know, to change his mind."

"Why?"

"Two things, really. For one, I am retired, you know—"

"No, I didn't. If I had known, I would have come to wish you well."

"Well, it was just a quiet leavetaking, no ceremony. Of

course, I expect to stay in Pittsville and keep my hand in now and then." David Wang had smiled. Only death would ever take him from the college and the town where he had been an institution for nearly forty years.

"The second reason is that I have a brother. I had not thought much about him all these years and then suddenly there was a letter inviting me to China. In the end, I came. A good idea, I guess."

Stratton had caught the uncertainty in the old man's voice.

"Is something wrong? Anything I can help you with?"

"I'm just a bit bewildered is all. Call it culture shock. You know, when I got off the plane, I was nearly too nervous to speak Chinese."

"I know the feeling."

Wang had touched Stratton's arm then, and they had both remembered the night by the fire in Wang's farmhouse when an angry and confused young man had spilled the bitter dregs of senseless war.

"My problems are nothing compared to the dilemmas you once had, believe me," said Wang. "But it would be nice to talk about them. I'll tell you what: I'm going to Xian to see my brother tomorrow. He's a deputy minister, you know. I'll be back around dark on Wednesday. I'll call you then. If you can break away from your tour, I'll show you the real Peking and we can talk as we walk."

"I wouldn't miss it."

Wednesday night Stratton returned from his walk to Bombshelter Park about nine thirty. David Wang never called.

CHAPTER 2

ALICE SCOLDED. Little Miss Sun, the China Travel International Service guide, implored timidly. Walter Thomas—or was it Thomas Walters?—a foppish Egyptologist from the Midwest, spoke vaguely of "fraternal kinship," whatever that meant. Stratton endured. When the atmosphere turned bitchy, he shrugged and walked away. The White Pagoda and a refurbished lamasery were not on his agenda that day. Stratton watched without expression while his colleagues, suitably armed with cameras in black leather cases and sensible shoes, obediently flocked onto their minibus under Miss Sun's set-piece smile. Then he went up to his room and squeezed forty-five minutes of exercise from the cramped patch between the cracking wall and iron bedstead. When, near ten o'clock, David Wang still had not called, he prowled the gloomy hotel corridors until he found the room that Jim McCarthy used as an office.

Dust blanketed stacks of books and haphazard piles of newspapers that overburdened a loose-jawed table. It carpeted the dials of an expensive radio atop a gray filing cabinet. It lay like virgin snow on the bright yellow shade of a lamp meant more for Sweden than China.

McCarthy lolled in a swivel chair, desert boots comfortably atop the burnished top of a huge partners' desk that Stratton identified instantly as a valuable antique.

Mechanically, McCarthy was ripping strips from a newspaper, laying them in a corner of the desk and tossing the discards in the general direction of the big straw basket.

"Hey, baby," McCarthy lured Stratton from the doorway. "Make yourself a cup of coffee. Or there's some Qingdao, if it's not too early for you." The massive head gestured toward a box-sized refrigerator on the floor.

"Thanks." Stratton spooned Brazilian instant into a hotel

13

cup identical to the one in his room, then added hot water from an identical pitcher.

"You teach art history. And karate, right?" McCarthy called.

"Why karate?" Stratton laughed.

"Sheila was admiring your whipcord body. I had a whipcord body, too—until I came to China." McCarthy patted his belly. "Is it fun, teaching?"

"I like it, I really do. It's not as exciting as being a foreign correspondent, but you do get hooked into the research. You find one piece here and another there and pretty soon you don't know where the hours went. Then, too, the vacations are nice and long. Most summers I go out west and help a friend of mine run a wilderness company for tourists—whitewater rafting, survival hikes, sissy climbing, that kind of thing. I should be out there now, instead of screwin' around here. But I really wanted to see China. Five cities, twenty-one days."

"Yeah, everybody ought to see it. Once. I wish I had— shh . . ."

McCarthy waved for silence and Stratton heard a familiar litany lancing through static.

". . . off the wall into the corner . . . Remy is in and Evans is around third . . . throw is to second but Rice is safe with a stand-up double . . . That'll be all for . . ."

"A baseball game?"

McCarthy laughed.

"Last night's game. We're thirteen hours ahead of the East Coast, remember. There's a game on almost every morning— Armed Forces radio."

"Pretty nice, if you're a fan."

"Naw, not me. Only been to one game in my life. My father took me to Briggs Stadium when I was a kid. About the third inning there was this foul ball and I reached up to catch it, you know, like on television. Broke two fingers. Never went back."

"If you're not a fan, why do you listen?" Stratton teased.

McCarthy heaved himself upright and planted both feet on the floor. Stratton, from the other side of the desk, imagined without seeing the spurts of dust.

"It's China, baby. In China, I'm a baseball fan because it helps kill the morning. In China, I read five or six newspapers a day and cut out things I might use six months from now, but probably never will. Savin' bits of string, but never finding the spool. For correspondents, China is purgatory, baby. The thing about this place that drives you crazy is that there are no facts; a billion people and not one goddamned fact. Did you know that everything here is a secret until it is published, even the fucking weather forecast?"

"Then what do you do for news?"

"I worry a lot." McCarthy grinned. "Particularly on Thursdays; that's when stories for the weekend paper are due. Today they want a political piece, ugh. I don't understand what's goin' on—that's normal—but I have reached the solemn conclusion that neither do the Chinese."

"Like how?"

"Like something big is bubbling beneath the surface. There are lots of little signs: people being suddenly reassigned or demoted, or simply disappearing—they could be forcibly retired, or dead—nobody knows. No one will talk about it."

"A power struggle," Stratton offered.

"Don't you know it. This place has been a circus since Mao died; probably before, too. When Deng came in with his pragmatists, the old hard-line Maoists got pushed aside. Now I'd say that the hard-liners were getting their own back."

"Most of the people who are being knocked down are the ones that Deng made respectable again?"

"That, for sure. But more than that." McCarthy lit a cigarette. "There's a hard-ass campaign under way right now against Chinese having anything to do with foreigners. You know the old song: 'We welcome your technology, but no blue jeans, please.' The idea that the decadent West will contaminate the heroic masses has been around for a long time, but now it's worse—ten times worse—than I've ever seen it."

Stratton was surprised.

"People have certainly been very nice to us. I've seen no hostility at all," he said.

McCarthy nodded.

"Right. The average guy is more interested in Western ideas and culture than ever. He hears the Party's antiforeign line and says to hell with it. But the guys who are getting axed are those whose jobs require the most contact with foreigners. They're falling like tenpins." McCarthy threw up his hands in mock despair. "Who's doing it? Does it means some sort of new madness like the Cultural Revolution is brewing? That's what my editors ask. And all I can do is to quote Confucius' greatest line.''

"What's that?"

"'It beats the shit out of me, baby.'"

Stratton laughed.

"I'll get out of your hair, but let me ask a quick question. I was supposed to meet a friend of mine today, a Chinese-American professor who's here on a personal visit. He never showed up. How do I go about tracking him down?"

"You sure he's here in Peking?"

"Almost. He was supposed to come back yesterday from Xian."

"Plane probably didn't fly. The national airline only flies when the weather is good. No joke."

"That's probably it. Still, I'd like to try. He's a very old friend of mine and I'd hate to miss connections."

"I could have the interpreter call the hotels, but it would be a waste of time. The one constructive suggestion I can make is that you ask about your friend at the American Embassy. If he's an academic type, they should have some record of him, an itinerary."

"Who could I ask?"

"The culture vultures would be most likely to know, but they are turds to a man. Try the consul, Steve Powell. He won't know, but he's the kind of guy who could find out."

"At the consulate?"

"Never on Thursday mornings. Steve plays tennis every Thursday. Over at the International Club, the courts they call the Rockpit. Do you know where it is?"

"I've passed it."

"I have to go out, but you're welcome to use the corporate bicycle."

"Corporate bicycle?"

"No correspondent is complete without one," said McCarthy, fishing a small key off a large ring. "Downstairs at the bike rack, license number oh-oh-two-seven-two. It's black, like all the rest of them. Do you know how to get there?"

"I have a map, thanks. Do you ride much?"

"Only in the line of duty."

Seen from a hotel window or a tourist bus, the infinite procession of bicycles is one of China's most impressive sights. On every major street, broad lanes are reserved for bicycles. Even in downtown Peking they outnumber the trucks and cars by a thousand to one. Alice and her friends rhapsodized about the bicycles. They could talk for hours, insulated in the air-conditioned bus, of the silent, measured stream, as massive and as unstoppable as the Yangtze. They found in the bicycles a symbol of the progressive New China. At faculty teas it would, no doubt, sound quite profound.

Stratton learned some different things before he had wobbled two blocks. For one thing, the Chinese bicycle, copy of old English Raleigh though it may be, is more tank than scooter. It weighs a ton, steers hard and pedals harder. McCarthy's corporate bike had no gears, and by the time Stratton passed the old imperial observatory he was sweating. What astonished him most, though, was the chaos into which he had plunged. Bicycles, he decided, as a pert young thing nonchalantly cut him off and he swerved to avoid a three-horse cart, were the ultimate bastion of Chinese individualism. To outsiders, the cyclists might look like an army of blue ants. To somebody who pedaled among them, the Chinese all had fangs. They veered without warning. They knifed through lanes of cross traffic with terrifying, expressionless élan. Chinese flirted as they rode. They hawked and spat. They sang and cursed.

The left turns were worst of all. The first time Stratton tried to make one he found he could not maneuver into the left segment of the bike lane in time. The second time he saw no way of getting across the oncoming flux of trucks and bikes. The third time he tensely negotiated the turn in the protective shadow of an old man who looked only straight ahead and miraculously emerged unscathed.

Twenty-five minutes later, Stratton pedaled past the iron gates of the International Club. He locked McCarthy's bike near a willow tree and walked to the tennis courts. Two players volleyed steadily on a pocked asphalt surface that looked as if it had not been repaved since Peking's last earthquake.

Stratton leaned on a chain-link fence and waited for a break in the game. It came on a gorgeous drop shot that brought one of the players, a stocky blond, lunging fruitlessly to the net. His opponent, a sandy-haired man in his early thirties, shouted in a southern accent: "Good try!"

"Mr. Powell?" Stratton called.

The sandy-haired player ambled to the fence. Stratton

introduced himself. He told the American consul about David Wang.

"Mr. Stratton, I usually don't hear about American citizens in China unless they get in some sort of trouble. Professor Wang is a man of some distinction, however, and I'll bet the culture folks have his itinerary."

"Yes, well, Jim McCarthy said—er—suggested . . ."

Powell smiled. "He said, 'Those culture vultures are cross-eyed, close-minded sonofabitches,'" he drawled in fair imitation. "Well, I suppose he's right. Tell you what, soon as I polish off Ingemar here, I'll make a couple calls."

Powell was an excellent tennis player and he ended the game with a fierce flurry. With a towel around his neck and his racket under one arm, he led Stratton into the main building of the club.

Stratton waited in the lobby while Powell used the phone in an adjoining booth.

"They're checking on your friend," he reported when he came out. "Have you read *Too Late, the King*?"

"Yes, of course." Stratton was impressed. It was not David Wang's best-known book, but it was his best work.

"I admired it very much," Powell said. "Clear, sharp, almost lyrical. We've got a copy in the library here."

"He's a special man. Very talented," Stratton said.

"Tell me more." Powell spread out the towel and sat down on an old leather chair.

"God, by the time I met David in the early seventies he'd already been around forever. He was born here in China, of course, but came to the U.S. to study just before World War II broke out. He never went back. By the time I entered graduate school he was famous in academia for his scholarship. I was"—Stratton hesitated—"just getting interested in Asian art. So it was natural to gravitate to Dr. Wang."

"He was originally from Shanghai, right?"

Stratton nodded. "An entrepreneurial family of the old sort. It had been making money, from salt or silk, opium or tea, from time immemorial. Toward the end of the nineteenth century both of David's grandparents, who were business rivals, I guess, got modern. David's father went to Columbia. His mother, who had studied at the Philadelphia Conservatory, was about fifteen years younger. When David's time came to go

off to school in the States, he was still a teenager. In the normal
course of events, he would have gone home and, as the eldest
son, taken over the business.''

"They were hardly normal times, were they?"

"No. Civil war between the Communists and the National-
ists. Invasion by Japan. Then the knockdown years until the
Communists finally won in forty-nine. I would guess that
David's father told him not to come back until it was all over.
And then, of course, the wrong people had won—if you were a
Shanghai millionaire. David bounced around, quietly ac-
cumulating degrees; money was never a problem, I gather, and
at the end of it all, there was nothing to come back to—the
Wang empire was just one more victim of revolution. Whether
he was cut off from his family or broke with them I don't know,
but he never mentioned them. He settled in at St. Edward's and
never left. I suppose he—"

"Excuse me. That'll be my boys." Powell caught the phone
on the second ring. Stratton stared out the window at weeping
willows in the overgrown courtyard.

When the consul returned, Stratton sensed there was no
news.

"We've got Dr. Wang listed at the Heping Hotel. The culture
officers had invited him to call or come by when he got back
from Xian, but so far no one's heard from him. Maybe he just
decided to spend an extra day or two at the digs."

"Maybe so," Stratton said, unconvinced.

"Our fellas are a little disappointed, too. They're looking
forward to meeting your Dr. Wang. You know about his
brother?"

"David told me he was a vice minister or something."

"A *deputy* minister, Mr. Stratton. Deputy minister of art and
culture. A big gun. His name is Wang Bin. He's in charge of
new archaeological digs and the big museum here."

Stratton said, "Maybe I'll just drop by David's hotel to see if
there's a message for me. What was the name again?"

"Heping," Powell said. "It means 'peace.' It's a nice place,
off the usual Peking trails. I can draw you a map . . ."

"No, thanks. David would be pleased if an old student
proved intrepid enough to track him down. In the meantime, if
you hear anything, could you call me? I'm at the Minzu."

"Sure," Powell said. "Good tracking."

Stratton nearly missed the hotel. It was tucked away in a lane barely wide enough for one car. Stratton left the bicycle in a parking lot near Wangfujing, Peking's main shopping street. An old woman with a can affixed a wooden marker with a number on the handlebars, handed him a paper receipt, and took a fee from among the aluminum coins Stratton displayed in an open palm.

It was a smaller hotel than the one he was in, and more graceful. Stratton did a full circle in the lobby looking for the front desk. There was the usual assortment of work spaces, but none of them identifiable. Finally, he chose one at random.

"Excuse me, could you tell me the room number for a guest named David Wang. He's American."

Three desks later a hunchback with a gray Mao jacket and some English took Stratton's request into an inner office. Through the open door Stratton could see him staring far-sightedly at what was obviously a handwritten guest register. Just as Stratton was succumbing to the sinking feeling that Wang had registered in his Chinese name—which he didn't know—the hunchback emerged. He had obviously found something.

"You wait," the man ordered.

Stratton watched curiously while the man trundled into a second office. There he spoke animatedly with another man whose face Stratton could not see.

It seemed to Stratton they were arguing.

Finally, the second man appeared alone. He had a hook nose and an obvious habit of command.

"The Wang man is not here," the Chinese said in labored English.

"Couldn't you check again? I'm a friend of his."

"Not here." The man turned away, walked back into his office and closed the door.

Perplexed, Stratton cycled slowly back to his own hotel. He had been lied to. Of that he was certain. Hook Nose had known something about "the Wang man" that he had chosen not to tell. Why would a hotel in Peking deny the presence of a guest?

Stratton was still thinking about it when he got back to his room.

The phone was ringing as he walked in.

"David?"

It was not David.

"Mr. Stratton, this is Steve Powell, at the consulate."

"Oh, hello. I went to the hotel and they claimed never to have heard of any David Wang—"

Powell interrupted brusquely.

"Mr. Stratton, I am sorry to have to tell you this. David Wang is dead."

CHAPTER 3

TOM STRATTON COULD SMELL the smoke. He could taste the cordite. He could see the gray shape, feel its struggle, hear its scream. He could sense the impatient clatter of the helicopter, hovering, waiting, anxious to be gone. Fire. Run. Run to the chopper, its rope ladder slowly dangling, the only lifeline he would ever get. Drop. Fire. Run from a black night and a devil-scorched patch of earth, all memory and no meaning.

Run, captain. Rope swaying. Lungs burning. Side burning as the black medic cut away the cloth and applied a salve. Eyes burning, exhaustion and shame, in the cramped cabin of a blacked-out aircraft carrier.

"You're sure there were no prisoners?" A man, a colonel, trying to be professional, sounding only disheartened.

"No POWs." A dirt-poor commune with a PLA company stationed on its fringes.

"Intelligence was so damn sure about the prisoners. They said there were American prisoners."

"Not anymore."

"How did they get on to you?"

"We made a mistake."

"Your team?"

"Gone, all gone."

"How long did they have you?"

"Not long."

"Bad?"

"Real bad."

"So what'd you tell 'em?"

"Said I was an East German, training with their Viet friends."

The colonel laughed at the idea.

"How'd you get away?"

"I got away."

"It was supposed to be a quiet recon."

"It wasn't quiet."

"Shit, you're telling me. Their radio is already screaming to high heaven. They say thirty-eight 'innocent peasants' are dead."

"Most of them were soldiers."

"They blame us; probably they'll get one of their pious friends to raise hell at the UN."

"Why shouldn't they blame us? We did it, didn't we?"

Stratton wrenched himself from a tangle of sodden sheets. His watch said 5:47. It was still dark in Peking. His eyes felt gummy, his mouth wooden. He glanced at the bottle of whiskey he had bought the night before in the hotel lobby. Less than half full, and still open.

He had not drunk like that for a long time. And he had not hurt like that for a long time. David Wang's death had triggered reactions and dreaded memories he thought he had buried for good.

From the street below came the muted whir of cyclists, harbingers of the morning rush hour. Stratton rejected his body's urging for sleep. His mind would not sleep. Naked, he lurched to the bathroom and turned on the hand shower, hardly noticing that the water was stone cold.

A wrinkled woman with blue-rinse hair and stiff new Hong Kong sandals sat across from Stratton in an anteroom at the U.S. Embassy. Sitting next to her, but obviously on a separate mission, was a slender middle-aged man with a leathery face, a smoker's face. He carried a suede valise.

"How is *your* tour?" the old woman said to Stratton.

"Not too good," he said hoarsely. News of David Wang's death had left him numb. Sadness itself was slow in coming. Another old friend dead and—as in Vietnam—Tom Stratton was a long way from tears. Instead he fought a deep, dull melancholy.

"We have a lovely guide," the wrinkled woman said. "Her name is Su Yee. Her great-grandfather helped to build the Great Wall."

Stratton managed a polite smile.

"Where are you from?"

"New York," volunteered the smoker. "I'm an art dealer."

"I'm from Tucson, retired there from Chicago," the woman reported. "My husband used to be a stockbroker."

Together they awaited Stratton's contribution. "I'm a teacher," he said finally. "I teach art."

"Asian art?" asked the man with the leathery face.

Stratton did not reply.

The art dealer hunched forward, and Stratton shifted uncomfortably. There was something felonious about the man. He was dressed well enough, but the fine clothes didn't match the tiny brown rodent eyes that scoured Stratton from head to toe in quick appraisal.

"Do you know much about Sung Dynasty sculpture?" the art dealer asked. His voice dropped to a clubby whisper. "I'm trying to cut a deal with some government types down in the Sichuan Province. They've got a little gold mine of a museum down there, but I can't persuade them to part with any of their artifacts."

"This is our first trip to China," the old woman interjected.

"Mine, too," Stratton said, glancing at the door to the consular office. Surely it would not be much longer.

"Where's your hotel?" the art dealer pressed. "Maybe we can get together for a duck dinner." He laughed a Rotary Club laugh. "Look, I've done a lot of work in Western Europe, the Mideast, even Russia. But this is new territory, and I don't know whose back needs scratching. Maybe we could help each other out."

"I don't see how," Stratton said.

The man held out his hand. "My name's Harold Broom."

Stratton guessed that Broom was the sort of man who carried business cards in his top shirt pocket, and he was right.

"I'm always looking for experts. Especially free-lancers," Broom said. "The more I know, the more I can take home." The smile was as thin and hollow as the voice. "And the more I take home, the more I spread around."

"No thanks," Stratton said. "I'm here on pleasure, not business."

"Too bad."

"I have a passport problem," said the old woman with blue-rinse hair. "I can't find my passport. I may have left it at the opera. My husband said there should be no problem, but I told him this isn't Europe. A passport is probably more important here. This *is* a Communist country."

"Yes," Stratton said. He was miserable.

The door opened and an American secretary beckoned. Steve Powell sat at a small desk in a tall room with one narrow window.

A gray file cabinet stood in one corner. On a table, in front of a cracked leather sofa, was a stack of American magazines.

"I'm sorry for making you wait," Powell said. "I've spent the last two hours wrestling with the Chinese bureaucracy. It is intractable on the most routine matters. You can imagine the problems we face with something like this."

"Can't be much worse than ours," Stratton said.

"Oh, but it is," Powell said cheerily. "Infinitely worse. I could tell you some incredible stories . . ."

"What happened to David?" Stratton asked. "When I went to his hotel all the manager would say is, 'Mr. Wang not here.'"

Powell nodded. "When you ask a question of a Chinese, expect a very literal answer. The man was telling you as much of the truth as you requested. Professor Wang became ill Tuesday night and was taken from the hotel."

"But David told me he wouldn't even be back in Peking until Wednesday evening."

Powell shrugged. He slipped on a pair of tortoiseshell glasses and opened a file. Stratton noticed that it was the only item on the desk. Powell was a neat young man.

"Tell me what happened to David," Stratton said impatiently.

"Death by duck."

Stratton's face twisted.

"Sounds funny, I know," Powell went on, "but that's what we call it. It's a new China syndrome: Aging, out-of-shape American tourist comes to Peking, hikes and strolls through the Forbidden City and climbs the Great Wall until he's blue in the face. Then he gorges himself on—what else?—rich Peking duck, gulps liters of Lao Shan mineral water and promptly drops dead of a myocardial infarction."

"A heart attack, that's all," Stratton said.

"Sure," Powell said. "Death by duck. We've had dozens of cases. It has nothing to do with the duck, I assure you. Just too much food, too much exertion. Might as well be Coney Island franks."

"Just like that." Stratton's voice was tired and low.

"After dinner, Dr. Wang apparently felt sick to his stomach. Several guests apparently saw him go up to his room. Two hours later one of the cleaning boys went in and found him there in bed, unconscious but still alive. Two medical students came and took him to a clinic nearby. The doctors apparently worked very hard but it was too late."

"It's all *apparently* this and *apparently* that. Aren't you sure?"

"Of course. I use the word as a reflex," Powell said uneasily. "This information comes from the Chinese government. I can't vouch for it a hundred percent, but on a matter like this, I see no reason to challenge the facts. It is, as I said before, fairly routine. Tragic, to be sure, but still routine."

"This is a maddening place," Stratton said. "The people at the hotel might at least have told me which hospital he went to."

"They probably didn't know," Powell responded. "It took *me* five phone calls to find out. It was a small but very modern clinic on Wan Fu Jing Street. It has everything most hospitals in Peking don't have—the machines, I mean. I'm sorry for the confusion, but if you've spent much time in Asia, you come to expect it."

Stratton nodded. He knew something of Asian confusion.

"Why," he asked, "was there such a delay in reporting the death to the embassy? Is that routine, too?"

The delay, Powell explained, was another matter. He opened a desk drawer and withdrew a new file; he put the first file away. Professor Wang's death was not treated as those of other American visitors, the consul continued, because of Wang's relation to a high-ranking Chinese official.

"It was a homecoming for Professor Wang, and apparently was a very moving reunion with his brother. In this file I have a note from the deputy minister himself—a rare communication, believe me—and it describes Professor Wang's visit to Xian, and his return to Peking with his brother. That night, unfortunately, he suffered his fatal heart attack."

"The deputy minister was notified before the U.S. Embassy was?"

"He *was* Professor Wang's brother, after all. And in his position, Wang Bin certainly would be entitled to all the information regarding his brother's death. Once that information was delivered to the deputy minister, we were officially

notified. Please don't make more of this than is warranted."
Powell sighed. He took off his glasses and put them on the
desk. "I was up half the night trying to reach David Wang's
relatives back in Ohio."

"There are none," Stratton said emptily.

"So I learned. No wife, no kids, just a roomful of books and
paintings."

"And a garden."

Powell glanced at his wristwatch. "I asked you to come this
morning because Wang Bin requested it. Apparently the
professor told his brother of your friendship and of your mutual
interest in Chinese art and culture. For obvious reasons, Wang
Bin will not be able to attend his brother's funeral in Pittsville.
But he would like someone to accompany the body back to the
United States."

Stratton rubbed his temples with both hands.

"In his note here," Powell said, "Wang Bin suggests that
you would be the perfect escort. Let me read you this one part:
'It would mean a great honor for the memory of my brother if
Mr. Thomas Stratton could accompany David's body to his
homeland for burial in the manner so requested by my brother.
I realize that this would be an inconvenience and a hardship,
but it would advance the friendship between our great peoples.
Please convey this humble request to Mr. Stratton, and please
assure him that he will be able to complete his visit to China at
any other suitable time, as a welcomed guest.'

"The deputy minister wrote that himself, in English,"
Powell said.

Stratton stood to leave. "Tell the deputy minister I'll be
happy to accompany David's casket to the United States."

"Excellent!" Powell was pleased with himself.

Stratton asked about the body.

"It won't be ready for transport for a few days."

"Where is it?" Stratton asked.

"One of the city hospitals. Capital Hospital, I believe."

"You're not sure?"

"I can find out." Powell was defensive again. "I'll leave
word at your hotel. But, as I said, I'm fairly sure it's at Capital.
That's where it was sent for the autopsy."

Stratton motioned toward Powell's file. "The autopsy
results?"

"Oh no. The stuff on the heart attack I got by phone this

morning. Through official channels . . . Anyway, the body
will be taken to the Peking Airport Monday morning."

"Fine," Stratton said. At the door, he turned again to
Powell. "I'm curious, though. Is Wang Bin certain that his
brother wished to be buried in the United States? Perhaps, after
all these years, he wanted to be buried here, in China."

Powell was a little perturbed. "I really couldn't say. I
assume his brother would know. And besides, nobody is buried
in China anymore. Nearly everyone is cremated. It's a helluva
thing, Mr. Stratton, but it's true. Apparently there's no more
room for any bodies—especially in Peking."

The important man rode in the back seat of the black
limousine. At each side sat a trusted comrade whose function,
simply put, was to do as he was told.

"The train is late," said the limousine driver, who wore
thick eyeglasses and gripped the wheel tightly with bony
hands.

"As long as everything is safe, I don't mind," said the
important man.

"I talked to the workers in Xian this morning," volunteered
the man at his left side. "They assure me that, as before, the
crate was placed in a separate boxcar."

"With a guard?"

"Several guards, Comrade."

The driver steered the limousine along the special lanes used
on Peking streets by privileged travelers. The bicyclists gave
wide berth to the long black car.

"You have done well."

"Thank you, Comrade."

Then, in a voice so low the driver could not hear, the man
said, "Has anyone asked questions?"

"No," replied one of the escorts, whispering. "No one."

"Excellent." The important man gazed out the window of
the speeding car and thought how fortunate he was, in these
times, to have someone he could trust.

CHAPTER 4

ALICE DEMPSEY KNOCKED on the door at eight sharp the next morning. At eight thirty, she knocked again. Stratton grunted.

"Surely, you're not still in bed!" she said through the door. "We leave for the Great Hall of the People in ten minutes."

Stratton groped for his watch. "I'll catch up," he mumbled.

He dressed and went downstairs to claim a cup of tepid American coffee in the hotel restaurant. Then he set off on foot for the Heping Hotel.

It has occurred to Stratton that David Wang's belongings would have to be gathered for the sad trip home—clothes, cameras, textbooks, souvenirs, and the ever-present journal. Wang was not a mellifluous writer, nor was he poetic, but he wrote down all he saw. His journals were meticulous, spongelike and even a bit silly; once he had visited Disney World in Florida and returned, sheepishly, with fifty-seven pages of diary. Tom Stratton felt a duty to recover his old friend's things.

Everything about Stratton attracted the eyes of the Chinese—his height, his blond hair, his thick reddish mustache. In Vietnam it had been much the same. He remembered the clutter and chaos of Saigon, the heady taste and thrill of war, the horror, the ultimate revulsion: bitter, black fear. Stratton waded like a bushy mutant among hundreds of Chinese in the broad streets, a pale stalk shooting up from blue fields. He thought back to the flippant, soft-life description of academia he had foisted on Jim McCarthy. A self-justification.

"I am an obscure college professor because that is as far as I could get from guns and killing," Stratton should have said. "I haven't got the balls to do anything else. I lost my pride, and something more, one terrible night a long time ago."

At David Wang's hotel Stratton was greeted by a polite young clerk who spoke poor but passable English.

"I am a friend of the gentleman who got sick here the other night," Stratton began. "I came for his things."

Stratton expected a discussion, but the clerk merely smiled and led him upstairs. The door to David Wang's room was not locked. "No one sleep here for three nights, I think," the clerk said.

The room was small, the walls white and recently repainted. Chinese tourist hotels are not luxurious by European standards, but they are functional. A blue woolen blanket was smoothed across a single bed, and a chest of drawers had been carefully dusted. Two fresh hand towels hung on a hook near a chipped water basin.

The room was ready for a new guest. There was no sign that David Wang had ever slept there.

"Do you remember Professor Wang, the man who stayed here?" Stratton asked the timid clerk. The man nodded vigorously. "I came for his things. Where are they?"

The clerk shook his head.

"His clothes, his books . . ."

"Men came and took things. Comrades clean the room, that's all."

Stratton checked the closet and found three wire coat hangers on a dowel. Stratton went through the bureau. In one drawer he found two handkerchiefs and a pair of blue cotton socks. One of the handkerchiefs was monogrammed with the initials D.W.

"The men left with suitcase," the clerk volunteered.

"When?"

"The day after Mr. Wang got sick."

Somebody tapped on the open door.

A small-shouldered American in khaki walking shorts stood in the hallway. He was gray-haired and pink in the face; around his neck hung a pair of small Nikon binoculars.

"Are you a friend of Dr. Wang's?" he asked Stratton. "My name is Saul Weinstock. I was here Tuesday night when he got sick after dinner."

Stratton stood up from the bed and introduced himself. "You were in the restaurant?"

"No, but I was in our room downstairs when I heard the commotion. A cleaning boy found Dr. Wang and shouted for help. That's when I ran upstairs. I'm a retired physician. Had a general practice in Queens for thirty-one years. My wife and I

are on a world tour. We met Dr. Wang on a walk through one of
the municipal parks."

Weinstock told Stratton that he had seen David Wang late
Tuesday afternoon, shortly after his return from Xian.

"He was tired, but he seemed in good health. We asked him
to join us for dinner because we wanted to hear all about the
reunion with his brother, but he declined. He promised to join
us for breakfast on Wednesday morning."

The clerk excused himself. Stratton closed the door and
motioned Weinstock to sit on the bed.

"Was David still alive when you got here?"

"I'm not sure, Mr. Stratton. Let me tell you what happened,
because it's been bothering me a great deal. After I heard the
room boy shouting, I ran up the stairs. As you can see, I'm not
a young man. But still, it couldn't have been more than two
minutes.

"Yet already there were two men in the room. They
identified themselves as medics—at least that's what they told
the hotel manager. I told them I was an American doctor, and I
showed them my medical bag. But it was no use, Mr. Stratton,
because they wouldn't let me in. One of the men stood there, at
the door, blocking the way. The other was here at the bed,
leaning over Dr. Wang. Now I saw some movement in the
professor's leg, and I'm almost positive I heard him say
something in Chinese."

Stratton asked, "Was he in pain?"

"Yes, it sounded that way. I begged to go in and help, but
the hotel manager insisted that I go back to my room. The
medics said everything was under control. After a few
minutes, they came out with Dr. Wang on a stretcher. A blanket
was pulled up to his neck. His eyeglasses were sort of propped
on his forehead, and his eyes were closed. I think he was still
breathing, but I couldn't be sure. His color was very poor. His
face was gray. I followed the medics downstairs to the car,"
Weinstock said.

"They had a car?" Stratton was surprised. Three-wheeled
bicycles customarily served as delivery wagons and ambu-
lances in the city.

"Not just a car," Weinstock added, "a limousine. They put
the litter in the back and roared off. And that was something
else that bothered me. There's a clinic just three blocks down
the street, near the Dong Dan market. It's a very modern

facility by chinese standards; it was included on our tour. I saw the cardiac unit myself—not great, but adequate for a heart attack. Yet the medics drove right past it, never even slowed down."

"Maybe it was closed for the evening."

"I don't think so, Mr. Stratton."

"Strange, isn't it?" Stratton mused. "Do you know who David had dinner with?"

"It was a small banquet in a corner of the dining room; all the people were Chinese."

Together they walked down the stairs. The whole hotel smelled of turpentine and cheap new paint. On the second floor, Weinstock paused on the stairwell, as if making up his mind. "Mr. Stratton," he said. "I've got something in my room that you should see."

Gerda Weinstock was caking her cheeks with makeup when the two mean walked in; she let out a tiny shriek and fled into the bathroom.

"She hates for anybody to see her until she gets her face on," Weinstock whispered. With bony knees rubbing on the wooden floor, he hunted under the bed. When Weinstock got to his feet, he was holding a black medical bag.

"Once a doctor, always a doctor," Stratton said.

Weinstock shook his head soberly. "No, this isn't mine. This is what the medics left behind in Dr. Wang's room. This is what I wanted to show you. I found it on the floor, near the bed. I opened it because I was curious. Professional curiosity."

Inside, lying in a shining heap, were dozens of identical gadgets: a small tool, perhaps three inches long, with a small arm that swung out on a tiny hing and flipped over to form a lever for the thumb. Pressing the lever make the sharp U-shaped jaws of the tool open and close silently.

"Do you know what these are?" Weinstock asked incredulously.

"Fingernail clippers," Stratton muttered.

"Fifty-four sets," the American doctor reported. "Made in China."

"I'll be damned," Stratton said.

"Some medics," said Saul Weinstock. "Some goddamned medics, huh?"

Stratton asked to keep the medical bag.

"Sure, just don't tell them where you got it. Please,"

Weinstock implored. "My wife and I don't want to get kicked out of China before we get to see Tibet."

"You're damn right!" came a voice from the bathroom.

Steve Powell lifted the doctor's bag from his tidy government-issue desk and shook it. The nail clippers clattered metallically inside. "You've got to admit it *sounds* authentic," he said to Stratton. Then, with a dry laugh: "Welcome to China, my friend."

Stratton ignored the consul's invitation to sit down. "I don't think this is funny," he said.

"Understand something, Mr. Stratton. These 'medics' who attended to your friend at the hotel—of course they weren't real medics. Forget the bullshit you've heard about the phenomenal modernization of Chinese medicine. It's still backward as hell. And try to find a fucking veterinarian in this town! The embassy wives have to send their precious French poodles to Hong Kong for a lousy distemper shot.

"These guys who took Wang to the hospital were, at the very most, first-year students. They could have been janitors just as easily. The doctor bag is a prop, as you no doubt figured out. They were lackeys. Their only job was to get the patient to a hospital."

Stratton asked about the clinic three blocks from the hotel. "It's supposed to be very good," he said.

"Maybe it is," Powell said, "but David Wang was the VIP brother of a deputy minister. The Chinese knew who he was, where he was and what he was doing. When he got sick, they took him to Capital Hospital, one of the most advanced hospitals in Peking, whatever 'advanced' means here."

Stratton sat down. "Yesterday you weren't so sure."

"Since then I've received a full report from Wang Bin's office."

As proof, Powell displayed a file folder. "You're probably wondering what happened to Professor Wang's personal effects." Powell rose. "Come with me. We'll do our own inventory."

The two men walked to a cordoned-off area of the embassy building. Powell flashed a plastic identification card at a Marine guard, who opened a gate to a stale vault. The consul used a tiny key to spring a metal drawer on a bottom row of locked cabinets. He removed three paper bags. Each had been marked in black ink: "D. Wang, Pittsville, Ohio."

"The Chinese authorities collected these from Professor Wang's room. They may have overlooked a couple of things, but I think you'll find most of Dr. Wang's valuables are intact."

Stratton dumped the contents on a small table in a dimly lit corner of the vault: underwear, shirts, pants, and white sun visor, and extra pair of eyeglasses, a Nikon 35-mm camera, a bottle of Excedrin, three tombstone etchings on rice paper, four books about China and Chinese dialects, three rolls of unused film and a shaving kit.

"Wasn't there a suitcase?"

"I suppose it was just too large for the drawer," Powell said. "Does everything else seem in order?"

"No," said Stratton. "Where is David's journal? He always wrote in a thick diary with a leather binding."

"His brother has it. Wang Bin asked us for permission to read through David's writings. We saw no reason to object. He has promised to return the journal before the body is sent to the States."

Stratton said, "And David's passport?"

Powell adjusted his glasses and pawed through the items on the table. The Marine stood stiffly at the door of the vault, his back toward the two men.

"It's not here?" Powell asked lamely.

"No." Stratton watched the consul's composure drain. The cool eyes fluttered.

"It must be here," Powell said. "Something so important."

"What are the regulations in a case like this?"

"Our regulations, or theirs?" Powell grumbled as he fished in the empty pockets of David Wang's neatly folded trousers. "Jesus, this is unbelievable. Just what I need. You say you went through the room as well?"

"Nothing much," Stratton said. "Socks, handkerchiefs. What happens if you can't find the passport?"

Powell had given up. He stuffed the sad remnants of David Wang's life into the paper bags. "Well, if we can't find it, then I have to write a report. That's about it. I'll have a few forms to fill out." He eyed Stratton with annoyance. "What *should* happen? I mean, Christ, the man's dead, isn't he? He doesn't need a passport anymore. A corpse travels on a bill of lading."

Back at the consul's office, Stratton waited while Powell

checked another office for David Wang's passport. Stratton sat
in a chair directly across from Powell's empty desk; there was a
different file on top now. It was light blue. Stratton could see
his own name on the tab. Instantly, he reached for it.

"Sir?" A woman's voice, behind him. "Sir, Please don't.
That's confidential, for Mr. Powell only."

Stratton faced a young woman who had emerged from an
adjoining office. She had long auburn hair and brown eyes, and
wore a dark blue dress with a round white collar. "You don't
have to sneak a peek," she teased. "You know what's in there.
Want some coffee?"

"Please." When she came back—"Watch it now, the cup's
very hot"—Stratton asked, "Where did that file come from?"

"Washington. By telex. It's routine. It would please both
governments to know that the person we're sending home with
Dr. Wang's remains is not a smuggler or a thief or a fugitive of
some sort. It's just a routine check."

"That's a pretty thick file," Stratton noted, "for routine."
The coffee was much too hot to drink, but it smelled glorious.

"You're a war hero," she said. "The Pentagon writes books
on its war heroes. In your case, they were happy to pass it
along. Proud even. Langley, too."

"Step right up and read all about it. Hurry, hurry."

"Sometimes Steve prefers a little synopsis," she said,
ignoring the sarcasm. "It saves time if I'm familiar with the
material. Don't worry, I've got clearance on stuff like this."

"You know *my* name, what's yours?" Stratton asked.

"Linda," she answered. "Linda Greer. I'm vice-consul."

Linda greer. He looked at her for a moment and wondered.
This hardly seemed the time, but . . . the only women he
had talked with for days had been Alice and her gaggle, and
little Miss Sun. Right now, he certainly could use some company.

"Would you like to have dinner sometime?" he tried.

"No, thank you, Mr. Stratton."

"A movie?"

"The embassy movie doesn't change for another two weeks,
and I've already seen it four times. Besides, you're leaving for
the States on Monday morning."

Stratton sat back in the chair and tested the coffee again.
Well, it was what he'd deserved. Linda disappeared. Powell
walked in and crisply stationed himself at the desk.

"I'll be looking into the passport matter. I hope to have some sort of explanation by the time you leave."

"Monday morning," Stratton said.

"Linda told you. Well, good. Did she tell you the itinerary? It's Hong Kong, San Francisco, Cleveland. The body stays on the plane in Hong Kong, but you'll have a customs layover in California. We're trying to get a diplomatic waiver from Washington on that now."

Stratton did not react outwardly. Powell shifted.

"Do you have a suit and tie?" the consul asked.

Puzzled, Stratton said: "I have a tie and a blazer. I suppose it's good enough for Pan Am."

"And for the deputy minister as well," Powell said. "He'd like to see you tomorrow morning. Nine o'clock. Any taxi at the hotel will take you. Here's the address."

Powell walked Stratton to the door. Stratton got the impression that this was a vital part of his job, walking tourists to the door.

"Linda says you were at Man-ling."

"Yes," Stratton replied.

Powell asked, "Was it as bad as they say?"

"Worse," Stratton said as he walked out. "I'm sure it's all in the file."

CHAPTER 5

IN THE HOTEL COURTYARD, amid gleaming rows of Chinese-made automobiles that looked like boxy stegosauruses, off-duty waiters played uproarious catch with a red Frisbee. Stratton sat on the stone front steps, elbows on his knees, palms supporting his face, a brown study. He watched without seeing. David Wang was dead and he did not know how to mourn him. Wang had come late to Stratton's life, and yet for a time Stratton had felt closer to him than he had ever felt to his own father. Stratton had the feeling, without really knowing, that he had been but one of a number of private reclamation projects Wang must have quietly undertaken over the years at St. Edward's. In Stratton's case, it had worked. Wang had molded a scarred young officer—no, that was a euphemism; a cynical young killer—into the shape of a civilized man who could honestly savor poetry and the whisper of breeze on a pine branch. Who could sleep deeply and rise remorseless, without scrabbling for a cigarette and a gun. Who could even, more than a decade later, return to China, feeling legitimate, almost comfortable, as a genuine if unheralded and rough-hewn college professor.

But Wang had worked too well, had he not? Stratton had slipped away from him, further every year. Two disparate clouds that had met improbably, intermingled and then sailed away to different horizons. Had he been back home teaching, word of David Wang's death might have provoked a few minutes of sharp but distanced regret, then hurried cancellation of classes and a trip to the funeral, complete, surely, with the trappings of a Catholicism that Wang knew and loved as much as the priests who would recite the final incantation. Here it was different. Was it cruel for Wang to have died in his native China? Or was it poetic? Regardless, Stratton felt grievously hurt by his death and fiercely protective of the body that lay somewhere in Peking, being prepared for a journey home.

37

How banal, yet how true. In their last gossamer encounter, David had seemed so well. . . .

An insistent horn snapped the reverie. Stratton levered up off the steps and strode into the parking lot. The passenger door of a tan Toyota opened invitingly. As he slid in, his gloom began to lift.

"I'm glad you changed your mind," he said.

Linda Greer smiled. She had changed into a beige shirtwaist dress, a fetching advertisement for her long, bronzed legs that scissored with a rustle of unseen silk as she expertly maneuvered the car into bike-laden streets.

"Usually when I say 'no,' it's because I mean 'no.' When I say 'no' and mean 'yes,' I am not above confessing my mistake. One look at your face in there, and I could tell you needed someone to talk to. And I am sorry about your friend."

He gave her a curious look, then settled back against the seat. She swung the car quickly around a yellow-and-red bus bursting with empty-faced workers on their way home, then pulled sharply behind a three-wheel motorbike spewing a noxious trail of black smoke.

"Ugh," Linda said. "And the Chinese wonder why the air is so bad."

They drove past the majestic Qianmen, once the front gate of a walled Peking. Linda turned to enter the gigantic square named after the gate. Stratton's guidebook said it was ninety-eight acres.

"Postcards hardly do the place justice," Linda remarked. "You could land a plane in here."

In the vastness of the square, a handful of Chinese on their haunches nursed kites through the light summer air. The handmade kites—frogs and princes, fat fish, and a clever troop of tiny sparrows suspended from the same string—danced against the backdrop of the Forbidden City, the network of palaces that had housed imperial dynasties for six hundred years. On the left stood the stark white mausoleum where the rubber-looking remains of Chairman Mao lay under glass. Beyond the mausoleum rose the Great Hall of the People, more massive than majestic.

"The museums," Linda said, pointing. "History on the right, the Museum of the Revolution, appropriately, on the left."

"They're huge. You could lose an army in there."

"That's fitting, too. The people across the street"—she waved a cool hand toward the Great Hall—"they're perpetually worried about losing a country."

"Many things are sacred in China, of course, but not history. History is for rewriting. Take poor Emperor Qin. For centuries, history officially shat all over Emperor Qin." Linda pronounced it 'Tsin.' "He was always the example of the most savage dictator, a kind of Chinese anti-Christ. He was the nut who commissioned the sculpture of seven thousand clay soldiers to guard him in the afterlife. And he was the maniac who once ordered four hundred Confucian scholars buried alive because they wouldn't admit that he was smarter. Buried alive, can you imagine? But in the new history, that's all forgiven. Qin is the man who unified China and so he's a hero—rehabilitated two thousand years later. And his celestial army is a national treasure. What the hell, easy come, easy go . . . Hey c'mon, Stratton, come back to me, huh?"

Normally, she would have had all his attention. Linda Greer was more than a passably attractive woman. Quick, witty, assured. Stratton had made a fool of himself over that kind of woman more than once. The setting she had chosen for dinner added to her allure, as she undoubtedly knew, as she tossed off crystal-clear Mandarin to a smiling waitress.

They sat on an ancient balcony overlooking a moat at the rear of the Forbidden City. It was, Linda had said, the oldest restaurant in Peking. The food, particularly a kind of shaved beef that was the house specialty, was superb. The fiery *mao tai* she had ordered when they arrived smelled like distilled sweat socks, but went down smoothly and kicked like a mule. The Great Wall white wine, heavy and a trifle too sweet, had initially doused the *mao tai* fumes, but, by the second bottle, subtly fanned them. Stratton should have felt mellow, but all he really felt was sadness.

"Tell me about Wang Bin," he said, in an effort to rouse himself.

"A year younger than David," Linda began. "A perplexing man. His pedigree in the Party—and that's what counts in China—is impeccable. Madame Wang, his mother, was one of China's earliest and most vociferous revolutionaries."

Stratton was surprised. "I knew that David's father was a

man of substance in Shanghai, but I can't recall that he ever mentioned his mother."

"She was quite a lady. She had the two boys, and then gave herself—physically as well as ideologically—to the Revolution. In the early days, Mao and his friends could always be assured of a warm welcome at the Wang mansion on the Bund in naughty old Shanghai. By the time Papa Wang discovered his wife was more than a salon radical, it was too late. She had left and taken Bin with her. That must have been soon after David went abroad, because in the normal course of events Bin would have followed close behind.

"Madame Wang become the mistress of one of Mao's chief lieutenants. She actually made the famous Long March. And Wang Bin went with her, every step of the way, one of Mao's teenage soldiers. By the time the Communists won control of the country in 1949, Wang Bin was a distinguished veteran, an up-and-coming young man."

"Fascinating," Stratton said, as a mental light clicked on. "In another year, he might have gone off to school with David and none of it would ever have happened. And two years earlier that might have been David's story, too, although I can't imagine David raising his hand to strike even his worst enemy—if he ever had one."

"Like most of Mao's soldiers, Wang Bin's education had been shut off by war—although I guess most of them would never have had much schooling anyway," Linda continued. "Bin would probably have stayed in the army and become one of those semiliterate genius-generals that still run the armed forces, but Mama Wang took a hand. He entered the University of Peking and became a major figure in the Party there."

"That must have seemed pretty tame after what he had been through. What'd he study, theology?" It was a pale joke, but a joke nonetheless.

"Fine arts, if you can believe that. Of course, he didn't stay long. During the Korean War somebody remembered that he spoke English—for the past two centuries all Shanghai Wangs have apparently spoken English—and back into the army he went as an interrogator of captured Americans. After that, there were a succession of jobs, mostly Party positions of increasing influence, although he did have an occasional artsy job here and there. I guess that's what did him in."

"Did him in?"

"Yes, sir. In the mid-sixties, along comes the Cultural Revolution—you know, Mao's attempt to revive a revolution that was choking on its own red tape. It was incredibly destructive madness, of course, turned the Chinese universe topsy-turvy for nearly ten years. In the midst of it, Wang Bin just vanished. Turned out he had been attacked by the Red Guards because he was an intellectual—crime enough in those days. He apparently spent four or five years slopping hogs in a commune out west. Didn't get rehabilitated until the mid-seventies."

"And now he's back on the track again."

"Well, not exactly." Linda Greer chose her words with care. "He is a powerful man. It looks as though his culture job is a kind of front for deeper Communist Party activities. He's rumored to have his own little band of enforcers to patrol his domain. You've heard about the political struggle that's going on around here, I'm sure."

"A little." McCarthy had given him a beginner's lesson. Stratton wished he had paid more attention.

"Well, as far as we can figure out, all the guys Wang Bin has ridden with over the past thirty years are being systematically shot out of the saddle."

"But not him," Stratton anticipated.

"Not him, at least not yet. Maybe not ever, who knows? He should be struggling for his political life and instead, while all sorts of political shit flies, he invites his long-lost brother to come from America—that certainly could be used against him—and spends all his time assembling an archaeological exhibit nobody but us cares much about."

"An overture to old Uncle Sam, right?"

"Maybe. I wish I knew."

Stratton emptied his glass, and refilled both of theirs.

"How long have you been a spook, Linda?"

Linda Greer blushed.

"I'm not. I'm a vice-consul."

"Sure you are."

"Not convinced, huh?" she tried again.

"Try that on some little old tourist lady who has lost her luggage."

"About five years, if you must know. And I am not a spook. I am a case officer."

"Then get off my case, officer." He watched her hackles rise.

"What do you mean by that?"

He reached across and took her hand.

"Linda, it took me all of five minutes to figure out that you didn't pick me up just because of my sad face, but I only just now realized exactly what it is you want. Linda, I was recruited and trained and conned and sent to the wolves by guys who were playing nasty games while you were still in Pampers. This is what I would call a transitory recruitment."

"Okay, wiseass, how does it go?"

"Something like this. Could Mr. Stratton, who is known to us and thought, on the basis of previous service, to be reliable, interject into his conversation with Wang Bin tomorrow questions that might establish Comrade Wang's view of the United States, such as: How does Comrade Wang foresee the development of relations between our two great countries in this time of great international stress? And, providing Comrade Wang seemed receptive to that particular conversation, perhaps expressing veiled admiration for the United States, a second approach might be made. And perhaps a third, and a fourth, each one a little deeper until one day somebody, say a beautiful, art-loving vice-consul, would hold her breath and try to recruit Comrade Wang." Stratton stared out over the sleeping canal. "Actually, it's not a bad gambit."

"Gee, thanks."

Stratton thought aloud. "Let's see, if Wang will deal and he wins this current round of intrigue, you're in clover—you've got a source at a high level. And if he loses, Wang might be persuaded to accept asylum in the United States—'defect' has a nasty ring to it, don't you think? He would be a man with a grudge against the guys who forced him out. He would provide great inside intelligence up until the time he left, and knowledgeable guesses about how things might go from there."

Linda Greer assayed a wan smile. "You could have been a great one, Stratton. It's all there in your file."

"And does the file also say that I left in such disgust that, if I had stayed, I probably would have blown my head off?"

"Or somebody else's."

"And no doubt the file also says I am now a straight-and-narrow, almost middle-aged college professor who hardly ever does anything more adventuresome than jaywalking?"

"That, too."

"So why bother?"

"A spur-of-the-moment thing. Nothing we set up. We thought the fact you deliberately came to China might mean you were bored, but we were willing to let it go at that. No contact. But suddenly you have natural access—much better than any of us could ever get—to a major player in the Chinese drama. So we thought we'd try—although we had a hunch you'd say no."

"And all this while I was supposed to think I was here in this romantic setting because of your vast powers of sympathy. Or was it my dashing figure and rugged good looks?"

She had the grace to smile.

"Stratton, Thomas Henry. D.O.B. et cetera, et cetera. Married the former Carol Webster, pediatrician. Rancorous divorce after nine years and one child, Jason, age six. . . ."

"He's nearly eight."

"Okay, Mr. Rugged Looks." Linda Greer took his hand with both of her own. "Will you do it, Tom?"

"What's in it for you, Linda? Little gold star on that pretty forehead? Big desk at Langley, maybe. One case is all it takes, right? I know how it works."

"Do you really?" She was hurt. Stratton instantly regretted the nasty jabs.

"How do you think I got this job, Tom? I got it because I'm good, and I've got some guts. And I've risked my ass once or twice, literally. I'm no war hero, and maybe I don't have your scars, Tom, but I've got a few little nightmares of my own. No ribbons, no plaques on the wall, just some pretty rotten dreams. And, yes, I want out of Peking. I want to work in a place where the twentieth century has arrived, where I can leave the city without a dog tag or a babysitter, where I can have a *life*, like a normal woman. So the answer is yes, I want this case. I want *him*. Wang Bin."

"Linda, I'm sorry . . ." But nothing gave way. No tears, no rage. Just a trace of color in her cheeks—and again the question.

"Tom, will you do it? Please."

"No," Stratton said. "I've already got my ribbons, remember?" A bloody stage, a pitchfork, a scream. He remembered.

"Nothing I can say or do to change your mind?"

"No."

"Shit."

They did not speak of it again. Leaving the restaurant, Linda Greer once again became an earnest tour guide. She drove competently on parking lights, dipping here and there into seemingly unpeopled alleys. Stratton had lost all sense of direction by the time Linda wheeled through a gate set in a twelve-foot brick wall. She nodded to two armed soldiers posted there, as though to trusted doormen.

"The diplomatic compound," she announced. "This is where I live."

Stratton waited.

She killed the motor and half-turned in the driver's seat. Her arm crawled up Stratton's shoulder and around his neck.

They kissed.

"That would be delightful, but the answer is still *no*."

"Mata Hari goes off duty after dessert," she murmured. "Besides, Peking is a lonely post, and you aren't bad-looking—in an almost middle-aged, professorial kind of way. You think you're the *only* one who needs some company?"

Stratton didn't believe a word of it, but he went.

CHAPTER 6

SHE DROVE ALONE THROUGH the night. The great city slept. Waxen pools of light marked a twenty-four-hour dumpling restaurant that was a nocturnal refuge of the young men and women who drove the number-one buses; a mindless twenty-mile route, back and forth endlessly, along Changan, and nary a turn. Her groin ached deliciously. Her mouth felt bruised. Maybe she had fibbed about going off duty, but she'd told the truth about one thing: she *had* needed the company. Peking was not exactly swarming with available American men. She yearned to be back in bed, but the digital clock on the dashboard read 3:15. Linda Greer was late.

She had roused Stratton with a lie, saying her reputation would be ruined if the night guards' report showed that a visitor to Miss Greer's apartment had not left. He had gone willingly enough—a goodbye kiss and a hug.

Her route led through the northern quarter of the city, and she knew it by heart. She turned right at a corner marked by a dusty bicycle shop and flashed her lights before a gray metal gate set firmly into the usual Peking-anonymous concrete wall. The gate creaked open at the urging of an old man in worker blue. She—or some other consular officer—was expected on duly appointed diplomatic rounds.

After nearly a year in Peking, she still did not understand why the Chinese had to do it in the dead of night. Was it distaste? Or left-over superstition that had survived the arrival of the Communist era? She had asked, at first, but all of her questions had been answered with a shrug. This is how it has always been done. After a while, she, too, had learned to shrug. By embassy tradition, it was a job reserved to the junior member of the consular corps. If that happened to be a woman, who also happened to be an intelligence officer, too bad. In another month, a new junior vice-consul would report for duty and Linda Greer would drive no more by night in Peking.

There were no preliminaries. The Chinese had no more liking for this chore than she.

"I am Miss Greer of the American Embassy. Where is Mr. Li?"

"Mr. Li is ill tonight. My name is Mr. Hu."

Linda nodded. Hu's on first, a pockmarked man with a cowlick. She was glad she had worn a skirt. Her panties were damp with the aftermath of love; no, of good old-fashioned hard-and-fast sex. For a wild moment Linda imagined driving to Stratton's hotel, rushing to his room on some pretext and . . . no, that would never do. That ruggedly aloof professor with the scarred body and great stamina was not for keeping; strictly a half-night stand. Still, it was better to think of him than to comtemplate her late-night diplomatic duty.

"I believe there are two," she said primly, waving a pair of manila folders.

Mr. Hu nodded. It was not unusual. The average was about twelve a year, but they tended to cluster in the peak tourist months. Twelve ducks.

The inner room was chilly, smelling of things Linda Greer never thought about. The welder, too, was new to Linda. She thought of asking Mr. Hu if the entire crew had been changed, but didn't bother.

"Friedman, Molly R., Fort Lauderdale, Florida," she read from the file.

Mr. Hu gestured. The lid was open. Linda looked, nodded.

"Wang, David T., Pittsville, Ohio." Her own voice seemed strained.

"We have already begun on that one."

"I am required to see it first."

"You were late."

"That is procedure."

"It is very hot."

A Chinese standoff. Linda could insist. They would shout and argue and, finally, with ill grace, they would probably snap the welds and open the lid. Linda had a sudden vision of herself, screaming like a harridan in Mandarin in the foreigners' morgue in Peking at the deadest hour before dawn. She shivered and surrendered.

"Very well," she said.

Mr. Hu nodded. The welder, a stocky, middle-aged woman, twirled a knob and ignited her torch.

Then, as procedure dictated, Linda watched in the eerie, smoking blue light of cascading sparks as the welder worked methodically, up one side and down the other. When she had finished, Linda checked to make sure that the labels were correct—that was really the most important part of her night's work. Neither coffin would be opened again, but it would never do to dispatch heart attack victim Wang—Stratton's friend—to Florida, or obese Mrs. Friedman, victim of complications of a broken hip on the Great Wall, to Ohio.

Linda Greer walked with cowlicked Mr. Hu to a small office. There, with a pen and a seal, she testified, in parallel English and Chinese documents that Linda May Greer, consular officer of the United States of America, had witnessed the sealing of two caskets and certified their contents. She drove home in the breaking dawn, trying to think of sex, but the images would not come and the effort left her feeling dry and brittle.

The setting was exactly as Linda Greer had predicted.

"It's a ritual, Tom. All official meetings in all parts of China are staged exactly the same way," she had said. "Maybe it's something they borrowed from the Russians early on—or from the emperors—but it is literally a case of 'See one, you've seen them all.'"

Wang Bin had sent a car to the hotel. A Red Flag, no less, one of those dying-breed hand-tooled lustrous black limousines that are such a conspicuous status symbol in China that they have their own relaxed set of traffic regulations. The driver wore white gloves and had no English. He deposited Stratton at the apex of a circular driveway at the entrance to the museum. A young man with bottle-bottom glasses sprang for the door.

"Welcome, Professor Stratton. My name is Mr. Zhou. Comrade Wang is waiting for you. Follow me, please."

They passed quickly through a marbled lobby bristling with watchers, turned left immediately, and left again at the first doorway.

The formal reception room was just as Linda had sketched it: long and narrow, filled by two lines of parallel overstuffed chairs and sofas in gray-brown wrapping. Between them ran a set of low coffee tables. Before each seat was a flowered tea mug, an ashtray and an ornate wooden box of tea leaves. On the wall was a large mural of the traditional dwarfed-by-nature theme.

Inside the doorway stood Wang Bin, a gently rounded ghost of his brother. From a few steps away, the resemblance to David was startling; nonplussed, Stratton faltered at the door. Wang Bin motioned him in kindly.

As they shook hands, Stratton saw the differences. Wang Bin's face seemed leaner and older than David's; the hair was shorter of course, but also thinner, and more liberally dashed with gray at the temples. The deputy minister's bearing, in a crisp gray Mao suit with a black mourner's band on one arm, was rock-hard military. But the greatest difference welled in the eyes. To look at David Wang's almost-almond eyes was to have seen wisdom, humor, compassion. In Wang Bin's eyes Stratton saw intelligence, strength—and something else. A certain intrepid determination that had no doubt stood him in good stead all these years.

Stratton and Wang sat at right angles in adjoining chairs and the interpreter took up a priest-at-confession pose to one side. Stratton's last private meeting with a Chinese official had been with a snarling, saucer-faced man who'd punctuated shouting questions with blows from a rubber truncheon. When the time had come to leave, Stratton had shot him, twice.

Wang Bin was speaking. Stratton leaned forward attentively, letting the sibilant Mandarin wash over him in uncomprehended waves. A girl in pigtails and a white jacket materialized. Gently, she eased the top off Stratton's tea cup and added boiling water from a thermos. She soundlessly recovered the cup. Tea leaves had already been placed in the cup.

". . . to meet a distinguished scholar such as yourself and hopes you are enjoying your stay in China," the interpreter hissed.

"Please tell Comrade Wang that I am pleased and excited to be in China. It is a fascinating country and my trip has been very educational."

A pause for translation. Wang's response. Then the translation floating back toward Stratton. An agonizing way to communicate, he reflected, about as lively as geriatric shuffleboard.

"Comrade Wang asks if this is your first trip to China."

"Tell Comrade Wang that, yes, this is my first trip. I have always wanted to come before, but it was too expensive." Stratton had told that same lie dozens of times. He would die proclaiming it. And why not? The first time he had come without a passport.

"Comrade Wang asks, What cities beside Peking have you visited?"

The conversation meandered like the Yangtze for nearly fifteen minutes; three offers of cigarettes, two cups of tea and banalities uncounted. Stratton let it wander. It was Wang Bin's ball park, and if he was in no hurry, neither was Stratton. The art historians had voted unanimously to spend their last morning in Peking—a rare, unprogrammed three hours—on a return visit to the Friendship Store.

"Comrade Wang says his brother spoke well of you to him. He said you were a treasured former student and a distinguished professor. Comrade Wang says he is pleased."

Stratton smiled.

"Tell Comrade Wang that David had many spiritual children like me and that some of them are truly distinguished. I am not, but I mourn David as I would my own father."

When the translation ended, Wang said something to the interpreter that brought him to his feet. Stratton, too, started to rise, thinking the colorless encounter ended. Wang stopped him with a gesture of his mourning-banded arm. When the door closed behind the young interpreter, Wang lit a cigarette and blew smoke at the ceiling.

"I would like to speak of my brother, Professor Stratton. I believe we can dispense with protocol," he said in nearly accentless English. Stratton did not comment on the language shift. Wang had never allowed the interpreter to complete a translation of anything Stratton had said.

"You will be returning with my brother to the United States, the land he made his nation. Many people will ask about his death. I will tell you, so you may tell them."

"I would like to know."

"Let me start with life, Professor Stratton. That is where all death begins, does it not? In life? Once we had been close, my brother and I, close in that special way that only brothers know. I can still see the cobblestone courtyard in Shanghai where we would play.

"We took piano lessons and studied our math and our English and when no one was looking we would sneak away to play by the river. We loved the river. So much life, excitement. Once we saw a knife fight betwen two sailors. Then came the day for my brother to leave. Back to the river, but this time in rickshas with trunks and my brother in a Western suit. We tried not to cry, but we cried and my father was angry. At first my brother wrote every week. After my parents had done with them, I would take those letters and read them until they entered my memory. But already the Revolution was beginning, Professor Stratton, and the letters became more infrequent. Soon I left with my mother to join the people's struggle. I heard no more from my American brother for many, many years. Some good years, and a few that were very bad. For several years my job was to collect night soil in a big barrel that I pushed on a cart. Do you know what night soil is?"

"Human excrement, collected for fertilizer."

"Yes, I am glad to see that you have done your lessons, Professor. Human excrement, to be collected by leaders in punishment when the Revolution is betrayed by fools. I know you have read of the Cultural Revolution, Professor, but it was worse than anything that is written about it. Much worse. Then came some good years, and now . . . who knows?" Wang Bin sipped some tea and lit a fresh cigarette from the butt of the old. "My brother . . . one may lose touch with a brother, but one never forgets him. Brothers are part of you, like parents. I have heard that when parents go to visit their grown children in America, they are asked to pay for their meals, Professor Stratton. Is that true?"

"Certainly not."

"I thought not. It is a lie then, published in our newspapers to make people less envious of America. Revolutions require many lies, you know." Wang Bin smiled without mirth.

"One day, I decided to write my brother. I cannot tell you why, exactly, except that he was my brother and we are—were—old men. That must have been three years ago; a friend in our embassy in Washington got me the address. At first, the letters were respectful, distant, like the opening moves in a game of chess. But, eventually, they became letters between two brothers. I invited David to come for a visit. Hundreds of thousand of overseas Chinese have returned for visits to their families in the past few years, from America, Canada, Europe, everywhere. Did you know that?"

"It must have been very emotional, your reunion with David."

"Oh, yes, it was. A wonderful experience, happy and sad. Last week, when I saw my brother for the first time in nearly fifty years, I wept. So did he, although Chinese do not display their emotions publicly. Americans are much more open about that, aren't they?"

"Yes, I suppose so."

"As David—that was not my brother's given name, but that is what he asked me to call him—as David may have told you, I was unfortunately not in Peking when he arrived, but in Xian, a city in the west. Do you know it?"

Stratton shook his head.

"A beautiful city where the emperors lived when Peking was still just a village. So David flew to Xian and there we reunited. We wept, and laughed, and at night after dinner we would go to his room, drink tea and remember; be little boys again."

"Did he show any signs of being sick?" Stratton asked.

"Only the excitement, at first. But then, perhaps it was the day before we returned to Peking, he complained of pains in his chest. We sat for a while and then continued our walk; we were in the park. He took a little pill, I think, and when I asked him if something was wrong, he laughed and said he had some trouble with his heart, but that it was not serious. His doctor had joked, David said, that the problem was just grave enough for him to take two or three little pills a day for the next forty years."

"I hadn't known that," Stratton said.

"Well, he tried to do too much, you see. He was so excited about being in China again and being with me. He tried to do too much, rushing everywhere. I tried to slow him down, but you know how David was. . . ."

"Yes. Were you with him the last night?"

"At the beginning. Some of my colleagues here had arranged a special banquet for us in honor of my brother—a Peking duck banquet. You will forgive my patriotism, Professor Stratton, but I am assured by men who know that Peking duck is the single finest dish in the world. It is also, for Chinese people, quite expensive. My brother and I were both moved by my colleague's gesture. It was a wonderful meal, one I shall remember always. Afterwards, I went with David back to his hotel, but I did not join him for tea. I had a meeting."

Wang Bin's eyes strayed to the ceiling.

"Someone came for me there to say that David had been stricken. I rushed to the hospital, but the comrade doctors said he was dead when he arrived. Heart, they said."

"I'm sorry," said Stratton.

"Your embassy has inquired about David's passport. The comrades at the hospital told me that intravenous solution had spilled on the passport during the attempt to save David. An apprentice, not knowing what it was, threw it away. He will be punished."

Stratton sipped some of his own tea. He had the overwhelming sensation that he was being lied to, fed a carefully contrived script. But what was the lie? And, more important, why?

"Tell me about America, Professor Stratton."

The request caught Stratton off guard.

"Well, how—I mean—what would you like to know?"

"I would like to know something of the truth, something between the lies of the Revolution and the lies of the American Embassy. It is not often that a senior Chinese official may speak frankly with an American without someone present to listen."

Better natural access than any of us will ever get, Linda Greer had said. Well, why not?

"I am partial, of course, Comrade Minister, but it is one of the few places on earth where a man is actually free. Think what you like. Do what you like. Which is not to say that it is a nation without problems. Many people never think at all, and even more talk without having anything to say. It is a beautiful and powerful and vigorous and violent country."

"Yes, I have always admired the vigor without understanding the violence."

"You must come to visit."

"I would like that, but my duties here and"—his hand waved at the window, toward the Communist Party headquarters across the massive square—"elsewhere do not permit it. But tell me about my brother's America. Tell me about the special place he will be buried."

"The Arbor," Stratton said. David's pride.

Soon after he had appeared at St. Edward's as a young assistant professor, David Wang had bought an abandoned dairy farm on the outskirts of Pittsville. When he hadn't been teaching, he'd begun to work the land. Not to farm it, or forest it exactly, but to manicure it, to build it into a place of beauty according to his own orderly view. David had planted stands of pine and maple, birches and oak, as well as exotic trees he grew from seed. A clear stream bubbled through the Arbor into an exquisite formal lake on the lee side of a gentle hill. David Wang had done most of the work himself, with simple tools. When he hadn't been in the classroom, he côuld be found on his land or deep in an armchair in the old white clapboard farmhouse that had no locks on the doors.

Over the years the town had grown; tract houses now flanked the Arbor on two sides and an interstate lanced through an adjoining ridgetop. But nothing molested the tranquillity and the beauty of David Wang's oasis, and nothing ever would. Gradually it had become a part park, part botanical garden, a place of fierce civic pride. Stratton could remember spring weekends when sixty people, from rough-hewn farmers in bib overalls to shapely college girls in cutoffs, would appear at the Arbor as volunteer gardeners. And how many St. Edward's coeds, over the years, had surrendered their virginity on an aromatic bed of pine needles? Stratton smiled at his own memories. Anyone was free to wander the land, and no one dared molest it. This was where David Wang wanted to be buried.

Stratton spoke haltingly at first, and then with a rush of details. The Arbor was a place of both beauty and meaning.

Wang Bin displayed such lively interest that for an instant Stratton wondered, absurdly, whether the deputy minister believed that his brother had willed him the land. Everybody in Ohio who knew about the Arbor also knew that David Wang had publicly promised it to the college.

As he talked, Stratton mentally weighed what he knew about David's death against what Wang Bin had told him. There was something . . .

And then he had it.

". . . would like to have enjoyed it at David's side," Wang Bin was saying.

"Yes, of course." But what did it mean, damn it?

Wang Bin looked at Stratton sharply, as though he had divined the wandering of a perplexed mind. From the table he took a leather-bound volume that looked like a diary. He handed it to Stratton.

"Here, this is my brother's journal. Apparently he was addicted to writing something nearly every day. I was interested in his first impressions of China. I would be grateful if you could take it with you." Wang Bin rose. "And I am in your debt, Professor Stratton, for agreeing to accompany

David's body. I am sure your presence will smooth the formalities. I am assured that the body has been prepared to the most exacting standards."

"Yes, of course."

"I know little of such things, Professor, since corpses are cremated in China, but I believe my brother would have appreciated a simple ceremony as quickly as it can be arranged. For my part, I think it is particularly fitting that he be buried in the Chinese coffin in which he makes his last journey."

"That should be no problem. But, look, about my accompanying the body. I'm not sure . . ." Stratton wanted some fresh air, some room to think.

"Why?" Wang Bin asked sharply. He made no effort to hide the strength behind the question.

Stratton improvised.

"This has been very emotional for me. The thought of David's body riding in the cargo hold of the same plane . . . I'm not sure that I'm up to it."

"It is all arranged, Professor. My car will call for you in ample time for the flight. Everything is taken care of."

"But . . ."

"You must." Stratton could taste the menace.

Later, Stratton would not remember leaving the museum, or whether he walked back to the hotel or had been driven. What he remembered with clarity was sitting on the bed, staring out the hotel window, puzzling, and the lie—and wondering why.

If you were a man in your sixties with serious heart trouble, would you go to China, where tourism is rigorous and health facilities are primitive by American standards? Perhaps, if it was to see a long-lost brother.

But, if you did go, would you remember those life-giving pills that you had to take two or three times a day "for the next forty years"? Of course. And if you took them with you, would you take them for the entire trip and a reserve supply, just in case? Again, yes.

And there logic exploded. Stratton had examined David Wang's effects with care. The only medication he had found was an unopened bottle of Excedrin.

CHAPTER 7

GRASS, LIKE NEARLY EVERYTHING else in China, is subject to political interpretation. Historically, the Chinese have taken a dim view of grass. In Peking's parks, the dirt is swept daily since cleanliness is prized, but gardeners relentlessly uproot any tuft of grass. Grass breeds disease, generations of Chinese have been taught. Additionally, Communist doctrine teaches that grass is decadent since it is usually associated with leisured classes and generates exploitation—one man hiring another to cut it.

In the pragmatic years, though, when the town fathers of Peking were allowed to gaze at their city without ideological blinders, they recoiled at what they saw. Peking, capital and presumed showcase of the most populous nation on earth, was a mess—overcrowded, disorganized, dreadfully polluted.

An emerging generation of Chinese environmentalists has sought to repair the wreckage by planting trees and, yes, grass. But history does not die without a fight. So it is that on some weeks students at Chinese elementary schools can hear a lecture one day from an earnest ecologist on the virtues of grass and another from a functionary of public health on the merits of its destruction.

Tom Stratton, amused by the ongoing struggle between tradition and modernization, had early on spotted a fresh plot of grass on the shoulder of a new highway overpass near his hotel.

It was on this hard-won and possibly temporary bit of green that he sat cross-legged in the heat of a summer's afternoon to read David Wang's journal.

AUGUST 10.
Peking overwhelms me, and it is only my second day. Walking the streets, I realized how cluttered and musty my

memories have become. As a child, I visited this city a dozen times, and for all these years, I have carried visions of its history and art, visions of brilliant colors and vibrant people.

Yet that is not what I have found so far. What has struck me, instead, has been the crush of masses of people—all seemingly in a hurry and all almost faceless amid the brownness of the city. Each block seems to have at least one noisy factory. Brick chimneys spew so much filthy smoke that hundreds of Chinese customarily wear surgical masks, called koujiao, to protect their throats and lungs from infection. For a city with so few automobiles and trucks, I have never seen, or breathed, such foul air.

I suppose that this is one of the prices that the government has chosen to pay for industrialization, and I must admit that I have seen several great technological accomplishments. This morning, for example, I made a trip to the Grand Canal, which stretches eleven hundred miles to Hangchow. It is the longest man-made waterway in the world and many Chinese believe that it is more of a masterpiece than even the Great Wall.

During my childhood, however, the Grand Canal never was fully utilized because it had become blocked with silt and impossible to navigate at many key ports. My father told me it had been that way all during his life; my grandfather, too, could not remember the Grand Canal in its prime.

Yet, I learned, under the Communists the canal has been redredged during the last twenty years and is now thriving from Peking to its terminus. The economic benefits of this must be incalculable for cargo transport, as well as agriculture. Yet I fear that the human costs of the intense restoration program also were incalculable; in that area, my guide provided no information.

Tomorrow, I meet my niece for the first time. Of course I am nervous, but I am also nervous about seeing my brother again. With so much on my mind, it has been difficult to absorb and appreciate the changes in this ancient place.

AUGUST 11.
The most disturbing thing just happened. When I returned to my room, I discovered that someone had searched my belongings. Nothing was missing, but several things are out of order. My passport, which I had left under a pile of undershirts, had obviously been examined and replaced. I found it in

another drawer. I complained to the room attendant, but he seemed uninterested. In all, it has been a stressful day.

This morning, at the former Democracy Wall, I struck up a conversation with a young man whose father had once been prominent in the Communist Party. Perhaps because the man could see by my clothing that I was an overseas Chinese, a huh chiao, *he spoke with surprising candor.*

He told me that his father had once enjoyed a promising career, that he had risen in the bureaucracy from a street cadre to being a Party officer of some standing. One night, while dining with several comrades at a restaurant here in Peking, the Party man recited a poem that he had written to celebrate the Cultural Revolution. It was an amateurish but lively verse that extolled Mao and glorified the progress of the Party. The last lines of his father's poem, the young man told me, said:

*And in the radiant future, all China's children
Will sing in freedom and dance in universal happiness.*

Several weeks passed, the young man recounted, and then his father was suddenly arrested by the army. He was stripped of his Party membership and charged with counterrevolutionary behavior. At his trial, the prosecutors charged that the man's poetry encouraged laziness and immorality. Why? Because good, strong Party workers would never have the time, or desire, for song and dance. Such frivolous things, the prosecutors said, belong only in the theater.

The man, whose name was Cheng Hua, was never given a chance to speak in his own defense. He was not even permitted to introduce the complete poem into evidence to demonstrate his loyalty and love for the government.

Cheng was sentenced to eight years in a prison camp. His son told me he is not allowed any visitors, but letters are delivered once every two months. One of his father's closest friends is the man who turned him in, the young man told me. This story made me profoundly depressed.

At lunchtime I met my niece, Kangmei. She is a beautiful girl of twenty-three, slender, with a luminous smile and a very quick mind. Unlike most Chinese women, she likes jeans and silky shirts—from Hong Kong, she told me. She was fascinated by my descriptions of the United States, so much so that I could scarcely get her to tell me anything about life in China. Of her father—my brother—she said little. "He is a man of power and achievement," Kangmei said—but, of course, this I already know.

She described her studies at the Foreign Languages Institute and impressed me with her flawless English. In a few months, she will graduate and assume a prestigious job as a government translator. Kangmei said she is looking forward greatly to the travel opportunities, and to meeting more European and American visitors.

Finally, near the end of our lunch, I asked my niece about the young man whom I had met at Democracy Wall. I told her his sad story.

"Such events were not uncommon," she remarked. "The boy's father was very unwise to reveal his poem, even to friends. Within the Party, many cadres rise and prosper by informing on fellow workers. Everyone should be cautious."

"But it seems so wrong," I replied.

"Your outlook is different," Kangmei said. "We who live here understand. There is freedom only for the old men who exploit the Chinese people."

As we talked more, I learned that my niece is a woman of firm opinions. She possesses a keen, questioning intellect—and I am heartened by it. We promised to meet again after I had seen Wang Bin.

AUGUST 12.

Today I walked down the Avenue of Eternal Tranquility, toward the western wall of the Forbidden City. I had a notion to visit the palaces, but first I stopped to buy a knitted hat from a vendor named Hong.

I noticed that one of his legs had been removed at the hip. Because of his youthfulness—he appeared about thrity—such a handicap seemed unusual. I asked him if he had been in a bicycle accident, which is common in the city.

Hong smiled and said no, he had lost the leg as a teenager. The year was 1966. His father was a prominent scientist. One of his colleagues, a Party member, was very jealous. He accused Hong's father of secretly passing scientific papers to pro-Western publications in Taiwan.

The Red Guards came to the scientist's apartment. Hong, who was seventeen and full of fire, took a punch at one of the intruders. The youth was quickly knocked to the floor, and beaten so badly with the butt of a rifle that his leg bones were shattered. His father was put in detention for eighteen months, and was freed only after his accuser was arrested—for lying about the loyalty of another fellow worker.

Hong told me that he bears no ill will toward the Red Guards. I find that difficult to believe.

Later this afternoon, I had a marvelous surprise by the lake at the Summer Palace. I ran into an old friend, Thomas Stratton. He once was a student of mine at St. Edward's, and now teaches art history at a college in New England. Tom is visiting China with a group of art historians and he is understandably eager to break away from the entourage as soon as possible.

I promised him a personal tour of Peking, as soon as I return from Xian. There's some wonderful Qing hung porcelain on display in a state gallery near the Heping. I think we'll stop there first.

Tomorrow is the biggest day of my trip. In the morning, I fly to Xian where I am to meet my brother at eleven sharp. After lunch, we will tour the archaeological site of the tomb of the Emperor Qin.

I'm thrilled about visiting this historical dig, but I'm even more excited about seeing Wang Bin again. He is only a year younger, but history and political fortunes have cast us centuries apart. Even without knowing him, I fear that we will be the inverse of each other. Perhaps not. Perhaps the journey backward to our Chinese childhood is not so great. It is easy to remember little Bin's face as a boy. But it has been fifty years since we were together in my father's home. And, in that time, I have not seen so much as a photograph. His invitation was so unexpected that I didn't know how to respond.

I think it will be a powerful reunion.

Tom Stratton closed his friend's journal and walked thoughtfully back to his hotel.

The words faithfully belonged to David, and reading them freshened Stratton's grief. It was so typical of his old friend, he thought, to be moved more by the people of Peking than its art or scenery. David Wang had not returned for the temples and tombs of China, but for the people like Cheng and Hong. Each day had brought new faces, new chances to learn: What is it really like? What have I missed? Should I have come back sooner?

But David Wang was a circumspect man; not all of what he saw and heard would be recorded in his notebook—of this Stratton was sure. The professor had probably altered the names of the Chinese to protect them from reprisals. He had also carefully refrained from political commentary that could backfire against his brother, the deputy minister.

But the journal ended too abruptly.

It contained no mention of David Wang's trip to Xian, or of his reunion with his brother. Stratton was baffled, for the professor unfailingly wrote in the notebook each night before going to bed. Why—full of such emotion, and dazzled by exotic sights—would David have forsaken this habit while on this most important trip?

Opening the journal again in his room, Stratton flipped to the last written pages. Something caught his eye. He retrieved a metal fingernail file from his luggage and slipped it between the pages, pressing toward the spine of the notebook. The binding easily gave way, and the pages separated in loose stacks.

Stratton ran a finger across the inside borders of the paper. It felt sticky. He held one page to his nose. The glue was pungent, and new. Someone had pried Wang's journal apart, and then glued it back together so it would appear undisturbed. No ragged stubs revealed where the missing pages had been.

It was a professional job, Tom Stratton thought. Almost perfect.

"Every time I see you, you're riding solo," Jim McCarthy said with a cannon laugh. "Your tour group really must be wall-to-wall losers, huh?"

Stratton accepted McCarthy's offer of a bottle of Peking-brewed Coca-Cola.

"Almost like home," the newsman said. "Now where did you want me to take you?"

Stratton said, "The Foreign Languages Institute."

"And what," McCarthy said, "do you plan to do there? Stare at the walls? Pose for pictures with a few soldiers outside the gate? It's a restricted area, baby. No Yanks allowed. It's definitely not on the tour, yours or anybody else's."

Stratton told McCarthy about David Wang.

"Death by duck, right? That's what Powell said, I bet."

"Yes," Stratton replied. "How did you know?"

"Because the bastard ripped the lead off one of my stories to steal that phrase. Fucking cretins at State, no imagination. Suppose I should be flattered."

"So there really is such a thing?"

"Sure." McCarthy pried open the Coke on a desk drawer handle and guzzled half. "Just your basic tourist burnout, really. The Peking roast duck dinner gives it a nice twist, though. I wrote the story two years ago and the stats have held up. Quite a few elderly Americans die every year in the great China adventure, but it's not a trend that gets much publicity. I remember one old geezer who arrived lugging a heavy suitcase and went home inside it."

"Huh?"

"His wife had him cremated and continued the tour—said he would have wanted it that way."

Stratton blanched.

"Hey, Stratton, I don't mean to sound like a total prick about it. I'm sorry about your friend, really I am. But what's it got to do with the Foreign Languages school?"

"David's niece is a student there."

McCathy whistled. "It's a tough school to get into."

"Her father is Wang Bin, a deputy minister. David's younger brother."

"Right, I remember now."

"The girl saw David shortly before he left for Xian to meet Bin. I want to talk to her, just to make sure everything was all right." Stratton decided not to mention the journal or the passport.

McCarthy said, "I'm not exactly a low-profile character in this town. More like the Jolly Red Giant. With me at your side, you don't stand a fucking prayer of getting in.

"But I tell you what. Go with my driver. He'll take you to the gate and haggle on your behalf. He speaks some English and he's worked miracles for me, but don't get your hopes up. You might have to settle for leaving a note—and then it could be another four weeks before you get an answer. I'm not kidding. Watching this government in action is like watching a bad ballet performed in molasses."

* * *

Stratton sat in the backseat trying to look important while McCarthy's driver argued with a guard at the Foreign Languages Institute. After several minutes, the driver, Xiu, shuffled to the car with a furrowed brow.

"It is not possible, Mr. Stratton."

"Why not?"

"He says it is a study hour. The students are in their dormitories and cannot be disturbed."

Stratton sighed. "Tell him I am a friend of the family. I have come to offer my condolences at the death of her uncle. I will be most insulted if I am not permitted just a few minutes."

Xiu nodded somberly and tracked once more toward the gatehouse. He came back smiling. "A few minutes, Mr. Stratton. Can you wait?"

Soon, a young woman appeared. The guard motioned toward the car and spoke rapidly. Then he waved stiffly at Stratton.

David Wang had not embellished his journal; his niece, Kangmei, was indeed a beautiful woman. Her jet-black hair, daringly long by Peking standards, fell past her shoulders. Her eyes were bright, and her features were elegant, almost regal.

"I was a good friend of your uncle," he began.

"Yes. Stratton," she said. Her eyes worked on him.

"David was a good man, a great scholar," Stratton said. "I felt I needed to—"

The guard shifted his feet and peered up into Stratton's face.

"You wish to talk?" Kangmei asked.

"If it's possible."

"It is."

"At my hotel?"

"Not a good choice, Mr. Stratton." Her English was excellent and self-assured. "Meet me in an hour at the Tiananmen Gate. Don't tell anyone. Have the driver take you back to the hotel, then walk."

Stratton eyed the guard anxiously.

Kangmei almost smiled. "Don't worry, they don't speak a word of English." Then she was off, her hair bouncing lightly. It was a Western walk. A wonderful walk.

Stratton was ten minutes early. Kangmei arrived precisely on time, the trait of a good Chinese. She parked her bicycle in a guarded sidewalk lot and locked it.

"Just like Boston," Stratton said.

"Excuse me?"

"Thieves, I mean."

Kangmei shrugged. "Bicycles are expensive. Come with me, Mr. Stratton. We are going on a tour of the Forbidden City."

"But I had hoped to talk—"

Again her eyes stopped him. "Please," she said, "we will talk."

At an imperial red kiosk, Stratton paid for his ticket with ten fen. Kangmei spoke to the cashier in Chinese and was allowed to enter without paying.

"I told her I'm your guide," she explained, escorting Stratton through the broad entrance tunnel. "I saw my Uncle David two days before he left for Xian. We had a very nice talk. He was very thoughtful."

"He mentioned you in his journal," Stratton said as they walked. "He was very impressed."

"Oh." She paused as a crowd of Chinese tourists passed them, chattering. When it was quiet, she asked, "Was he important in the United States?"

"Yes, in his field. And popular. He had many friends."

They approached a group of Americans, Kodaks clicking. They were led by a Chinese guide with her hair pulled back in a prim bun.

Kangmei said, in a louder voice, "This is the Meridian Gate, the entrance to the grounds of the Inner Palaces. It is the biggest gate in all the Forbidden City, built in the year 1420 and restored again in the fifteenth and seventeenth centuries. Every year, the reigning emperor would ascend to the top of this structure and announce a new calendar for the people of China . . ."

Stratton applauded. Kangmei blushed. "Please don't make fun," she whispered. "You must behave like a tourist and I like a guide. For me to be with you under any circumstances would be very serious."

The competing tour group moved away. Kangmei walked Stratton across a paved courtyard to a marble bridge over a clear, slow-moving stream.

"The *Ji Shui He*," she trilled.

"Did you and your uncle talk about politics?" Stratton asked.

"A little. He seemed to understand that China cannot be analyzed in a week, or understood. I don't think that's why he came, Mr. Stratton. Some of his questions could never be answered. They are not relevant anymore. Not to my generation." A family of alabaster ducks splashed noisily in the stream.

"They were good questions, just the same," Stratton said.

"Yes," Kangmei said softly. "Very good. It was odd, seeing my uncle. He looked very much like my father; there is an alertness about both of them. Uncle David was more direct, of course. My father cannot afford to be so candid. Not with all the rumors of a new political campaign. We live with that concern, and it makes people like my father more cunning than David. No one can be sure what the future holds, so we must constantly be watchful. This, Mr. Stratton, is the Hall of Supreme Harmony."

A group of Chinese schoolchildren swarmed around them. A plump teacher in a blue Mao tunic recited a history lesson and the children listened attentively.

"The statues on the terrace are made of bronze," Kangmei said in her drone-guide voice.. "On one side are storks and, on the other, giant tortoises. A sundial on the eastern side of the terrace represents righteousness and truth; on the west side is a grain measure, which symbolizes justice . . ."

"Did you memorize all this stuff?" Stratton said under his breath.

"We learn English at the Institute," Kangmei explained when the school tour was gone. "Those who perform well may someday become translators. The very best will receive diplomatic assignments. And travel." She ran a girlish hand through her hair, and Stratton noticed for the first time the glint of red nail polish, expertly applied. "So the answer is yes, I memorized this 'stuff,'" she said acidly.

They climbed the stairs and entered the hall. The columns were extravagantly carved with gilded dragons. In the middle stood the emperor's throne, surrounded by incense burners.

"How did David feel about seeing your father?" Stratton asked.

"The first time we spoke, he was very excited."

Stratton took her elbow. "The first time? You saw David more than once?"

"Yes," Kangmei replied. "Once before Xian, and the night of his return."

"The night of his heart attack?"

"The night he died, yes," she said.

"And how did he seem?" Stratton pressed.

"Upset. I guess the reunion was a disappointment. He and my father argued. There were bitter words. The tour of Xian was cut short by a day and the two of them returned to Peking."

"What did they argue about?"

"I'm not certain." They were alone in the Hall. It was too dark for pictures so the Americans had moved on, a fidgeting, pink-faced horde.

Kangmei said, "Do you listen to music at home?"

"A little," Stratton answered, off balance again.

"The Rolling Stones. Do you listen to the Rolling Stones? A friend of mine, another student at the Languages Institute, got an album smuggled to her from Hong Kong. It's a Rolling Stone album; during *xiu-xi*, our daily nap breaks, we sometimes sneak down to the music room and play it on the phonograph. The name of the album is '*Goat's Head Soup.*' Does that have special meaning in America?"

Stratton laughed. "No, not at all. Do you like the music?"

"Very much. It's good dancing music. My friend and I dance together when we play the record. We have to be careful, though. We could be expelled over something like that." Kangmei's voice dropped. "I would love to have some records."

They walked down marble steps and faced another pavilion. "As an art expert, you will appreciate the exhibit in this hall," Kangmei said. "Bronze chariots and their warriors, taken from the Han tombs."

"No, thank you," Stratton said. "It's time for me to go."

They retraced their steps toward Tiananmen. Kangmei kept her eyes on the pavement.

"Mr. Stratton, David and my father argued about the artifacts at Xian," she said. "David did not go into detail. But he said that my father was doing something wrong. Immoral was the word my uncle used. He was horrified his brother would attempt such a thing."

"He told you this—"

"After dinner last Tuesday night. He had left a message for

me at the dormitory. I rode to the hotel after my father and his group had left. I met Uncle David in the lobby."

"He seemed in good health?" Stratton asked.

"Fine. Just angry. As we walked down Changan Avenue, he stopped to curse at the cadres who were following us. My father's little watchdogs. Uncle David walked right up to them and called them something nasty in Chinese," she said, blushing. "I admired his courage. The cadres said nothing. They just disappeared into the crowd."

"Some pages were missing from David's journal. And his passport is gone," Stratton said.

"Oh," Kangmei said.

"Something's wrong with all this. Do you believe your uncle died of a heart attack?"

"I have not thought about the how, Mr. Stratton. His life is over, and I'm sad. I wish I had known him better and longer. I'm very sorry that he and my father quarreled."

After they left the steps of the Forbidden City, Kangmei walked briskly to the lot where her bicycle was parked.

"Thank you for meeting me," Stratton said.

Kangmei nodded as she lithely swung onto the bike. "I'm glad that you are going with Uncle David's body. It's a long trip back to America and it is only right that he should be with someone who cares."

I cannot bury my friend so easily, Stratton thought, and not under a cloud of riddles.

"I'm sorry, Kangmei, but I won't be going after all," he said. "My tour group leaves for Xian tomorrow, and I've decided to join them."

Her expression never changed. It didn't have to.

"Tourists always take the early train," she said, and rode away.

CHAPTER 8

STEVE POWELL OFFERED HOT TEA all around. Linda Greer shook her head politely. The station chief said yes to a small cup. The Marine who served them closed the door carefully as he left.

"What do you make of it?" Powell said.

Linda scanned the note once more, then passed it across the table to the station chief. It was the handwriting of a man who was trying hard to be neat, but obviously would have been more comfortable with an academic's scribble:

> *"Dear Mr. Powell,*
>
> *"Please inform Deputy Minister Wang Bin that I have changed my plans and, therefore, will not be able to accompany David's body back to the United States. I regret the inconvenience this might cause, but such a journey would be too emotional for me at this time. When I return to the United States, I will pay the proper respects to my dear friend at his gravesite in Ohio. In the meantime, I've decided to join my tour group on the trip to Xian this morning. David Wang would understand and I would hope his brother does, too.*
>
> > *"Sincerely,*
> > *Thomas Stratton."*

The station chief tossed the note on the table and shrugged. "Linda?"

"He's bummed out. Just doesn't want to make the long flight with his buddy's corpse," she said. "Can you blame him?"

"That's the way I read it, too," Powell said. His tone suggested that the meeting should be over. The station chief didn't budge.

"Shit, if it's such a big deal, we can send a Marine back with the body, can't we?" Powell asked.

"Finding an escort is not the problem," the station chief said impatiently. "The problem is Stratton. He's not the kind of guy we want running all over China without a tether. He'll get in trouble. He'll get *us* in trouble."

"He'll be all right," Linda said. She glanced at Powell, who was obviously in some distress.

"I can call him now," the consul offered. "Lay on the guilt. Tell him it will be an international insult if he doesn't go home with the professor's body. He'll understand. He knows the system; I saw his file. He used to be a pro."

"He used to be a killer," the station chief muttered. "Now I wish you hadn't hit on him about Wang Bin."

"It was your goddamn idea," Linda Greer snapped. "I told you he wouldn't go for it. All it did was get his antennae up."

The station chief, a gray-skinned man with baggy eyes and thin dark hair, nodded tiredly. "It was a risk," he conceded. "And I take the responsibility."

Powell was getting frantic. "I don't understand."

"It's not important now," the station chief said. "What is important is that Wang Bin is going to be pissed off at a time when we don't want him pissed. He's going to suggest that Mr. Stratton has offended the People's Republic and is not so welcome here anymore. He's going to want to know more about Mr. Stratton and we cannot afford to let him find out *anything*. Is that clear, Powell?"

"Man-ling was a long time ago," the consul remarked.

"To the Chinese, it might as well have happened last night," the station chief said sharply. He leaned back, waiting for another remark from the consul.

"Steven, it's a matter of lousy timing, that's all," Linda Greer intervened. "Stratton could have helped us with Wang Bin, but he didn't want to. Now he's headed off to the countryside, upset about his friend's death, suspicious when there's no reason to be—"

"It was a goddamn heart attack!" Powell said in exasperation. "I told him, death by duck."

"I know," Linda said.

The station chief stood up. "Powell, see if you can smooth Wang Bin's feathers. Apologize on behalf of the embassy. Tell him Stratton meant no offense. Offer a fucking dress guard of

Marine escorts if you have to. And remember, we want the old guy to *like* us. Just in case.

"Linda, you think your dinner friend will really stick with that tour group?"

"I think so," she answered coldly, trying not to blush. The Company kept track of everything, didn't it?

"Any other reason he'd go to Xian?" the station chief asked.

"History," Linda Greer replied. "That's all."

The Americans piled their luggage on the steps of the Minzu Hotel. Stratton offered polite good-mornings to Alice Dempsey, Walter Thomas, and the other art historians who milled and paced and tested their cameras on passing Chinese. Naturally the gaggle of brightly dressed foreigners attracted a crowd outside the hotel, and Stratton was mildly embarrassed. He melted back into the lobby to wait for the bus.

"Are you coming to Xian?" It was Miss Sun, the pert, ceaselessly cheerful tour guide.

"Yes, I'm looking forward to it," Stratton replied.

"Yesterday you missed beautiful White Pagoda," Miss Sun said. It was not a reprimand, but there was concern in her voice.

"I'm sorry," Stratton said. "I had a personal matter."

Miss Sun seemed embarrassed. "I did not mean to intrude in your business, Professor Stratton."

"It's quite all right. Your English is coming along very well, Miss Sun. You've been practicing," he said warmly.

The tour guide smiled gratefully.

"Tom's going to be a good boy, aren't you, Professor?" Alice Dempsey had a way of inserting herself into conversations that made Stratton want to punch her. "I promised Miss Sun I'd keep an eye on you at Xian, Tom. If you'd read the tour book, you'd know about the travel restrictions outside of Peking. Can't just go roaming the hills, digging for pottery and chatting with the townsfolk. You'll get us all in hot water."

Stratton scowled. "Don't worry, Alice."

"Mr. Stratton?" A thin man with thick glasses and a fresh-bought Mao cap called out across the lobby. It was a man Stratton knew only as Weatherby, an art history teacher from a small college in San Francisco. Weatherby was delicate, anemic-looking; he approached in tiny, diffident steps.

"Tom Stratton?"

"Yes."

"There are two men out front who say they've come to pick you up," Weatherby reported.

"Here we go again," Alice Dempsey muttered.

"I do not understand," Miss Sun said, her voice rising.

"Me neither," Stratton said. "There must be a mistake."

"They've got a car," Weatherby said dramatically.

Stratton walked out of the lobby and down the steps. A jet-black Red Flag limousine was parked in front of the hotel. Two cadres in starched blue uniforms stood near the front bumper, talking in whispers. At the sight of Stratton, they turned and bowed slightly, from the neck, in unison. When the cadres looked up, they wore official smiles.

"Where is your luggage, Professor?"

"On its way to Xian."

"Oh. Very bad." The taller of the two wore thick eyeglasses set in heavy black frames. His teeth were crooked and yellow.

The other cadre, a plump young man with fat rubbery lips, said, "Mr. Stratton, we came to take you to airport."

"But I'm going to Xian by train. With my group."

The cadres conferred, brisk Mandarin whispers.

"We take you to airport," repeated Crooked Teeth, unsmiling. "Plane leaves for America."

In Chinese, Miss Sun asked, "Where are you?"—the equivalent of an American, "Who do you work for?"

"Ministry of Culture," Fat Lips replied curtly, and then again in English for Tom Stratton's benefit. "Deputy Minister Wang Bin sent us." And then more, to the tour guide, in Mandarin.

"He says you are scheduled to fly back to America with the body of your friend," Miss Sun said to Stratton. "I very sorry, Professor. I did not know of this tragedy. I did not know that the deputy minister had made this request of you."

"Miss Sun—" Stratton began.

"Comrade says your plane leaves soon," she said. "I'll get your suitcase from the bus—"

"No!" Stratton said. "Miss Sun, please tell the comrades that I sent a message to Deputy Minister Wang this morning, informing him of my change in plans. The U.S. Embassy was notified at the same time. Everything is fine. I don't wish to leave China today. I wish to stay with the group."

Miss Sun translated. Fat Lips frowned and traded glances with his partner. They replied breathlessly, together: "This is a most urgent matter. The deputy minister is anxious. Mr. Stratton is expected at the airport soon; we know nothing of any messages to the embassy. Our task is to take the professor to the plane. There is no other choice."

Miss Sun understood. "*Wei*," she said neutrally, and walked away.

Stratton saw that the other Americans were filing into the Toyota bus for the ride to the train station. From a window seat in the first row, Alice Dempsey glowered out at him.

"We take you to airport," Crooked Teeth announced with cheerfulness. "Come now."

"No," Tom Stratton insisted. The cadres were well trained in the Chinese art of stubbornness. The next stratagem, he knew, would be guilt. Americans were suckers when it came to guilt.

"We must go," Fat Lips said worriedly. "It would be bad not to go, Professor."

"Arrangements are ready for you," the other cadre added. "The deputy minister—"

"It's impossible, comrades. Thanks just the same, but my bus is about to leave." Stratton turned away and hurried along the sidewalk. The green minibus was idling. The driver tapped on the horn three times.

"Coming!" Stratton shouted, breaking into a trot.

Then he felt an arm on his sleeve. Angrily, he whirled to face Crooked Teeth. The other cadre jogged a few steps behind, puffing.

"Come now," Crooked Teeth said. This time is was a command, and there was nothing polite about it.

"What is this?" Stratton demanded.

Inside the tour bus, the Americans watched the confrontation with shock. Stratton towered over the cadres, shouting down into their impassive faces.

"Fuck off!" is what he said.

"My God," sighed Alice Dempsey.

"He's nothing but a troublemaker," mumbled Walter Thomas. "He's going to spoil this for all of us."

"He's a little upset, that's all," Weatherby said. "He's just upset about his friend."

The other Americans craned for a glimpse of their colleague haggling with the government cadres. Miss Sun quickly moved to the front of the bus and whispered to the driver: "Go now."

As the tour departed for the railway station, Alice Dempsey

saw Stratton being guided down the sidewalk toward the limousine, a resolute Chinese at each elbow.

"I missed the fucking bus," Stratton was growling. "Get your hands off me, comrades."

"All is arranged," Crooked Teeth said as they walked.

Stratton sneaked a backward glance over his right shoulder as the minibus turned down Dongdan Street and disappeared. Fat Lips slipped away from Stratton's side long enough to open the door to the cavernous Red Flag.

"Okay," said Fat Lips, with a shove.

"No okay," said Stratton, uncorking a nasty left jab that snapped flush in the cadre's face. Fat Lips fell backward like a domino. His head cracked on the rear fender.

Instantly, Stratton stumbled forward, gasping. His right side cramped from a kidney punch; he caught himself with both hands on the Red Flag and spun around. Crooked Teeth coiled in a crouch, snarling. His cap was on the pavement. Other Chinese pressed in a growing circle, yammering excitedly. The fight did not last long.

Crooked Teeth feinted a punch, then spun forward on one leg, aiming a powerful kick at Stratton's neck. It was a prosaic maneuver, and Stratton deflected it from memory. Deftly, he seized the cadre's ankle in midair, and seemed to hold him there—flustered and grunting—before delivering a decisive punch to the poor man's testicles. Crooked Teeth fell in a blue heap, bug-eyed, semiconscious.

Instinct warned Stratton to run, but he could hardly move. The bystanders formed a wall—hundreds of them, packed shoulder to shoulder in front of the hotel. Soon the police would arrive.

Sideways, Stratton edged through the heaving crowd with deliberate slowness. Stratton resolved to keep calm, to stop the fear from reaching his eyes, where people could see it. Obviously, the Chinese in the street were confused; some hastily moved out of the tall American's path, while others stood firm, scolding. The worst thing would be to run, Stratton knew, so he held himself to a purposeful walk; a man with someplace to go.

After three blocks, Stratton appropriated an unlocked bicycle and aimed himself on a wobbly course toward Tienanmen Square. He had no map and very little time. The Square was the heart of Peking, a central magnet, lousy with tourists.

Somebody there surely would be able to tell him the quickest way to the trains.

Inexorably, Stratton was drawn into a broad, slow-moving stream of bicycles. He had hoped that the clanging blue mass would swallow him and offer concealment—but his stature and blond hair betrayed him. Among the Chinese he shone like a beacon.

From somewhere a car honked, and the cycling throng parted grudgingly. Stratton dutifully guided the bike to the right side of the blacktop road. He heard the automobile approach and he slowed, expecting it to pass. Instead it lingered, coasting behind the two-wheeled caravan.

Puzzled, Stratton turned to look. It was the Red Flag limousine, so close he could feel the ripple of heat from its engine. Crooked Teeth was at the wheel, fingers taut on the rim; his battered eyeglasses were propped comically on his nose. He looked like Jerry Lewis.

Next to him sat Fat Lips, gingerly daubing a scarf to a gash on his forehead. Neither of the cadres showed any anger, only eyes hardened in determination.

Stratton pedaled like a madman. He weaved and darted from street to sidewalk, stiff-arming cyclists who dawdled and elbowing himself a narrow, navigable track through the horde. The tin bells on a hundred sets of handlebars chriped furiously in protest as Stratton plowed through a lush pile of fresh cabbages. In a racer's crouch, he doubled his speed, his chin to the bar. He gained precious yardage while the Red Flag braked and swerved, dodging Chinese pedestrians who had raced into the street to retrieve mangled vegetables.

Finally, Stratton broke free of the mob and barreled into the cobbled vastness of Tienanmen Square. Behind him the limousine came to a jerky stop on the perimeter road. The cadres got out and stood together, smaller and smaller as Stratton pedaled on.

Then came small voices. Dozens of them crying, "*Buzhen*! *Buzhen*!" Stop. And then Stratton remembered: Bicycling is strictly forbidden inside the great square. Quickly he dismounted. He found himself in a sea of schoolchildren, dressed in blue and white uniforms with brilliant red scarves. They walked in formation, bright-eyed, singing, toward Mao's tomb, stealing secret glances at the tall foreigner with the Chinese bicycle. The youngsters had stopped shouting the moment Stratton dismounted. He smiled apologetically and set a course for the ornate main gate at the far end of the square. Looking back, he no longer could see the limousine. Perhaps his escorts finally had given up.

"You, mister!" A young Chinese waved at Stratton. A plastic badge identified him as a guide from the China International Travel Service.

"Please no ride bicycle in the. Square," he said firmly.

"I'm very sorry," Stratton said. "I am late for a train. Can you tell me which way to the railway station?"

The young guide pointed east. "Left at the Tienanmen. About five blocks."

"Thank you."

"Where is your suitcase?" the guide asked.

"At the train. I overslept," Stratton said.

The guide eyed him curiously. "You need a ticket to enter the station."

"It's in my luggage." Stratton waved, moving off. "Thanks again."

"Is that your bicycle?" the guide called.

Stratton waved again and kept walking. His eyes fanned the crowds for a sign of the two cadres. The square was immense. Still, Stratton knew, he could hardly be invisible.

In the center of Tienanmen, at the Monument to the People's Heroes, a class of teenaged boys listened to a political speech. Someone had placed a wreath of red and gold paper flowers at the base of the statue. The speaker paused briefly while Stratton passed, then resumed an ardent, high-pitched denunciation.

Finally, Stratton reached the tree-lined avenue bordering the end of Tienanmen. It had taken twenty minutes to cross the great square. He mounted the bicycle, praying that the train would be late in departing.

Pedaling quietly, he was absorbed quickly into the flow of traffic. The bright sun gave life to the brown buildings, and the trees shimmered green. Stratton's heart beat cold when the big car roared up behind him. He was incredulous; the resourceful cadres wore their familiar expressions.

Recklessly, Stratton broke from the pack and veered south down a side street. With the limousine close behind, he raced through the Old Legation Quarter, gracious Colonial-styled embassies long since converted to warehouses, clinics, banks —buildings to serve the workers. And, between them, drab and monotonous apartment buildings, sterile and new, lifeless in the shadow of the Forbidden City.

He tucked the bike down an alley so narrow that his knuckles scraped against the flaking walls. The cadres merely circled the block and waited at the other end. Crooked Teeth tried to position the limousine to block Stratton's path, but the American managed to skitter by, jumping a curb so violently that the basket snapped off the bicycle and clattered to the pavement.

"Stop!" Fat Lips cried in English.

But Stratton heard a train. He was back in the safety of traffic. Ahead, a busload of tourists turned south. Stratton followed. The railway station was but two blocks away. Another whistle blew.

This time it was the cadres who found a propitious side street. The railway-bound minibus passed, with Stratton not far behind. Crooked Teeth punched the accelerator.

By the time Stratton spotted the long black car, it was too late. The Red Flag clipped the bicycle's rear tire. Stratton spun clockwise. He hit the pavement to the sound of glass tinkling around him. A headlight. Through half-open eyes he watched the twisted bicycle skid away, kicking up sparks as it bounced.

Stratton forced himself to his feet. He had landed brutally hard on his right shoulder. The sleeve was in shreds, and his arm was bloody. His left hand felt for broken bones.

"Now!" said a triumphant voice behind him. "Time for airport."

Stratton lurched into a run.

"No, no!" Fat Lips scuttled back to the limousine. "Stop!" he yelled as Crooked Teeth started the car.

And Stratton did stop—when he got to the bicycle. The chain had been torn from the sprockets and hung from the hub of the rear wheel. He picked it up.

The limousine pursued with a needless screech of the tires. Stratton stood motionless, his arms at his side. This time the cadres showed no sign of slowing down.

Stratton's left arm shot up and windmilled above his head. The steel bicycle chain hit the Red Flag like a shot, and pebbled the glass in the cadres' faces. The car weaved erratically through the cyclists, hopped the curb and parked itself violently around the trunk of a Chinese elm. The radiator spit a hot geyser into the branches.

Stratton trudged the last leg to the train station in a stinging fog.

"You're darn lucky the train's late. What happened to your arm? What was all that fuss back at the hotel?"

"Nice to see you, Alice," Stratton muttered.

The group was gathered fitfully outside the entrance. There had been the usual delays. Miss Sun had gone inside to make the necessary inquiries. The Americans were outnumbered by large groups of Chinese travelers who waited patiently with cardboard suitcases. A crate of two hundred live chickens perfumed the air.

It was Weatherby who came up with a first-aid kit. Stratton was grateful for the disinfectant and bandages.

"What happened?" Alice repeated.

"I had a little bike accident."

"You're lucky it's just a scrape," Weatherby said.

"You don't know the half of it," said Stratton.

Miss Sun bounced down the steps. "Okay, we go now," she said brightly.

Then she saw Stratton. "But you went to the airport."

"No. I straightened everything out."

"You come to Xian?"

"Yes," Stratton replied. He knew it wasn't what little Miss Sun had wanted to hear. She had pegged him as a troublemaker back at the hotel. "You have my ticket?"

"Yes, Professor," she said, scanning the promenade for some sign of the diligent cadres.

"Then let's go," Stratton said.

Miss Sun led the way. Once inside the railway station, the art historians filed up a long escalator toward the trains. Stratton made it a point to be first.

The train to Xian was half full. As the Americans walked along the platform toward the soft-class cars, Stratton glanced up at the faces of the Chinese who were already aboard.

An old man with an elegant gray beard, squinting at the tourists. A plump matron with a baby on her shoulder and a toddler in her lap. A dour soldier.

And a stunning young woman with long black hair, tapping gently on the dingy window. Stratton smiled.

Kangmei.

From his private office in the national museum, Deputy Minister Wang Bin could gaze at the Forbidden City, a grand horizon, serrated by the gold-tiled rooftops of a dozen ancient temples.

His thoughts were sour. History taunted him. The architecture was inspired, ripe with passion. The city was full of such masterpieces.

But where did they come from? The ages, Wang Bin reflected sadly. The dynasties. Where could one find such imagination now? And, worse, how could it flourish?

The thin man in the stuffed chair waited until the deputy minister turned from the window. "I'm deeply sorry we were not successful," he said in Chinese. "The cadres were clumsy, and their actions were dangerous. I would punish them but . . ." He clasped his hands together.

"Both dead?" Wang Bin asked.

"One, yes. The other is badly injured."

Wang Bin asked, "Did Stratton leave on the train?"

"Yes," the thin man said. With nervous hands, he lit a cigarette.

"Liao and Deng are on their way to Xian?"

"The plane leaves in an hour," the thin man reported. "Their documents are in order. No questions were raised. Officially, they are joining the inventory team at the tombs."

Wang Bin rigidly walked to the sparse desk and sat down. His voice tightened. "This is very delicate, you understand, Comrade Xi? Stratton has put us in a fragile posture. He is no ordinary tourist, I assure you."

Xi was soothing. "Deng is a trustworthy man. Have you ever known him to fail? In two days the threat will be gone, I am certain."

"I hope so," Wang Bin said, rising. "Now send in my visitor."

"The embassy has sent Miss Greer. She wants to apologize formally for Mr. Stratton's inconsiderate change of heart. They have even offered to send an American soldier back with the casket." Xi grinned. "It's ironic, isn't it?"

"A thoughtful gesture," Bin said sarcastically.

The deputy minister was halfway to the door when Xi reminded him: "Comrade, your mourning band. Don't forget."

CHAPTER 9

"ONE OF HISTORY'S MOST PATHETIC lines was uttered in this city," J. Paul Prudoe was explaining. "It occurred in 1911, as the last dynasty, the Qing, was falling. The Qing were Manchu, of course, and the majority of Han people hated them as barbarian invaders. The Manchus imposed their rule in Xian with an army of occupation that occupied its own quarter of the city. When the people rebelled against the Manchus in 1911, there was a fearful slaughter. Many Manchus died. There was an English hospital here then and a few Manchus wound up there with dreadful self-inflicted wounds.

"An English doctor asked one of the wounded soldiers—his name is not recorded, alas—why he had attempted to slit his own throat. The soldier replied: 'Because the wells were full.'"

J. Paul Prudoe, erect in a stiffly pressed safari shirt and hair-by-hair perfect Van Dyke with an artful sprinkling of gray, paused for effect. He surveyed the room. Around him, twenty-three art historians waited expectantly.

"'The wells were full.' Starting with the commanding general, an old man who realized that defense was hopeless, the Manchus had thrown themselves down the wells to avoid capture. The wells were thirty-six feet deep, and when they were full, a warrior's only honorable escape was to slit his throat. Subsequently, of course, the city is famous for the so-called Xian Incident, when the Communists caught Chiang Kai-shek in a farmhouse during the Civil War, but let him go. During the last days of that war, the giant man-made hill—the tumulus of Emperor Qin, dead for more than two thousand years—was literally an armed camp, fortified with machine guns and snipers. How the muse of history must have smiled at that."

J. Paul Prudoe was the envy of America's art historians. He

spoke with the zeal of a revivalist, the slick, contrived passion of a corrupt politician. His presence on the tour, tramping through museums and riding the buses like any ole AAH, was the celebrity magnet that had drawn so many of his nominal peers to China in the first place.

Stratton, slouched and alone at the rear of a reception room in Xian's Renmin Daxia Hotel, disliked Prudoe's showmanship as much as he despised his pop art scholarship.

"Now that I have your attention," Prudoe went on, preening, "let me talk about the Xian that really interests us, or Changan, as it was called then."

Stratton slurped his tea loudly enough to draw annoyed glances and an unspoken reprimand from Prudoe himself. Pompous ass. Stratton tuned out.

They had arrived before dawn, twenty hours from Peking. Twice Stratton had walked through the train looking for Kangmei. Twice guards had turned him back from the hard-class section of the train reserved for Chinese only.

But she found him on the platform at Xian. They had shared a few quiet minutes in a corner of the terminal as the train disgorged its passengers with billowing steam and a slumbering pace.

"I have come to help," Kangmei had said.

"But . . ."

"You want to know what happened to make my father fight with my American uncle. So do I. Alone you will never find out. I can help."

"How? How can you even be here? Don't you need a special pass?"

"Listen to me, Thom-as," she said with sober, almost childlike earnestness. "In China, many things are possible for Chinese. Not for foreigners"—she tapped him lightly on the chest—"but for Chinese."

Stratton smiled. She was proud of herself.

"China is the most wonderful land on earth, Thom-as, but it has been betrayed too many times. Everywhere there are old men who rule only because they are old, or cruel, or because they are friends of other stupid old men."

The crowd on the platform was beginning to thin. From somewhere near the terminal entrance, Stratton heard a petulant woman—it could only be Alice Dempsey—in full bay. "Now where can he have gotten himself to?"

"The old men sit on the young," Kangmei continued. "They are jealous because we have studied and they have not. They cling to power, betraying China and their own Communist ideals. These tired old men are everywhere, Thom-as. And everywhere there are also angry young people who believe in the New China. There are millions of us. We talk not to the stupid old men, not to the government, or the Party. We talk to one another. In Peking, in Shanghai, in Canton, here in Xian—everywhere. My friends and the friends of my friends. They will help me to help you."

"Stratton? Ah, there you are. Will you come on, please? Everyone is waiting. How can you be so rude?" Alice Dempsey's bray carried across half a hundred Chinese heads and echoed off the vaulted terminal roof.

Kangmei grabbed his arm.

"Go, Thom-as. In two hours, I will come to your hotel. Be ready."

With an empty smile for Alice, Stratton had docilely ridden the bus to the tourist hotel.

". . . at Ban Po, a few miles out of town, we will see a well-preserved village belonging to the Yang Shao culture from about 6000 B.C. Xian did not come into its own, though, until the third century before Christ. The famous Emperor Qin, who unified China and built the Great Wall, had his capital here. We'll visit the new digs around his tomb east of the city . . ."

It certainly was something to think about, Stratton reflected. If anybody could actually harness the energies of the educated Chinese young people . . . no, "harness" was a bad word. "Unfetter" would be better. Unfetter the young millions, let them think and act and build without the constraints of a revolution grown old before its time. Would they yank China headlong, breathless and excited, into the twenty-first century, or would they produce some monstrous new revolution? The last time the young had been mobilized, it had been by Mao, and that little adventure—the Cultural Revolution—had cost China a decade of development and a generation of young people who discovered too late that being revolutionary too often meant being uneducated as well.

Two thoughts occurred to Stratton simultaneously. The first was that if Kangmei was willing to help him, then she was openly at odds with her own father. The second was more chilling than revealing: If Kangmei's network of disaffected young people was any more than a nebulous and idealistic dream, if it had any form at all, any organization that posed the slightest threat to the state or to the Party, then it was only a question of time until authority in all its multibludgeoned wonder fell on it like a ton of bricks. Such was the historic international lesson of communism. Hungary, Czechoslovakia, Democracy Wall, Solidarity . . .

". . . successive dynasties built successive capitals in and around present-day Xian. At the beginning of the Tang Dynasty, Changan was a metropolis of over one million people, six miles square and girded by stout walls breeched by eight gates. The Tang palace was nearly a mile square inside the city and protected by a wall nearly sixty feet thick at its base. Enough remains to keep us more than busy for the two days we have." An avuncular smile.

Stratton knew exactly what he wanted to accomplish in Xian. It had been his reason for not flying home with David's body: He wanted to know what had happened between the two brothers and if, by any means, it could have led to David's death.

Stratton must have sighed aloud, for it drew J. Paul Prudoe's ire.

". . . forest of steles, pagodas, pottery and a celestial army. Professor Stratton?"

Stratton stood up. "May I be excused, please, Mr. Prudoe? I have to go to the bathroom."

He left the art historians to mutter at his insolence and walked out into the early morning sunshine. In the courtyard of the hotel, draped around the open door of a gray Shanghai saloon, stood Kangmei.

"Are you Professor Stratton?" The smile was dazzling. "Good morning, and welcome to Xian. I am Miss Wang and this is Mr. Xia. We are your guides. Please get in."

The rail-thin Mr. Xia, it turned out, was a legitimate China Travel Service guide. That he was one of Kangmei's young allies went without saying, for she too wore the same guide's red identification pin on her white cotton blouse. Kangmei's friend smiled a lot and spoke little, although his English proved to be quite good. Xiao-Xia, she called him.

Leaving the hotel, they drove through handsome, wide streets with little traffic. At one clutter of shops, Stratton did a double take. There on the sidewalk, in English, was a sandwich board announcing "Xian's First Exhibition of Abstract Art."

"I never saw anything like that in Peking," Stratton said. Kangmei and the guide laughed. The third Chinese, the driver, was a lugubrious soul with sharp features. He gave no sign of understanding, no English.

"And you never will," chirped Kangmei, radiant with excitement. "Abstract art—what would the old men say to that? That it was counterrevolutionary, of course. Here it is different. Remember, Thom-as, that the farther you get from Peking, the more relaxed are the people and the easier the rules. I would like to show you the south someday, where my mother's family lives. You would think Peking was in another country."

"There are fewer police here," confirmed Mr. Xia, the guide.

They drove toward what seemed to be the center of the city, a giant tower that stood as a high-hatted civic sentinel.

"Where are we going?" Stratton asked.

"That is for you to decide," Kangmei replied. "But you must see the Bell Tower. It is very old, very famous." She gestured ahead.

"Once it was the center of the Tang imperial city, in about the ninth century," said Mr. Xia in reflexive patter-for-tourists. "It was restored again after Liberation. From the second story, there is a fine view of the city—"

Stratton cut him off. "Kangmei, what I really want to know is what your father and your uncle fought about. I want to go to some of the places they might have gone together; someone might have heard something. I will see the sites of Xian some other time."

"I see," she said doubtfully, and lapsed into a lengthy exchange of Chinese with Mr. Xia.

"It will be difficult, Thom-as. There are so many places. And what do we say?"

"We say that I am a friend of the distinguished American brother of Deputy Minister Wang. Anything like that will do, and there can't be all that many places. What exactly is your father's responsibility here?"

She thought about that one.

"He is everything and he is nothing. There are many cultural places in China, and they are usually controlled by local authorities. Until the old men in Peking get interested in one of them. Then it is my father's job to carry out their wishes. At least, I think that is how it works. My father does not confide in young daughters."

"All right. Between you and Mr. Xia, you must be able to think of some things special here that have interested the old men in Peking. That is where we go."

"It is a good plan, Thom-as," she said. There followed another Mandarin interlude. "There are five or six such places."

They visited the historical museum, a fourteenth-century temple, a thirteenth-century drum tower and Big Goose Pagoda south of the city, originally built early in the seventh century by the Tang, or was it the Sui? They walked the Ming city walls, and visited the neolithic site at Ban Po. Dynasties and centuries began to run together for Stratton. At each stop, Stratton and Mr. Xia would do a quick tourist round and Mr. Xia would ask to see the comrade in charge so that a distinguished American visitor could pay his respects. None of the comrades seemed overworked. To a man, they all poured gracious tea and exchanged compliments interminably. Three of them knew of Comrade Wang from Peking. None had ever met his distinguished brother. By midafternoon, Stratton wondered whether his patience or his bladder would burst first. Kangmei attended none of the interviews. Instead, she wandered around, "talking to the young people," as she put it. It was hard for Stratton to know whether she was devoted more to seeking information or to recruiting for her cause.

"So much for the Taoist Temple of the Eight Immortals." Stratton sighed as he sank back into seat cushions already dank with his sweat. "Now what?"

"The Qin ruins to the east of the city. It will take us about thirty minutes to get there, Thom-as." She ran light fingers across his cheek. "Do not be discouraged."

They drove through an intensely cultivated valley, past communes that seemed rich by Chinese standards. Suddenly, the car turned sharply onto a narrow strip of asphalt that looked as if it had been laid as an afterthought. Through gaps in the fields of chest-high corn, Stratton could see a large cone-shaped hill off to the right.

"That is Mount Qin, the tumulus," said Mr. Xia. "It was looted three years after the emperor's death, when the dynasty fell. It took an army three days and three nights to carry away treasure from the tomb. The new excavations have not reached it yet, so it is not known what the grave robbers may have left. The current excavations are all here, to the west of the tumulus."

"What's that?" Stratton nodded toward a squat, two-story building with a big chimney about a quarter mile off to the left.

"That is a factory belonging to the commune. They make Tiger Brand sewing machines." Mr. Xia smiled. "The factory wants to expand, but the local authorities will not allow it because it is not known what is buried around the factory, or even under it. The factory owners say they do not care about old things: It is the commune's land and the commune has an obligation to provide a good life for it people."

"Sounds like the kind of squabble we have at home between environmentalists and developers," Stratton said. "What happened?"

"The dispute went all the way to Peking. There is no decision yet," said Mr. Xia.

Stratton turned to Kangmei. "By 'Peking' does he mean your father?"

She nodded.

To honor a cruel emperor reviled for two thousand years, but latterly proclaimed a hero, the Chinese had created an instant museum.

Kangmei vanished in search of young co-conspirators. Mr. Xia led Stratton into a large building with a vaulted roof that looked like an airplane hangar. Once inside, the guide went off to look for an official with whom Stratton could drink tea. Alone, Stratton pushed through two polished doors and into the main chamber.

It was like changing centuries.

Stratton stood about fifteen feet above the dig in a skylight-lit hall the size of a football field. His first thought was that it was the cleverest and most awesome museum he had ever seen. To protect the excavation while simultaneously exploiting the discovery as a tourist attraction, the Chinese had simply erected the museum over the dig.

Below Stratton, in roofless chambers that extended in four files, lay the Emperor Qin's celestial army. Stratton stood on a concrete platform, which was shaped like a square U with two wings stretched out parallel along the files. In the pit, a modern army of chinese technicians worked with brushes, dust pans and hand shovels. Stratton stared into the chamber where three hundred clay soldiers stood.

They were magnificent. He had seen pictures, of course—who had not?—but even that foretaste had left Stratton unprepared for their true majesty.

The figures were life-sized, nearly six feet tall. They had been molded from gray river clay by master craftsmen, dead for twenty-two hundred years. Stratton stared with breathless fascination at the nearest warrior, a kneeling archer. The detail was extraordinary.

The archer wore a topknot, pulled tightly to the left side of his head and held with a band. Stratton could count the hairs.

The archer's ears clung close to his skull. The eyebrows were high and stylized, as though they had been plucked. The nose was broad, classically Chinese. The warrior had affected a finely combed mustache and a tuft of hair on his chin. On the face, mirthless and resolute, were flecks of blue and red paint mixed two centuries before Christ was born.

The archer wore a studded jerkin that reached below his waist and ended high on the biceps. It afforded protection from sword slashes, while at the same time allowing mobility with which to wield a bow. Below the waist, the emperor's soldier wore a skirtlike loincloth, leggings and stout, square-toed sandals.

Nearby, a second archer wore the same uniform, but his face was different—rounder, a trifle older, no mustache. Every soldier, Stratton noted with awe, had a different face—in eternity, as in life.

Stratton paced the arms of the platform. Here lay a terracotta arm jutting out from the red clay. And there, a headless torso, being dusted by a young woman with intense concentration. Toward the back of the vast hall, new chambers had been carefully outlined in chalk, but had so far been unmolested. Working at their current painstaking pace, Stratton reckoned, it would take the Chinese technicians at least another ten or twenty years to exploit the dig completely. Stratton was fascinated. He could have stayed for hours. Too soon, Mr. Xia was at his side.

"Director Ku will see you for a few moments, but you must hurry. It is nearly closing time."

Reluctantly, Stratton followed him out of the chamber.

"Mr. Xia, do you realize that this might be the most important archaeological discovery of this century?" Stratton asked.

"Yes, so many American friends have told us. The soldiers excite them very much, but there are many other discoveries as well."

"Can I see them?"

"I am sorry, but only the soldiers are open to the public."

Director Ku was a roly-poly individual with a ready smile and the callused hands of a worker. Stratton squatted on the inevitable overstuffed chair and tried not to drink the tea.

The pleasantries went quickly enough. Ku, Stratton suspected, was not a man to keep his dinner waiting. Even the set speech that seemed to come with every Chinese official's job seemed to sail by: the discovery had been made in 1965 by peasants digging a well. During the Cultural Revolution, not much happened. Since then, the work had proceeded systematically, entirely in the hands of Chinese specialists; no foreigners were welcome. Test excavations were still being dug. So far, scientists had positively identified an armory, an imperial zoo, stables, other groups of warriors, the tombs of nobles sacrificed to mark the emperor's death, the underground entrance to the tumulus and exquisite bronze workings, including a chariot two-thirds life-size.

"I did not know about the bronzes," said Stratton. "Can they be seen?"

"They are in Peking," came back the translation. Stratton saw what he thought was a flash of annoyance on the director's lined face. Annoyance at the question? No, more likely at the thought that Xian's precious treasures had been preempted by the central government.

"Explain about my friend and his brother, Xiao-Xia, but this time don't ask if they were here. Say that my friend told me he would always remember the hospitality he received here."

At the translation, Ku's face lit. He reached into his breast pocket and extracted a silver ballpoint pen.

"The director says he remembers your friend very well. He calls him the 'gentle professor' and shows you the pen he was honored to receive as a gift," said Mr. Xia.

Bingo. But now what?

"Ask the comrade director if it would be possible for me to

see the special excavation that my friend and his brother
visited. Be sure and use Kangmei's father's name."

That provoked a quick exchange in Mandarin before Mr. Xia
finally said: "He asks if you have permission."

A direct hit. "Tell him yes."

Mr. Xia looked quizzically at Stratton.

"Do you really have permission?"

"Of course."

Stratton barely concealed his impatience at the Mandarin
that followed. If he could see what David had seen, he might
understand why the brothers had quarreled. Ku, who obviously
took no pains to hide his own distaste for Peking, might even
tell him. For him, Peking probably meant Wang Bin.

"The director regrets that the excavation is only opened
when Peking advises him that an important visitor is coming.
He regrets that the responsible offcials in Peking did not inform
him you were coming, but, he says, perhaps in a day or two it
will be possible."

Damn. What that meant was that the director would check
with Peking.

"I would be grateful," Stratton said. "Ask him if my
friend—"

"The director also apologizes, but explains that he now must
supervise the closing and meet with the technicians to discuss
tomorrow's work schedule." Mr. Xia interjected.

"Shit," said Stratton. It escaped. Mr. Xia looked perplexed.
Stratton flushed. "Say we are sorry for interrupting his work.
Thank him for his hospitality and say we will return to look at
the special excavation when the details have been arranged."

Darkness was falling and large numbers of workers had
already left the site on a wheezy bus by the time Kangmei
returned to the car.

"It happened here, Thom-as." she erupted. "My father and
my uncle had an angry discussion, shouting. A young worker
told me; he is a cousin of a friend of mine who also studied
languages."

"What was it about? Why did they argue?"

"I do not know. My friend could not speak long. But later I
will see him. He will tell me then."

"Kangmei, that's terrific."

Kangmei bubbled excitedly as the car returned to the old
imperial city. After darkness had fallen, and she was sure Mr.

Xia would not see from the front seat, she grasped Stratton's
hand and clasped it tightly.

Stratton ate alone in the restaurant of the sprawling hotel
complex, careful to time his arrival and departure to miss the
art historians. To his astonishment, the food was awful. He
retired to his room with wizened tangerines and a bottle of
mineral water. He was half asleep, near ten o'clock, when the
phone rang.

"Thom-as," she said without introduction. "In two minutes, you must walk to the end of the corridor with the vacuum
bottle in your room and ask the floor attendant for more hot
water."

Stratton understood; he was to be a decoy. "Are you sure
that's wise?"

"Please."

Stratton obeyed, remembering to empty the thermos. The
attendant, drowsing over the color pictures in a back copy of
Time that a tourist must have left, smiled and obligingly padded
into a kitchen with the bottle, leaving the hall unwatched.

When Stratton returned to the room, Kangmei was waiting.
She embraced him. Her tongue played a sparrow's tattoo
against his teeth. It was Stratton who broke the embrace.

"Kangmei . . ." he said uncertainly.

"It is so exciting," she said. "My friend told me everything, Thom-as, everything." She sat on the narrow iron-
framed bed, leaving Stratton standing absurdly above her,
thermos suspended.

"Would you like some tea?" he asked weakly.

"Yes, please."

Stratton turned and busied himself elaborately with the tea
leaves. He tried to ignore the rustlings behind him. Was she
getting into bed?

"Here is what happened," she began. "My friend saw it.
There is a special place near the emperor's tomb, Thom-as. It is
not controlled by the workers there, but by Peking directly—
my father—and it makes all the Xian people very angry."

"What kind of a place?" Stratton asked.

"My friend called it a special place. No one may go there
without permission. When my uncle came, my father took him
there. My friend was there to help; it is covered with reeds and
cloth most of the time. My father and my uncle went down into
the hole on a ladder, into a long tunnel. They were gone a long

time. When they came out again, they began to argue. My father tried to grab my uncle's camera. 'No, no!' my uncle kept saying. My father grew very angry. They shouted. Then my father ordered the hole covered and they drove away."

Stratton was thinking furiously. If the chamber with the common soldiers was an international sensation, then Wang Bin's private dig could be a literal gold mine. Stratton had a vision of gold swords encrusted with jewels, of bronze and gold helmets, chests of gems: an emperor's legacy.

"My father wanted my uncle to help him steal something, Thom-as, didn't he?" It was the voice of a little girl.

"It's possible," Stratton said. He turned, a full teacup in each hand.

Kangmei lay naked on the bed. The light from a single dim-watted bulb painted her the color of brushed ivory. She wriggled, and the shadowed V between her legs became a beckoning S. She reached for him, arching her back.

"Kangmei, we can't . . ."

"Thom-as," she whispered. "Do you know what Kangmei means in Chinese?"

"Mmm?"

"It means 'Resist America,' Thom-as. My father was very patriotic before he become a thieving old man. Shall I resist America, Thom-as?"

Her little-girl laugh broke the spell.

"Kangmei," Stratton said more sternly than he felt, "you are David's niece, and I'm nearly old enough—"

"To what?"

"To know better," he said. She was a spectacular woman, and certainly older than some of the students with whom he had dallied in his early years as a teacher. "You are very beautiful, and I want to," Stratton said lamely, "but it would be wrong. Do you understand why?"

Kangmei seemed to wilt. Stratton, feeling a fool with a teacup in each hand, watched as tears sparked in her eyes. She clawed for the sheet and drew it up to her chin.

"Oh, Thom-as, I meant nothing wrong, but you . . . there is so little time, and I am very excited. Also a little frightened."

"So am I," Stratton said, and kissed her lightly on the forehead.

She took the tea, and he sat primly by her on the bed,

stroking her hair as an uncle might, or a lover-to-be. When at last Kangmei fell asleep, Stratton curled stiffly in a hard-bottomed chair, wondering if he yet knew enough to lay murder charges against her father.

CHAPTER 10

THE MEN NAMED LIAO and Deng moved away from the streetlight and into the shadows. Their discussion was brief, disturbed.

"You are sure it was her?" Teng asked. He was the older of the two; brawny, leather-faced, he wore his Mao cap pulled tight on his head, the brim snug on his eyebrows.

"I am certain," Liao replied. "This changes everything." He lit a cheap cigarette and glanced across the street at the hotel. His eyes moved up the wall to an open window. A faint bulb gave a burnished light to the inside of the room; no shadows moved. Liao was hatless; his black hair was cropped extremely short. In a robe, he could have passed for a Buddhist monk. His round face was youthful, but humorless.

"When she leaves . . ." he said.

"And if she doesn't?" Deng asked. "Perhaps we should contact Peking."

"I don't think we should wake the deputy minister." Liao shook his head.

Deng scowled. "This foreigner is important."

"That's why we're here."

"But so is the daughter important. It is a grave matter," Deng insisted. The brim of his cap bobbed as his brow furrowed. "We can't wait all night. I say we grab the girl. As for the American, we have our instructions."

Liao sighed. He had an intuition about complications, and this assignment troubled him. "We'll have to report this to her *dan-wei*."

Deng said, "Why? Let Lao Wang handle it. He is her father." And then he thought for a moment and said, "You are right. We must report it. Even if the deputy minister tells us not to." Deng and Liao had heard the same rumors. Today the old

91

man was a power broker, but he could just as easily be shoveling cowshit in Hunan tomorrow.

"We do as we're told," Liao said finally, "and a little more. The deputy minister does not have to know whom we talk to. China comes first."

Stratton drowsed, half-sleeping, in the hard chair. When he heard the doorknob jiggling, he figured it was one of the floor attendants. They all had passkeys, and no compunction about barging in on the slightest pretext.

It would not be wise to be found in the same room with a Chinese woman. Stratton padded barefoot across the floor and reached for the door. Two men stood there in the darkness. One held a sack of some kind in his right hand, away from his body.

"Yes?" Stratton said, stiffening.

The young man bowed, then rammed the heel of his hand into the tip of Stratton's nose. The American fell in a heap, gurgling blood.

From the bed, Kangmei yelped and sat up. The men stared silently at her naked figure before they closed the door behind them.

Stratton awoke in darkness, heaving for air. His nostrils were clogged with blood, and his face was clammy and wet. Two strips of industrial tape had been pasted across his mouth, forming an X that nearly blocked his desperate breathing.

He was in a closet. He smelled clothing—his own—and the canvas from his duffel. Through throbbing eyes, he noticed a weak sliver of light at the base of the door, near his feet.

Stratton tried to move. His hands were free, but his legs were bound tightly at the ankles. Voices, male and female, seeped through the door. The conversation was singsongy Mandarin, and Stratton understood none of it. The male voices were cold and conspiratorial and the female voice was full of fear. Kangmei.

He struggled to his knees, grunting, using his hands to feel in the blackness. If these thugs were so efficient, he wondered, why hadn't they tied his hands as well? Why leave him free to explore the darkness for a way out—

And then one of Stratton's hands found what it was supposed to. It was as big as a baseball bat, yet taut and rippling. It was smooth to the touch, not oily, and it made a hushing sound as it glided across the floor of the dark closet.

Stratton froze, and the amplified beat of his heart filled his ears. The creature had stopped moving; it was not bothered at all by the darkness.

Stratton cowered. He felt that the thing could actually sense his pulse, and feel the heat of his terror.

"You are stupid men. Leave us alone!" Kangmei clutched the cotton sheet to her neck. Her knees were drawn protectively to her chest.

"Your father sent us," Deng said from under his brim. "Not for you, Kangmei, but for your American friend. He is a dangerous man, an enemy of the state. He is trying to use you to obtain information that would harm the deputy minister."

"Lies!"

"We did not know you were with him," Liao said in a nervous whisper. "And you can be sure that we will not make a public matter of this . . . incident."

Kangmei's eyes flashed toward the closet, and the knot of hemp rope that secured the door.

"You know what would happen if this episode became known," Liao continued. "You would lose your place at the language school. There might even be punishment at a labor camp for rehabilitation."

"What do you want?"

Deng nodded toward the closet. "The foreigner is our only interest. If you need to know more, ask your father. We are here to do a job. I am sorry that you had to become involved in this, Comrade."

"Think of the shame and embarrassment for the deputy minister," Liao said.

"Thom-as was a friend of my uncle. He is an art teacher on tour," Kangmei said. "That is all."

"We see what we see, Comrade," Liao said.

Kangmei flushed.

"Put on your clothes. You will come with us and say nothing of what happened here," Liao said.

"And what is happening?" she demanded.

"Very unfortunate," Deng said. "Mr Stratton, the American tourist, purchased a rare poisonous snake from a street vendor. His plan was to smuggle it out of China to the United States. It was a king cobra, the most terrible snake in the world, Comrade. Zoos in America would pay handsomely for a specimen—and the one *meiguoren* wanted to smuggle was certainly large and healthy."

"Unfortunately," Liao broke in, "the American was careless. The snake bit him. He fell forward, shattering his nose on the floor—see here." With a blue canvas shoe, Liao daubed at a blood smear on the wood.

"But the fall didn't matter," Deng said. "He probably was dead already. One drop of the king cobra's venom can kill a horse."

Kangmei stared at the empty sack in Deng's hand and began to whimper. She dressed with her back to the cadres.

"Come now, we will take you away," Deng said. "In the morning, we will notify the deputy minister. If you behave, my friend and I will leave the explanation of this up to you. It is not our place to tell the deputy minister that his daughter is a common whore."

"A traitorous whore!" Liao barked, pushing her toward the door.

"But Thom-as!" Kangmei cried.

"We will come back in a little while," Deng said, "to arrange things."

"Yes," Liao said with a satisfied smile. "The snake will require special attention."

Tom Stratton inched into a corner of the closet and balled up like some gangly, naked autistic child. He ached and he itched, but he dared not stretch or scratch. Every motion was a clue, and every tiny noise a magnet for the huge killing machine that shared his darkness.

He knew a little about cobras: that their vision was excellent, their sensory reflexes keen, all filtered through a magical flicking tongue that could find a rat or a lizard or a camouflaged toad in the blackest of Asian jungle nights. Man was not prey; he was an enemy. The cobra, Stratton knew, would not attack unless cornered and threatened.

It was a small closet, but Stratton gladly surrendered most of it to the reptile. During the argument outside the door, it had moved back and forth, brushing silkily against his feet and legs. Occasionally, its shadow crossed the floor in such a way that it obliterated the crack of light beneath the door. In those moments of total darkness, Stratton would close his eyes, for he feared an unseen strike at his face, and strained to listen for the cobra's breathing. He could hear nothing. In and out, the tongue was reading him, measuring him, taking his temperature . . . all in silence.

It was a superb creature, a mystical creature.

When the door to the hotel room closed, and Kangmei and her captors were gone, the snake seemed to settle down in a corner of its own. In his mind's eye, Stratton could see its thick olive coils—and the hooded head, motionless and erect.

After an hour, Stratton decided that the snake was as relaxed as it was ever going to be. He edged on his buttocks across the dusty floor, inches at a time, pausing several moments between moves. From the corner where he imagined that the cobra slept there came no sound.

Stratton eased himself up to the door. His right hand spidered slowly across the wood until it found the knob. He twisted and pushed—but the door would not budge. Stratton tried again, this time with his shoulder as a buttress. The door held fast. The problem was breaking it down without arousing the cobra.

Stratton's knees cracked loudly as he struggled to his feet. The ankle ropes had been a cinch, even in the darkness. If he could just get out of the goddamn closet, he would be free.

He was careful not to move his legs; instead, he pivoted from the waist up, ramming the door with his upper body. Stratton could feel the hinges weaken. He rammed again, a bayonet-thrust without the sword. And once more with all of his hundred ninety pounds.

On Stratton's third try the snake struck. He heard the hiss and felt the passing breath. Stratton froze. The cobra struck again, biting air. Six inches to the left and the fangs would have pierced Stratton's groin.

The cobra was angry. The sweat, the heat of human exertion, the blood racing through Stratton's body as he pounded the door—all this had ignited the snake's primal reflex.

Instinctively, Stratton jumped to his left, crashing into a suit of clothes that hung from a dowel. The snake followed. Once, ssshhhhhh, in the air. Again, closer, a deadly sibilance two inches from Stratton's ear. And once more, higher and longer . . .

Stratton pressed his head against the wall; he held himself there to stay out of range. Now he heard a different sound. The cobra was struggling in front of him, thrashing wildly in the folds of clothing. Stratton knew instantly what had happened.

Its fangs were hung in the fabric. The beast was stuck like a dart on cork.

He reached out and found the snake. He grabbed it like a rope, working upward, hand-over-hand toward the frantic lethal head. Stratton found the cobra's hood. It seemed enormous, but it folded smoothly in his grip. Stratton kneaded his way to the head.

Both hands yanked the cobra down to the floor of the closet. Squeezing its neck with all of his strength, he threw his body on the writhing coils. The cobra took twelve and one-half minutes to die. Stratton knew. He counted every second.

"Thomas! I hear you in there." Alice Dempsey paced the hallway outside the hotel room. Her voice dripped with annoyance. "You missed breakfast again, and you're about to miss the bus." Alice despised disorder; Stratton embodied it. In her mind, she had already composed a stern letter to his dean. The trip was a farce as far as Stratton went. He had disappeared for days at a time. He had openly taunted his colleagues. He had insulted the Chinese and even fought with them, for God's sakes. Stratton would live to regret his inexcusable behavior.

"Come on!"

Alice knocked again. This time the door swung open on its own. Two Chinese strangers stood there. One wore a Mao cap pulled down low over his eyes.

"Where's Mr. Stratton?" Alice demanded. She sensed trouble.

The man with the cap shrugged and said nothing.

"Do you understand English?"

The other man, younger than the first, shook his head no. Alice took a step inside. The bed had been slept in, but the room held no sign of Stratton. The drawers in the bureau had been drawn half open. The closet door was ajar—it too was empty—but something caught Alice's eye: a length of heavy rope hung from the outside doorknob. In one corner of the room appeared to be another length of rope, brownish green in color, and glossy, as if it were made of plastic. Curious, Alice stepped forward for a closer look.

She let out a hoarse scream when she saw that the coil of rope was actually a large dead snake.

The man with the Mao pointed to the reptile and then tapped his chest proudly.

"You killed it?" Alice gasped.

The man nodded excitedly and pointed to his friend. Then he performed a brief pantomime, clubbing at the floor with an imaginary truncheon. Then he pointed at the cobra again and grinned.

Alice returned a nervous smile. "Well, you both are very brave. But where has Mr. Stratten gone? Have you seen him?"

The men's faces were blank.

"*Weiguoren*," Alice said, laboring over each syllable.

"*Wei*," answered the man in the Mao cap. It was as good as a shrug.

Alice bowed goodbye and left the room, grumbling. No one on the bus would believe *this*.

Stratton poured himself a large cup of hot tea and drank it quickly; the train would lurch to a start any second, and he didn't want the steaming cup to spill in his lap. That the soft-class compartment was unoccupied was his second stroke of luck this morning. The first had been talking his way onto the Peking-bound train. His papers showed that he was not routed back to Peking, and the clerk at the station had noticed the discrepancy at first glance. She had called for an interpreter, who had explained that Stratton could not leave Xian until the date prescribed on his papers. Stratton had responded with a hideously graphic story about food poisoning from some bad snails; he even interrupted the discussion and ran to the restroom, pretending to be sick. It was a good performance, and both the clerk and the translator had solemnly agreed that he should return to Peking at once for rest and medical treatment.

Now, alone on the train and seemingly safe, Stratton had time to think. David—dead at the hands of his own brother. Kangmei—arrested, maybe worse. Then there was the deputy minister, Wang Bin—frightened enough to order the murder of an American tourist. But why?

At the dig, Kangmei's friend had observed Wang Bin struggling for David's camera. This puzzled Stratton, for the site had been photographed extensively, and the pictures had been published throughout the world. Evidently David had found something extraordinary—something forbidden.

The inventory of his belongings provided by the American Embassy listed three unexposed rolls of film. To Stratton, the explanation was simple: Wang Bin had confiscated all the film his brother had shot during his homecoming.

A shrill chorus of military music exploded from a scratchy speaker in Stratton's compartment. He groped for the dial and tried to turn it off; the marching song faded, but it would not die. He glanced at his wristwatch and noticed that the train was already ten minutes late for departure.

Stratton was uneasy. Next time, he knew, Wang Bin's methods would be less diabolical, but more dependable than a killer snake. Once back in Peking, Stratton would make a beeline for the embassy and enlist Linda's help.

A waiter knocked lightly on the door of the compartment. He brought Stratton a hand towel and a small lumpy pillow. Stratton thanked him and said, "Are we leaving soon?"

"Soon," the waiter answered politely. He stared at Stratton's swollen nose as he backed out.

"Is there some kind of mechanical problem?"

"Soon," the waiter repeated, disappearing.

Through the window Stratton scanned the empty station ramp. The train was loaded. Any minute now . . . he sighed, and stretched his legs on the long seat.

Stratton toyed with his newfound scenario. Wang Bin had invited his brother to China, hoping to recruit David into a smuggling scheme. As a courier, perhaps, for ancient artifacts. Or maybe Wang Bin simply needed a trusted person to act as a broker for the priceless contraband back in the States.

Together they visited the Qin tombs. Wang Bin gave David the grand tour—maybe more. David took some pictures. Wang Bin made his pitch, but David rebuffed him. The deputy minister was enraged, panic-stricken. Stratton could easily imagine Wang Bin's reaction if David had threatened—as he probably did—to report his greedy brother to the authorities in Peking.

Stratton recalled Kangmei's conversation with her uncle on the night of his death: *He said that Wang Bin was doing something very wrong. . . . He was horrified that his brother would attempt such a thing.* Yes, that old professor's indignation would have been volcanic. And what if, Stratton wondered, David had learned something so scandalous that it could have sent the deputy minister to prison?

Wouldn't that be enough to make one brother murder another?

Stratton finished his tea and set the empty cup on the table. The train still had not moved, but in his ruminations Stratton had forgotten his impatience.

He was sure now. He had figured it out.

To Wang Bin, it must have seemed a simple scheme, wonderfully pragmatic. Faithful brother David returns home from his China trip, a sword or vase or delicate clay mask packed in his personal luggage. The proper-looking receipts would be provided, of course—and where would one ever encounter a customs officer expert enough, or bold enough, to challenge such artifacts?

Once safely in the United States, any large museum would pay magnificently and ask precious few questions. David would be delighted for his cut, however small. After all, who can retire comfortably on a meager university pension?

As for the rest of the money, Wang Bin's share: a bank draft to a numbered account in Zurich, and from there, a transfer to Hong Kong. There were a few creative ways to get it actually back into Peking, but Stratton figured that Hong Kong would have been close enough for the deputy minister.

A neat scheme, Stratton thought, until David Wang balked. Then there was only one thing his fearful brother could do.

Stratton stood up and stretched. Powell would never believe it. With Linda Greer, he had a better chance. By now, she would have learned of his escapade with the cadres in the Red Flag limousine. Her feelers would be out on the street; friendly eyes would be looking for him. Stratton figured that Wang Bin was not the only person who now wanted him out of China.

He was not frightened for himself, but he worried for Kangmei. Because of who she was, she probably would not be killed. Still, her life could be ruined. There was no telling what her penance would be. In Kangmei's case, Stratton reflected sadly, there would be no one to intervene.

Someone tapped on the door.

"More tea?"

"No, thank you," Stratton said, surprised at the sound of hard-learned English. "Can you tell me when we're leaving?"

The door opened. "Now," said the man in the Mao cap. He pointed a Russian-made pistol at Stratton face. The American raised his arms. Liao followed Deng through the door.

The three men stood awkwardly together in the small compartment, Stratton awaiting directions. He could not believe they would shoot him on a crowded morning train.

"Where to?" he asked after a few moments.

"Off train," Deng said, but he didn't move.

"Nose broke," Liao said with a perceptive sneer. He pointed at Stratton's face.

"Yeah, well, I'm sorry about your pet snake," Stratton muttered.

Deng lowered the pistol from Stratton's head and held it at waist level, trained on the American's midsection.

"I'll go quietly, don't worry," Stratton said. The Chinese traded glances. "How long are we going to stand here?" Stratton asked.

"Go now," said Deng, pulling the trigger.

The bullet lifted Tom Stratton and propelled him backward into the wall of the compartment. His head cracked against a steel bunk and he rag-dolled forward into a heap on the floor. Day became night. The Chinese demons screamed in Stratton's ears until his mind went limp and cold in a terrible sleep.

CHAPTER 11

"WE'VE GOT A PAIR OF NASTY little problems on our hands, don't we?" The station chief drummed his pudgy gray fingers on the desk. He let out a sigh of disgust. "Wang Bin *and* Stratton."

Linda Greer was reading a file. She wore glasses, forcing herself to fix on the words. She fought off despair.

"Why did the deputy minister want your friend out of the country so badly? Think of it: We tell him quite politely that Mr. Stratton will not be accompanying his brother's body back to the United States—and what does he do? He sends a couple of goons to the hotel. Why?" The station chief did not wait to hear any theories. "Because he *knows*. Linda, somehow Wang Bin got hold of Stratton's service record. He knows about Manling."

Linda shook her head slowly and set the file on the desk. "It's more than that. It's got to be."

"Damn, the coffee's cold already. Why does it have to be more than that?"

"Suppose Wang Bin knows about Stratton's brief incursion back in 1971," Linda began. "Wouldn't it be easier, and more effective, to make a formal request: 'This man is an undesirable and we would like him to leave China at once'? A sticky little deportation problem, nothing more. We've handled stuff like that in the past. Now this," she said, motioning toward the file, "is pretty clumsy, sir. Chasing Stratton all over the city with a goddamn Red Flag, then trying to run him over in the street . . . that's not the style of this bureaucracy, sir. It's too messy. Reckless. Something like that might happen in Moscow—"

"In a blue moon!" the station chief huffed.

"—but never in Peking. The police or the PLA could have captured Stratton in a matter of minutes."

101

The phone rang once. The station chief spoke briefly and hung up. "So what are you saying, Linda? That this was a private matter between Wang and Stratton? An informal abduction?"

"Something's going on, and it's damn sure not just a matter of honor. My guess is that Wang Bin sent those two clowns to grab Stratton, not to kill him. But when it looked as if he would get away, they panicked and tried to run him down."

"Now one is dead and the other's a cabbage. Jesus!" The station chief grunted as he flipped through his copy of the file. "And our Mr. Stratton is missing in action. What a fiasco!"

Linda Greer said nothing. The possibilities were too depressing.

The station chief looked up and asked, "Think they caught up with him at Xian?"

"Yes."

"Me, too. Think he's dead?"

"Probably. We had someone interview some of the other Americans on that tour. They saw Stratton at the hotel yesterday morning, but he didn't stay with the group."

"Naturally."

"He left with two Chinese, a young woman and a man."

"And?"

Linda took off her glasses and folded them. "This morning, when one of the Americans went to Stratton's hotel room, he was gone. Gone without a trace. The woman who discovered him missing is the same one who gave us the story about the snake."

The station chief smiled slightly, remembering the bland entry in the file, rated "very reliable."

"Ah, that would be the busybody Mrs. Dempsey. She also found the Chinese in Stratton's room. Just tidying up, I suppose. What kind of snake?

"She didn't know," Linda said. "By the time our people got there, the room was clean. There was a little blood on the floor, though. Most of it had been scrubbed away—"

"Was there enough to—"

"Yes. O positive. Same as Tom's." Linda Greer felt very tired. She wanted to go back to her apartment and soak in the bathtub. She wanted to cry.

"Oh dear," the station chief muttered. He gazed out the window; the setting sun painted the tiled roofs of Peking a burned yellow and turned the haze into a pale lemon curtain.

"I took the liberty of filing formal inquiries with China Travel, the tourism bureau, and the others. . . . I don't expect to hear anything, but at least we're on the record as far as procedure goes."

"Yes," the station chief said. "Good thinking. Let's meet again tomorrow. Noonish. In the meantime, say nothing to Powell. I'm sure he's picked up whispers about that insane goddamn bicycle chase, so just tell him we're checking it out."

Linda Greer collected her purse and briefcase, and headed for the door.

The station chief cleared his throat. "Linda," he called in a softer voice. "I'm sorry about Stratton."

"Thanks."

"What do you suppose he was after?"

"I haven't the slightest idea," she replied truthfully.

For three days the freight train creaked south through plains and farmland, skirting the rugged mountain ranges that rule China's interior. The trip was hot, the train old and plodding, led by a spanking new steam locomotive.

Tom Stratton lay in a boxcar that smelled of ammonia and cow manure. His arms and legs were trussed, and a burlap sack had been tied loosely over his head and upper torso. A dirty wad of gauze had been tightly taped over the nearly circular wound in his thigh. Deng's aim had been perfect; the small-caliber bullet had missed Stratton's hip bone and passed harmlessly through the fat of his upper leg. The blow on the head that had come with the fall had been a bonus for Deng and his partner; it had then been a simple matter to explain the unconscious American tourist being carried off the train in Xian. He had fallen in the compartment and badly cut his leg. He needed medical attention immediately.

Tom Stratton woke hours later to the clanging of rails, the lurching of the boxcar, and the tickle of a small animal scampering across the sack that cloaked his head. It was night. His thigh ached painfully. Stratton guessed that his bunkmate was probably a rat, and he rolled over to frighten it away. His head twirled and his ears rang as he moved; undoubtedly he had been sedated. He lay still and inhaled vigorously, the burlap puckering at his mouth with each breath. The stale air was heavy with musk, but in it there was a sweet tinge of wheat and maize. Stratton's stomach growled in recognition.

Eventually, he squirmed into a sitting position, propped up against a sack of what smelled like potatoes.

It was a small moral victory. Sitting up, Stratton felt a little less helpless. He wondered why they hadn't just killed him. No esoteric stuff—cobras and the like—just a good old-fashioned bullet in the brain. He felt slightly nauseous but resolved not to throw up in the sack. As the hours passed and his body cried for water, Stratton began to pray that they would not leave him there to die in a vegetable car with a horde of hungry goddamn rats.

The panel door of the boxcar clattered open and daylight exploded in Stratton's face. He had managed to work himself out of the burlap, in the darkness, but could see nothing. Now the sudden brightness blinded him. Rough hands yanked him upright by the hair. A terse command in Mandarin, and then in English: "Drink!" Stratton gulped strange-tasting water from a wooden mug. Within minutes, he grew dizzy and passed out.

Deng and Liao were in a foul mood; neither had relished a trip to the south. Peking, with its fine restaurants and all its cadre privileges, was infinitely preferable to a muggy peasant farm village. Down here the lines of authority were less clearly drawn, Deng grumbled; respect seemed to diminish with each kilometer away from the Imperial City. At every stop there had been questions: Where are your papers? What are you doing here? Where is your *dan-wei*? In his agitation, Deng handled the sleeping form of Tom Stratton with something less than gentleness.

"I thought we would be finished with this in Xian," Liao said as they heaved Stratton onto a flatbed truck. "The orders changed. I wonder why."

"A good question for the deputy minister," Deng said. "He will be here soon."

Wang Bin leaned back and blew a smoke ring toward the ceiling. "Tell me about the American."

"I will not," his daughter said hotly.

"You will! You are too old to spank, Wang Kangmei, but you are of an age where other punishment can be more terrible. You still have a future today, but there is no guarantee. Tomorrow, who knows? I would not be the first senior Party official to forsake an errant child."

Kangmei folded her arms across her breasts and stared at the floor.

"Did you sleep with him?"

"He told me all about Uncle David. He wished to see the tombs at Xian, the dig you are so proud of. What harm was there in showing him?"

"He asked many questions, did he not?"

"Not as many as I asked him. Father, I was merely curious. About Xian, about my uncle. I was distraught because he died only days after we first met. Can you understand that?"

"Did you—"

"No! I did not sleep with Stratton."

"Deng and Liao told me you were in his room." Wang Bin's eyes dropped. "Naked in his bed."

"They are vicious liars, Father. They came to *my* room, and dragged me from my own bed. They took me to Stratton and began to interrogate us. They hit me, Father, and said terrible things. Stratton tried to stop them and they beat him up, and locked him in a closet—"

Wang Bin raised a hand. "You are a foolish girl, and a bad liar. For that, I suppose, I should be grateful. Your eyes confess everything, Kangmei. Now I ask you: What of the family honor? Whoring with a foreigner—such behavior aggrieves me, and insults the entire Wang family. I shall not mention what it would do to your mother."

"I *told* you—"

"It probably will not be possible to keep this quiet for very long. Today the loyalties of Liao and Deng belong to me; tomorrow, who can say?" Wang Bin watched his daughter's eyes grow moist. Her posture remained erect, and her face defiant. "Kangmei, this fascination you nurture for America has become a dangerous and disturbing thing. You are in serious trouble. This Thomas Stratton is no simple tourist. He is a cunning man, a former soldier. He has been to China before, and he has killed Chinese. He is a spy, Kangmei, and you, his tool. The shame you have brought to our family . . . it saddens me."

"No!" Kangmei cried. "You are wrong, Father. Stratton was a friend of my uncle, that it all. He mourns David Wang as a friend mourns, deeply and sincerely. This I know. I've done nothing shameful—"

"That is enough," Wang Bin said coldly.

"No!" Kangmei was on her feet, shouting and crying at once. "How can you treat a daughter like this? The thugs who beat me, attacked me in my bed—*they* should be in jail, not me. Yet I am dragged from my room, tied up, gagged, and thrown in a dirty cell with dangerous criminals. Why, Father?"

Wang Bin laughed shortly and stubbed out his cigarette. "Your pitiful cellmates hardly qualify as dangerous criminals. They are petty thieves, my daughter, that's all. They're being punished for pilfering from the archaeological sites—nothing valuable: trinkets, really. But it is important to set an example for the others. Stealing cannot be tolerated at such historic places. However, these people are not truly dangerous, so stop the tears."

Kangmei asked, "Must I go back to the cell?"

Wang Bin circled the small desk and slipped an arm around his daughter's trembling shoulders. "No," he said. "We're going on a trip."

Kangmei pulled away and faced her father. "Where?"

"South," he replied, "to a small village. Kangmei, there is something you must do for me—and for yourself. To erase what has happened is impossible. But it is still possible for you to repent, to have a future, and perhaps even a good position in China. You *must* do as I say."

"And if I refuse?"

Wang Bin raised his hands in a gesture of feigned indifference. "Then I will not hesitate to put you on the first train to Tibet, where you can grub potatoes for the next five years."

Tom Stratton awoke to the hum of flies circling his head. His cheek pressed against an earthen floor, and the cool smell of clay filled his nostrils.

As he righted himself, the bleak room spun briefly. His arms and legs were free. His thigh throbbed, and by the dismal condition of the bandage, Stratton knew that his captors had not changed the dressing.

His cell was spartan: a single wooden chair, straight-backed, handmade, with a crude hemp seat; a solitary bare light bulb, fixed in the rafters; a large ceramic bowl, crusted with stale rice and scum, buzzing with insects; and a single window, at eye level, crisscrossed in a loose pattern with barbed wire.

Tom Stratton was alone. He paced the dimensions of the room at eight feet by twelve. The heavy door was made of intransigent timber. Stratton knew it would never yield to his shoulder.

Peering through the window, which measured about a foot square, Stratton expected to see a military compound with marching squads of People's Liberation Army soldiers, or at least some uniformed police. Instead he saw a newly paved road and a large parking lot half-filled with trucks and bicycles; beyond that, a banana grove carpeted an entire hillside. A lorry painted dark PLA green trundled down the two-lane road and stopped in the parking lot no more than fifty yards from Stratton's cell. He watched a quiet but affable procession of Chinese jump down and form an orderly group. The men wore sturdy gray or brown slacks, starched shirts open at the neck, while the pigtailed women wore loose-fitting pants and white cotton blouses. Their clothing was too fancy for work. Stratton assumed that the visitors were local tourists.

The truck rattled off, and the Chinese marched dutifully toward the building in which Stratton was being held. They crossed only a few feet from his cell, talking in pleasant tones, until they finally passed out of Stratton's sight.

He decided that his dungeon definitely was not part of a regular Chinese jail.

Stratton moved to the corner of the room that garnered the most light from the small window. There he peeled off the soiled bandage and examined the bullet hole in his right thigh. The dime-sized wound was black and scabbed, but the vermilion halo around it announced that infection had set in. Stratton's only piece of clothing, a short-sleeved sports shirt, was rancid from the long train ride, and of no use as a sponge. Reluctantly, he rewrapped his injured leg with the same dirty gauze, and sat down to wait for his keepers.

They arrived without pleasantries, an hour before dusk; three men, lean, unremarkable, impassive at first. They wore no uniforms, which surprised Stratton. One of them, who carried a rifle with a bayonet, motioned Stratton out of the cell.

He was led to a small courtyard whose boundaries were marked by tangled hedges. Red bougainvillea plants radiantly climbed the walls of the otherwise drab buildings that formed the complex. The place reminded Stratton of a monastery.

The men stopped in the middle of the courtyard. Stratton faced them. He was naked from the waist down, and filthy. His mustache was flecked with clay, and it smelled.

"Could I have a pair of trousers?" Stratton asked.

His escorts glanced at each other. They spoke no English. The one with the rifle suddenly raised it to his shoulder and aimed at Stratton's dangling genitals.

"Pah! Pah!" he barked, pretending to pull the trigger. "Pah! Pah! Pah!"

His comrades sniggered. The rifleman lowered the gun and his face grew stoic once again.

Stratton lifted his arms from his sides. "You missed," he said, pointing. "See?"

Self-consciously, the escorts averted their eyes. From across the plaza came the sound of many voices. Stratton realized that the workers at the compound had been summoned to witness a public humiliation—his own.

As the Chinese filed through the courtyard, they bunched into a confused knot at the side of the half-naked American, standing at attention in the day's final shadows. A few jeered. Others laughed and pointed. Then, some of the women became upset and began to leave. The men also soon wearied of the spectacle.

Stratton was too exhausted to be embarrassed, but the three guards wore satisfied smiles.

After the workers had gone, the men took Stratton outside the compound to an alley. One of them twisted the handle on a water faucet, and a stream of cold water shot out. The man with the bayonet pointed at the swelling puddle.

Stratton obligingly stripped out of his shirt and removed the bandage from his thigh. He squatted beneath the faucet and closed his eyes. The frigid water was invigorating, but his injured leg stiffened in protest. While his feet and his buttocks rested in the murky puddle, Stratton was careful to keep the wound clean. He pressed his scalp to the mouth of the faucet, and let the hard water rinse the grime from his hair.

"*Gou!*" commanded one of the watchers. Enough.

Stratton stood up and smoothed his hair back. Then he slipped into his shirt.

One of the escorts held out the rag that had served as his bandage.

"But it's too dirty," Stratton objected.

The man with the gun stared back blankly. Stratton wrapped the fetid gauze around his upper leg and tied it with a small knot.

With a sharp shove to the small of his back, Stratton was directed to his cell. One of the jailers followed him inside just long enough to ladle two scoops of rice into the food dish, and to replace a rusty tin can full of water on the earthen floor.

The door closed heavily, and night swallowed Stratton's room with a humid gulp. Outside, in the tropical orchards, birds whistled. The hills were dotted sparsely with yellow lights from distant communes.

Stratton waved the flies off the bowl of rice, and put a cold lumpy handful in his mouth.

He decided that the march to the water faucet had been a good sign. Certainly the bath had not been meant for his benefit, so it could mean only one thing. Soon he would have a visitor.

Probably an important visitor.

CHAPTER 12

JIM MCCARTHY PARKED in a dark corner of the crowded lot at the Peking Hotel. His station wagon was fire-engine red—the journalist's mobile protest against the drab sameness of Peking. Every now and then, when China weighed too heavily, McCarthy would roll down the windows, plug in a Willie Nelson tape as loud as he could stand it and—gawkers be damned—cruise at high speed into the ancient hills around the city.

McCarthy made sure the driver's door was unlocked. He trudged up the circular driveway and through the automatic doors that admit foreigners only to Peking's best hotel. To the left of the lobby lay a broad marble passageway that had been converted with plastic tables and chairs into a brightly lit lounge. The Via Veneto, denizens called it sarcastically. The cafe, a grudging Chinese concession to the influx of foreigners that had accompanied the late '70s opening to the West, had, perforce, become the center of social life for transient foreigners in Peking. Sooner or later, everyone wound up drinking instant coffee at the ersatz cafe. McCarthy had interviewed a movie star there, an ice skater and a famous novelist, each one of them self-impressed and self-righteous—*doing* China.

That night there was only a middling crowd. McCarthy nodded to a pair of African diplomats. He chatted briefly with some members of a British lawyers' tour and watched in amusement while well-heeled businessmen of three nationalities sniffed around a lady banker from New York. She had lived in the hotel for two years and would die there on full expenses, if the Chinese allowed it, having long since discovered one of the secrets of revolutionary Peking: It is nirvana for ugly Western women. In New York, the lady banker would have trouble getting a tumble in the raunchiest

110

singles bar. In puritan Peking, without local competition, she never slept alone. McCarthy ordered a cognac at the bar and watched the circus.

After about ten minutes, he walked back to the car and drove toward the poorly lit northern quarter of the city. On an empty side street, he pulled to the curb.

"Come out, come out, wherever you are," he called.

From the backseat, a passenger untangled himself from the folds of a car blanket and climbed into the front seat.

McCarthy lit a cigarette, watching in the rearview mirror as the side lights of another car appeared. Things they never teach you in journalism school, he reflected sourly.

As the other car approached, it slowed. Its headlights flashed, bathing the station wagon from behind. McCarthy reacted.

The station wagon surged from the curb with a peel of rubber, dumping McCarthy's passenger awkwardly between seat and door. McCarthy turned right. The other car followed. For ten tense and silent minutes, he played hide-and-seek until at last he found the main road that tourists took to the Great Wall. His foot went to the floor. The following car, Chinese-made, more for touring than sprinting, dwindled and finally disappeared. McCarthy relaxed.

"It's nice to see you, Little Joe. How're things?"

The passenger smiled, dangling a child's sandal from its strap. In the dashboard half-light, it looked like a dead white hamster.

"I found this in the blanket."

"Shit, I've been looking for that for two weeks. Thanks." McCarthy passed over the pack of cigarettes. "Sorry for the bumpy start, but we had friends."

The passenger dragged deeply, opening the window to let the smoke escape.

"It is no surprise."

He was a slender youth in his twenties with a tousled thatch of black hair and sharp cheek bones. He wore a cheap open-necked white shirt and baggy olive-green trousers. A school-boy's satchel sat primly on his knees. Over the past year, since a casual meeting at an art exhibition arranged by the American Embassy, the shy youth had become McCarthy's best Chinese source.

"Shall we go to my place for a few drinks and some music?

The kids are all asleep, Little Joe." It was a name the boy had assigned himself. McCarthy didn't know his real name, or where he lived. He knew only about the young man's dreams and that his information was good.

"Tonight is bad, Lao Jim. The army, the police, the watchers all have instructions to be particularly alert about contacts with foreigners."

Among foreigners who knew any Chinese willing to risk it, the procedure for getting a guest into the walled diplomatic compound was almost routine: bundle them down in the back and drive smiling through the gate. The PLA soldiers seldom did more than wave; in the winter, they simply peered out from their hut and wrote down the special license numbers reserved for *weiguoren*. Except for taxis with passengers, normally registered vehicles were forbidden to enter the compound.

At first, Little Joe had been reluctant, and then thrilled, at the prospect of cheating the security system. In recent months, he had become more cautious, resorting finally to hurried phone calls to arrange meetings at "the usual place"—the hotel parking lot.

"How are things, Little Joe? Are we hearing the same rumors?" McCarthy coaxed.

The youth lit a fresh cigarette from the butt of the old.

"Special security units are being assigned to the embassies—uniformed and plainclothes—beginning two days from now. I think they expect some attempts to defect."

"Why?"

"The old Maoists are winning control. They will purge several hundred officials in Peking in the next week. Did you hear that rumor?" Little Joe not only spoke good English, but also had a subtle sense of humor, rare in a Chinese. He was a friend to be treasured.

"Among others," McCarthy lied.

"Well, I have seen the list, and it is true."

"Any names I would recognize?"

"Possibly." He named two or three. "Most of them, though, are second- or third-rank people, administrators and—how do you call it?—technocrats."

"What have they done?"

"Just like the others who have already been purged. They are skilled at what they do and have great experience in dealing with foreigners. The Party thinks they are more loyal to their own jobs, or to their ministries, or to their foreign friends, than to the Party itself. The Party allows no other lovers, as you know, Lao Jim."

"Is it true? About their loyalties?"

Little Joe laughed. "What do you think?"

"I'd say yes. A lot of people dislike the dull old men."

"You are right. It is not their loyalty to China that is the problem, but their reliance on the Party. The people I am talking about run factories that are profitable or bureaus that are too modern. They make decisions without asking the Party each day if it is permitted to eat rice for lunch."

"I know the kind of people you mean."

Little Joe nodded. "Yes, they are the best of China and the young people who work for them are fantastically loyal—these men are seen as the true future of the New China."

"To purge them will have a great effect on morale, won't it?"

"Will you never understand China, Lao Jim?" The Chinese laughed at his own question. "They will be purged not because they are efficient, but because they are corrupt. That is what the accusations will say, and that is what many people will believe. That Manager Hu used his position to enrich himself; that he stole money, or the factory's car; that he accepted gifts or bribes from foreigners; that he had a foreign bank account; that he smuggled goods from China under false documents. The list of charges is endless. The Party can say anything it likes. No guilt is necessary. The accusation is enough—for the Party."

McCarthy saw what was coming.

"No good news for you, huh?"

"I have been denied permission to travel—no families of leading cadres may go abroad to study any longer. That is the ruling."

"I'm sorry."

Little Joe had worked three years to pass the exams and polish his English. When McCarthy had first met him, the young man had boasted of a scholarship offer from an American university. "I am going to study language and literature," Little Joe had said. "Can you lend me some books to read before I go?"

It had been a year of yes-maybe-come-back-tomorrows. And then the bureaucracy had reneged.

"I have been assigned to work in the Number Five Locomotive Factory. I am to be a cook."

"Jesus, that's awful." They were on the tree-shaded street where Little Joe usually got out. McCarthy stopped the car and reached around for a package on the back seat. "It's easy for me to say, but try not to be discouraged, Little Joe. Keep reading and studying. Here, take a look."

McCarthy flipped on the dome light and the Chinese quickly riffled through his gifts—back copies of *The Economist, Time* and *Newsweek* and some paperback books.

"I couldn't find *Twelfth Night*, but I got *Merchant of Venice*. And here's one by Graham Greene, *Monsignor Quixote*. It's great."

"Quixote . . . Cervantes, right?"

McCarthy nodded.

"Well, he wrote in prison. I guess I can read in prison." Little Joe gestured. He meant everything around him.

"*Zaijian*," said Little Joe, and vanished into the night.

Pensively, McCarthy drove home. Poor bastard, he thought, another one of the good young ones being devoured. But a damned good source. Apprentice cook he might be, but Little Joe was still the son of a general.

"I trust the accommodations are satisfactory," Wang Bin said from the doorway. "I would be offended if such a distinguished guest were not comfortable."

Stratton stared dully at him from a pile of dirty straw at the far corner of the room.

Bathed in sweat, he rolled clumsily to a sitting position. Wang Bin sneered. "Your leg is all bloody. You should be more careful, Professor."

"Fuck you."

"Stand up."

"I can't."

On mincing steps, as though afraid of dirtying his highly polished shoes, Wang Bin advanced into the room until he stood over Stratton. His foot lashed out, striking Stratton's shin. Stratton bit back a moan.

"That is just the beginning, *Professor*." He spat as he spoke, hitting Stratton between the eyes. "I regret only that I shall not be present for the end. It was planned for Xian, but you were lucky. A train station is too public, and a bullet is too merciful for a man who rapes my daughter."

Stratton felt the spittle course down his face. He tensed for a spring. Movement caught Stratton's eye. Framed in the doorway stood one of the jailers, a pistol leveled at Stratton. With an explosion of breath, he allowed his body's tension to dissipate. Revenge alone was not enough. There must also be escape. There would be another time.

"I will tell you where you are, since you will never leave," Wang Bin said. "It is a museum on the outskirts of the city of Nanning. It is a backward place, Nanning, but it has some lovely Ming Dynasty pottery."

"You know where you can put your pottery."

"Oh no, Professor Stratton, there are better uses for it. For you, there is no use at all. Except as an example of revolutionary justice. Has anyone listed your crimes for you? No? An oversight, I'm sure."

Wang Bin rocked with his hands behind him, a student reciting his lessons.

"You are accused of theft: of the personal effects of my distinguished brother. You are accused of murder: of one of my trusted drivers in Peking, and of assault against another, who may still die."

Wang Bin's voice was rising in pitch, like a factory whistle.

"You are accused of kidnapping my daughter." He spat at Stratton again. "And of rape of my daughter.

"You are guilty of all charges, *Professor*." Wang Bin's face was flushed. "The sentence is death. There is no appeal. People's justice. Do you know how executions are carried out in revolutionary China, Professor?" Wang Bin's mouth twitched. "The condemned man is forced to kneel, with his hands tied behind his back. His executioner stands behind him. At the signal, the executioner advances one step, brings up his gun and in one motion, delivers a killing shot to the back of the head. Sometimes a pistol is used, but in your case, I think a rifle is more appropriate. A rifle leaves no room for mistakes."

"It will never happen," Stratton said slowly.

"You think not?"

"I know it. You are bluffing. This isn't a real jail, and you have no authority. This is your operation, *Deputy Minister*, and yours alone. The Chinese government has nothing against me—but a great deal against you."

"I am a servant of the Revolution," Wang Bin said, self-mockingly.

"You serve only yourself. You are a thief and a murderer."

"Stratton, you are like so many of your countrymen, much noise but no wisdom. You know nothing."

"I know that you have been stealing artifacts from the dig at Xian. I know that you asked your brother to help you smuggle something out. He refused. You argued, and later you killed him in Peking. Poison, I would say. There will be evidence, you know. Poison stays in the bones; any pathologist can find it. It remains only to exhume the body."

Wang Bin laughed.

"Fool! You understand nothing. My brother was of great assistance to me, yes, although he did not know it. I did not need him to smuggle contraband, Professor, but to bring me something. Something perfectly legitimate. He did it willingly."

"I'll bet."

"There is one other thing you should know, fool: My brother is not dead." Wang Bin hurled the words with ferocity.

"He's dead and you killed him. You can lie to me, but I doubt if your own government will be impressed. I have written a letter—everything I know about David's death, including the fact that you killed him. It is somewhere safe. If something happens to me, then it will be opened and forwarded to the Chinese government."

Wang Bin paused to consider.

"A letter, perhaps, with one of the members of your tour group, given to him before leaving Xian."

Stratton said nothing. That is what he might have done—if the document really existed.

Then Wang Bin smiled and Stratton knew his desperate ploy had failed.

"I think the letter is your invention, but if it exists, it cannot trouble me. For me, the time is ready. And your time is finished, *Captain*."

Stratton looked at the arrogant Chinese without expression.

"Does it surprise you to hear your old rank? It should not. We are thorough people, we Chinese, patient people with long memories. We have files for everything. There is a fat security file in Peking with your name on it, and a black ribbon across it. The ribbon is a special distinction. It means kill on sight.

So, in addition to all your other crimes, you are a spy. It will be a great pleasure to kill you, a service to the Revolution—my last gesture."

"How?" Stratton was too nonplussed to invent a denial.

"How did we ever know the name of the dashing captain of intelligence in Saigon who always undertook the most dangerous infiltration missions? The hero of many medals who led raids into North Vietnam and, once, even into China?

"How simple Americans are! Heroes are never truly anonymous, Captain, and soldiers can never be trusted with secrets. Can they? Think back to Saigon. Many Americans knew the true identity of the secret 'Captain Black.' Can you believe they never talked? To their girls, to friends when they were drunk. It took some time, the file says as much. But within a few months, North Vietnamese intelligence knew you were Captain Black. After your raid into China, they shared their information—we were allies then, remember. The Vietnamese wanted you very badly, and after your slaughter of innocent peasants, so did we. Too bad you left Saigon before the assassination teams could find you."

"You got the wrong guy," Stratton said without conviction.

"I think not. Your death, at least, is something for which the Revolution will thank me. Goodbye, Captain. I hope you will find hell even less hospitable than China."

Wang Bin stormed from the makeshift cell. Stratton heard the heavy wooden bar fall against the door. He lay for a long time on the fetid ground, thinking, listening.

Then, painfully but surely, he pulled himself to his feet. He hurt, but not as badly as he had led Wang Bin to believe. Teeth clenched, moving with the jerky uncertainty of an old man, Stratton began a series of painful limbering exercises. As he bent and swayed, Stratton replayed the conversation with Wang Bin. If the mind is too occupied to register pain, then there is no pain.

The man was angry, and he would be merciless. That was the bottom line. Yet there had been bits of information within the conversation that Stratton might use. He began to gnaw at them.

He was in the south of China. What he had seen of the vegetation Wang Bin had confirmed. Guangxi Province, Stratton tried to superimpose the train ride on a map of China.

South for three days. He couldn't be far from the coast. If he could get to the sea and steal a boat . . .

There had been puzzling things, too. David's unwitting role had been to bring something, Wang Bin had said. That was an obvious lie. The brothers had argued in Xian only after David had learned that Wang Bin wanted him to smuggle.

"My brother is not dead," he had said. A second lie, even more senseless than the first. Of course David was dead—he had been murdered.

There was a third riddle. Stratton's death was to be "my last gesture" to the Revolution. What could account for that strange phrase?

Gingerly, he began a series of knee bends. Down-two-three-four. His leg howled in protest. Why tell lies to a condemned man? Senseless. Unless . . .

"Oh, Jesus."

Stratton spoke aloud to the emptiness of his cell, the words forced from him by sudden realization. What if Wang Bin had been telling the truth?

Stratton saw it then. Not entirely clear, but in terrifying outline. Solid, diabolical, imminent.

On one point, Wang Bin had been right.

Stratton was a fool.

In frustration, he hammered at the walls of the cell. Then he snapped a leg from the wooden chair and with its point began to scrape at the crude mortar between the bricks. It was irrational, and he knew it. Still, it was not a time for reason. It was a time for fury. Stratton scraped like a man demented.

Wang Bin sat with his legs crossed in an overstuffed armchair, waiting for his tea to cool. On the table before him sat four vases, each exquisite, each more than five hundred years old.

An aide in bottle-bottom glasses came silently into the room. He sprang forward to light the deputy minister's cigarette.

"Will we be needing our guest any longer, Comrade?" the aide asked quietly.

"One more day, I'm afraid, Lao Zhou." Wang Bin was perturbed. "I wish it could have been done on the train. If only his embassy had not started asking questions. I *must* know what he told his people, if he told them anything. One more day . . . then he must vanish completely, do you understand? No trace."

"It will be done. He is a dangerous enemy of the state." The frail-looking young translator with weak eyes was the most sadistic killer Wang Bin had ever encountered.

"You will tell me everything he says. It is vital . . . to the Revolution," Wang Bin said. "I would like to be there myself, but I must return immediately to Peking. Go make the arrangements."

When the aide had gone, Wang Bin extracted a green and white envelope from the breast pocket of his Mao jacket. The telegram had arrived with breakfast and he knew its contents by heart.

YOU ARE REQUIRED TO APPEAR BEFORE THE DISCIPLINARY COMMISSION OF THE PARTY.

It gave a time and a date: tomorrow.

He had been expecting it. And it might have come sooner. Once again, it seemed, those idiots in Peking were determined to wrestle long-suffering China back into the Middle Ages. A few months before, such a summons would have paralyzed Wang Bin with terror—as it was intended to do. But he had foreseen it this time, and he was ready. Now there was just fleeting irritation at the dreadful cost to the nation and his own comfort. Let them writhe, he thought. Let them devour their own entrails if they wish. Comrade Deputy Minister Wang Bin would never again collect night soil.

This new peace of mind had its price, of course: an odious alliance with the American art dealer Harold Broom. His name had come to Wang Bin from an underground buyer in Hong Kong. Broom had been highly recommended, not for his taste—he had none—but for his resourcefulness. It was a trait that Wang Bin had come to appreciate, though he could not help but despise Broom for his crude arrogance.

Their short relationship had been curt, clandestine and efficient. So far. A visa problem smoothed over. A travel permit expedited. Quiet favors.

Yet there were watchers everywhere, Wang Bin well knew. He doubted that the Disciplinary Commission had learned the truth about Harold Broom, but such news would not shock him. He was ready for anything.

By the time the aide returned to confirm the travel arrangements, Wang Bin had already decided.

"We will take the first one and the fourth one," he said, pointing to the smallest of the four vases.

"Yes, Comrade Deputy Minister. But the comrade director of the museum will be very upset. They are among the best pieces."

"Tell him they are for permanent display in a place of honor in Peking."

"Still, he will not like it."

"Tell him it is for the good of the people. The Revolution demands it."

"Very well, Comrade Deputy Minister. But he is a hard man. He will want a receipt."

A hard man who thinks a receipt will protect him.

"A receipt," said Wang Bin. "By all means. Have the director prepare a receipt and I will sign it."

CHAPTER 13

HAROLD BROOM ARRIVED ten minutes early at the gleaming white mansion in the River Oaks section of Houston. He leaned against his rented Lincoln for five minutes, admiring the tall pillars and polished marble steps. At the door he was met by a Mexican houseboy in a stiff high-collared waiter's jacket, who motioned him inside. He led the art dealer up a spiral oaken staircase to a second-floor office where the customer waited.

"Well, hi there!" the Texan said. Even by Houston standards he was young for a millionaire. He wore a flannel shirt, pressed Levi's, lizardskin boots and the obligatory cowboy hat with a plume. When he shook Broom's hand, he gave a disconcerting little squeeze before he let go.

Broom sat down and said, "This is a helluva homestead."

The Texan grinned. "You like it?"

"Oh yeah." Broom noticed three king-sized television screens mounted on one wall, each flashing a different program. The corners of the office were occupied by stand-up stereo speakers. The Texan kept a video display terminal on his desk to watch the Dow Jones; behind his chair, Broom noticed, stood an arcade-sized Pac Man machine.

The Texan jerked a thumb at it. "Bored with it already," he said. "I've got an order in for an Astral Laser."

"Swell," Broom said. It was sickening: all this money and no brains. "Could I have a drink?"

"I don't see why not." The Texan poked an intercom button near the phone and shouted, "Paco! Two bourbons pronto."

"It's *Pablo*," a teenaged voice replied with unmasked annoyance.

The bourbon was excellent. Broom savored it, while the Texan sucked it down loudly. "Nectar," he said. "Pure nectar!"

Broom reached into the suede valise on his lap and extracted a glossy black-and-white photograph. He glanced at it before handing it across the desk to his host.

"There it is," Broom said with parental pride. "The real McCoy."

The Texan was radiant. "Broom, you've outdone yourself, I swear to God. I know better than to ask how you did it."

Broom took this as a compliment, and he forced a modest smile.

"If it arrives in this condition, it will be . . . awesome." The Texan clicked his teeth, as if leering at a centerfold.

Broom said, "The photograph was made moments before we packed it. I took the picture myself. That's the genuine item, and it's all yours. Guaranteed."

Pablo poured more bourbon. Broom drank up, basking in luxury and triumph. He was elated to be out of China.

"Harold," the Texan said, "I've gotta be sure. This is the only one?"

"Absolutely," Broom lied. If the Texan only knew.

"The price is—"

"Two hundred and fifty thousand now. Another two fifty on delivery. And don't worry. I'll be delivering it myself."

"You damn well better," the Texan growled, reaching for his checkbook. "For the kind of commission you're getting, Broom, you damn well ought to show up pulling a ricksha."

The *xiu xi* is China's most revered institution. Indeed, a worker's right to rest is enshrined in China's constitution. Nowhere does it say that all China shall sleep between noon and 2 P.M., but that is how it seems. If the Russians ever come, it will be at 1 P.M., when only the rawest Chinese recruits will be awake to oppose them. In Peking, office workers sleep on their desks. In the countryside, peasants sleep in the fields. If airplane crews find themselves on the ground at noon, they will not fly again until after lunch and a *xiu xi*. The more senior a cadre, the better-appointed and more private the place of his *xiu xi*, and the longer he sleeps.

The Disciplinary Commission had cited Wang Bin for 1 P.M. It was a calculated insult, and he knew it. At noon, Wang Bin lunched with senior aides in a private room of the staff restaurant at the Peking museum that was his headquarters. Conversation was furtive. One or two of the men who had been with him the longest mentioned things that had occurred in the

Deputy Minister's absence in the south: The Qin exhibition had been dispatched to the United States on schedule. From Xinjiang in China's desert west, the museum was to receive the mummified corpses of two soldiers perfectly preserved in the dry air these six hundred years; they would require a special room with stringent humidity controls.

Mostly, though, the aides avoided meeting Wang Bin's eyes. Their discomfort amused him. They knew. Deliberations of the Party are secrets closely held. But when the ax is about to fall, everybody knows. Peking becomes a village in those times. When the arrival of soup signaled the last course, Wang Bin pointedly looked around the table, studying his aides individually, making no secret of it. He was rewarded with the sight of six heads, bent uniformly, like acolytes, slurping their soup, seeing only the bowl. He wondered which of them had informed against him, and which would give testimony—if it came to that. The answer was obvious, and it saddened him: all of them. Poor China.

Rising, Wang Bin raised a tiny crystal glass of *mao tai*. "To long life and happiness," he proposed. "*Ganbei*."

"*Ganbei*," the aides responded, and each drained the fiery liquor in one swallow.

"*Xiu xi*," said Wang Bin. He found savage delight in the uncertainty that caused. One of the aides even looked at his watch. It was precisely one o'clock. So they even knew the time. Spineless sons of a turtle.

Wang Bin slept deeply on a daybed next to his office for more than an hour. The train from the south had been crowded and slow, arriving in Peking just after dawn, and he had rested little. Again and again, he had replayed the climactic acts of the drama he had forged. It would work, as long as he could keep time on his side. He had not expected the Party's summons so soon. Another day or two might have made all the difference. Wang Bin sighed with finality and prepared to meet his inquisitors.

Precisely at 3 P.M., Wang Bin presented himself at a side entrance of the Great Hall of the People. To those who knew it existed, it was the most dreaded doorway in Peking.

"You are late," said a severe young receptionist without preamble.

"I was detained on the people's business. Please tell the comrades that I have arrived."

"You will wait," the young man instructed. "The comrade will show you where."

He gestured to an orderly who led Wang Bin to a high-ceilinged reception room big enough for fifty people. It was empty, except for one straight-backed wooden chair in the precise center of a beige carpet. Wang Bin nearly laughed aloud. It was so transparent.

"Bring tea," he snarled to the orderly.

No tea came, nor any summons for nearly two hours. By the time Wang Bin was led into a red plush room usually reserved for Central Committee meetings, the two-wheeled afternoon rush hour gripped Peking.

Once more, intimidation. Another crude chair facing a long, highly polished table where three men sat: two wizened Party cadres and a PLA general, to lend authority. The army, after all, belonged not to the nation but to the Party, by decree of the same constitution that had enshrined the *xiu xi*.

Wang Bin knew all three men. The two Party ancients were willows, professional survivors who had devoted an empty lifetime to swaying back and forth with changing political winds. The general was something else again. Wang Bin had soldiered with him once, when they had both—like their cause—been young and strong.

The three old men comprised the Disciplinary Commission. To their right sat a younger man in his forties. His black hair leapt impulsively from his skull. His eyes burned with the unmistakable fire of a zealot. The prosecutor. At a desk of their own sat two sexless women stenographers.

"You may sit," said the elder of the two Party hacks. That made him the president of what was technically a commission of inquiry, but only by euphemism. It was as close to a trial as Wang Bin would see, if he was smart. Everybody in the room knew it. Everybody also knew that Wang Bin had already been found guilty of whatever it was they were about to charge him with. All that remained was the sentence.

"I prefer to stand, Comrade," said Wang Bin.

"You will sit," snapped the prosecutor.

"Oh, let him stand if he wants to. What difference does it make?" The general sighed from a mouth half-hidden by a hand that supported his face.

"Proceed," said the president.

"This is an inquiry by the Disciplinary Commission of the

Communist Party of the People's Republic of China against Wang Bin, Party member since 1937, expelled in 1966 and rehabilitated blameless in 1976."

The prosecutor read like an automaton in a high, singsong voice.

"Based on information received, and from direct observation, the Party accuses Wang Bin of conduct inimical to the best interests of the Party and the state."

Wang Bin tensed. How much did they know? Everything hinged on the innate stupidity of the bureaucracy. They would list the charges chronologically, with the most recent first, Wang Bin knew, to shake the confidence of the accused by showing how vigilant and up-to-date the watchers could be.

"One. You are accused of meeting secretly, privately and without authorization with a foreigner for purposes inconsistent with the best interests of the Party: namely, Harold Broom, an American citizen; five counts.

"Two. The same accusation applies to another American, one Thomas Stratton, with whom you met secretly in your office in Peking in violation of the Party code of correct conduct.

"Three. You are accused of misuse of Party property, namely one Red Flag limousine, damaged severely while assigned to you.

"Four. You are accused of the misuse of Party funds in paying for a decadent art exhibition attended by foreigners in state property, namely a museum, under your custody.

"Five. You are accused of conspiring against the best interests of the state and the Party in personally securing an entry visa for an American citizen, namely David Wang, without authorization, and of abandoning your post to travel and to meet secretly with David Wang.

"Six. You are accused of receiving unauthorized gifts from a foreigner, namely propaganda materials from the Embassy of France . . ."

Wang Bin stared at a streak of grease on a chunky window behind the commission table. He tried to remain detached. He tried to keep from laughing. The "propagnada materials" had been a set of art books for the museum library.

And how typical. The Party, in a frenzy of self-consuming self-righteousness, could not see fire, but invented smoke. What he was accused of was making his ministry fairly open, semiefficient and less backward than most in the Chinese government. His true guilt was unmentioned, unknown, invisible to zealot cadres who found termites in healthy trees, but never noticed that the forest was burning. Wang Bin fought back a sneer. *If you really knew my crimes, comrades, my friend the general would end this charade with a single shot—and I wouldn't blame him.*

It was amazing. The prosecutor seemed immune to breathing. He read without pause, increasing shrillness his only concession to an indictment of forty-seven different crimes over seven years.

"Forty-seven. You are accused of meeting privately with a foreigner, namely Gerta Hofsted, in the dining room of the Peking Hotel and charging your ministry for the meal when in fact it was paid for by the foreigner."

My, my, how thorough. A lunch seven years before with a West German anthropologist. She had never noticed when he pocketed the receipt, but obviously a waiter had.

The prosecutor shut up as suddenly as he had begun. Wang Bin remembered a joke a Russian had told him back in the days when Russia and China were allies. About the factory worker who left every night carrying a heavy load of sand in a wheelbarrow. The KGB knew he was stealing something. They tasted the sand. They sifted it. They sent it away for analysis. The results were conclusive: plain old ordinary worthless sand. It took them months to realize the worker was stealing wheelbarrows. *Marxist myopia.*

"One other matter has come to the attention of this commission," said the moribund cadre who sat next to the president. "It is not within the province of this investigation since the accused is not a Party member, but it does reflect on the failure of Comrade Wang Bin to inspire his own family to live according to Party principles." The cadre sucked, hollow-cheeked, at his tea.

"The commission has evidence that Wang Kangmei, daughter of Comrade Wang Bin, left her unit without permission, that she traveled without permission to the city of Xian, and that there she engaged in sexual relations with a foreigner."

"She was abducted," Wang Bin blurted, and instantly regretted it.

"This commission is forwarding the relevant testimony to

the Public Security Bureau for action," the cadre intoned without expression.

That was the cue for the prosecutor. He jerked back to his feet.

"In view of the seriousness of the charges, I call for a full trial and a sentence of life inprisonment at hard labor."

It was a formality. Still, in the calculated silence that followed the prosecutor's demand, Wang Bin began to sweat.

"The commission agrees with the prosecutor's request," said the president.

Again, the old men allowed a cruel silence to build. Wang Bin braced for the sound of the door opening, the rush of air, the footsteps of the guards summoned by a buzzer beneath the table.

"However," the president began.

At last! Wang Bin felt a sudden release.

"In view of Comrade Wang's long service to the Party, this commission will waive a trial in exchange for Comrade Wang's admission of guilt, a self-criticism, his removal from all state and Party posts and his reeducation through labor in . . ."— he consulted a printed list in front of him—"Jilin Province."

It was a sentence of slow death. Manchuria. Backward and cold, so bitterly cold and primitive he would not survive two years there.

"Jilin," said the second cadre.

That left the general.

"Hunan," said the general. "And as an office worker. He is an educated man."

Hunan was backward, too, but warmer. To work there as a bookkeeper on a commune would be dull, but not dangerous, almost like retiring. Such were the fruits of a fifty-year friendship between men who had once fought together.

The two hacks dithered for a while—Jilin was what their paper decreed—but the general proved implacable.

"Hunan." The president surrendered. "You have twenty-four hours, Comrade, in which to inform the commission whether you wish a trial or will accept the Party's mercy."

Wang Bin squared his back and strode from the room.

Twenty-four hours. He had counted on that. It was time enough.

CHAPTER 14

STRATTON'S MAKESHIFT CHISEL splintered after only an hour. A cone-shaped pile of concrete dust and a faint groove in the mortar were all he had to show for his furious scraping. There was no way out of the cell. Stratton snapped another leg off the wooden chair and rubbed one end back and forth across the rough wall until a sharp point was formed. Then he buried the stick in a corner. Another corner was used for defecation. A third corner he reserved for sleeping.

He curled up, facing the wall, and shielded his eyes with one arm. That night, for the first time, the jailers had left the light bulb burning in the rafters; insects darted and danced around it. Stratton closed his eyes and thought of his parents. For thirty-one years his father had driven a UPS truck in Hartford, while his mother had reared five children. Now the Strattons were retired, living in a small apartment in Boca Raton, Florida, entertaining grandchildren and feeding the ducks in a man-made lake behind the high rise. Tom Stratton had visited his parents only twice in their new home. He telephoned once a month from wherever he was. He had promised them postcards from Peking, but of course he had forgotten. They wouldn't be worried, not Dale and Ann Stratton. They knew their youngest son. The restless sort, his mother used to say. Pity the poor gal he marries, and pitied she had.

The flat horn of a truck jolted Stratton into daylight. He unfolded, stretched his arms, and watched through the window as the first morning visitors arrived at the small museum. It had been more than a day now since his keepers had brought fresh rice or water. Stratton was famished. He considered pounding on the door on the remote chance that he had been forgotten, but rejected the idea. He knew he was a VIP. Whatever awaited him had been carefully planned by Wang Bin.

The day passed slowly, and Stratton napped intermittently,

using sleep as a substitute for food. Finally, late in the afternoon, he heard footsteps in the hall outside the cell. He sat up, and shrank into the shadow of the cleanest corner, his sleeping corner.

Two men entered the cell. Stratton recognized one of them as a jailer, one of the men who had paraded him to his public bath.

The other was a wan, slightly built Chinese who wore bottle-bottom eyeglasses. He squinted at Stratton until he became accustomed to the light.

Each man carried a large tin bucket.

"Stand," ordered the man with the eyeglasses.

Stratton obeyed. The two men heaved the liquid contents of the buckets on the floor in a large puddle at Stratton's feet. The odor assaulted him and he tried hard not to gag.

"Pig manure," said the same man, again in clear English. "Kneel."

"Why?"

"You will not argue. You will not ask questions. You will do as I say. You are unfit to speak in this room. You are unfit to stand. So you will kneel, and you will be completely silent."

Stratton did not move. The man with the bottle-bottom glasses circled him disdainfully, eyeing the American as if he were a roach.

"You have broken this chair!"

"No, it fell apart."

"Liar!"

"Liar!" shouted the jailer, chiming in.

"An accident," Stratton repeated.

"My name is Comrade Zhou," said the man in the glasses. "We have met before."

"Oh, yes. You were Wang Bin's interpreter in Peking," Stratton said.

Zhou lifted the mangled two-legged chair as if examining it. Then he swung it over his head and brought it crashing down on Tom Stratton's shoulder. Stratton pitched forward, face down into the warm pig dung. A small hand seized his neck, and another clutched his hair. Roughly, he was jerked off the floor, and propped on his knees like a mannequin.

"I will repeat this one more time," Zhou said. Now he was squatting in front of Stratton, glaring into the American's dripping face. "You are unworthy to stand in the presence of any Chinese citizen, do you understand? You are worse than the shit on this floor. You are a murderer and a thief, a destroyer of Chinese property, a corrupter of young women, a spy . . . and, I think you should know, Stratton, that you have no secrets here. We know everything about you!"

Stratton made no response. He breathed through his mouth only. He closed his eyes. He fought to neutralize all his senses, one by one.

"We have come here to give you the opportunity to confess your crimes, Comrade Stratton. Do not be afraid, and do not be foolish. Many thousands of Chinese have profited from such expurgation. They lived to tell about it, however. I cannot promise the same for you."

"What is this, a struggle session? You're sick," Stratton said.

Zhou nodded. "Ah, you've heard of this. You have read about it, I suppose, in some perverted imperialist book. China is the subject of many books in your country. China is a popular subject among American scholars. You came here posing as a scholar, did you not?"

"I am a tourist."

"Liar!" It was the jailer again. He knew the script.

"Do not continue with these lies," Zhou said. "I know your country very well, Stratton. I know the American people, I even know the language. I studied for two years at Yale University." Zhou laughed. "It's amusing, in a way. In the many years since my return to China I have never once had the opportunity to interview an American criminal. You are my first. I am grateful to Comrade Wang Bin for the chance to serve China in this way. He tells me you are a treacherous spy."

"He is mistaken, Comrade Zhou. I am merely a friend of his brother."

"You are a liar," Zhou replied.

"Liar!" screamed the jailer. It was the only English word he knew.

"Liar!" Zhou yelled.

"No."

"Now it is time to confess," Zhou said. He left the cell, and returned shortly with a written Chinese document. "Please sign this now."

"What does it say? Could you read it to me?" Stratton said, stalling.

"Of course." Zhou motioned at the jailer, who slogged out

of the cell. He and another jailer returned carrying three
wooden chairs. One was placed directly in front of Stratton,
and that is where Zhou sat. The first jailer took the second
chair, to Zhou's left, but equidistant from the kneeling
American. A third chair was placed on Zhou's right. It was
empty.

"You have been found guilty of numerous crimes against the
state," Zhou began. "This is the list. It is lengthy.

"To begin with, you lied on your visa application. You said
you had never been to China before, Stratton. Therefore you
are charged with presenting false information to immigration
officials.

"Secondly, you are charged with the theft of personal
articles belonging to Mr. David Wang. These items were stolen
from Mr. Wang's hotel room in Peking nearly one week ago."

Stratton stared at the earthen floor and shook his head.

"You are charged with the murder of Huang Gong, a
limousine driver in Peking who was killed while serving the
state. Additionally, you are charged with the attempted murder
of another comrade, Ni Zanfu, who was seriously injured in
the same tragic episode."

"They tried to run me down," Stratton protested.

"Liar!" screamed the interrogators in unison.

"There are two more crimes which are the most serious,"
Zhou went on. "One of them is the abduction of Wang
Kangmei, the daughter of the deputy minister. We will discuss
that in a moment. But I first should like to ask you about the
crime of espionage against the People's Republic. On March
18, 1971 . . ." and Zhou began to read the document:
" 'Thomas Stratton, then a captain with the Special Forces
Intelligence section of the United States Army, illegally entered
the Chinese town of Man-ling with a squad of armed soldiers
and assassinated thirty-eight innocent peasants.' "

Zhou paused and glanced up from the paper. "You came
back to China this year for the purpose of continuing your
terrorism and trying to recruit Chinese citizens for your
criminal espionage. You are a dangerous agent of the United
States government, and you must be punished according to the
laws of the Chinese state. Now . . . are you willing to
confess to your crimes, Mr. Stratton?"

"I cannot, Comrade Zhou." Stratton stared at the frog-eyed
face. Zhou's thick eyeglasses looked like a cheap prop for

some stand-up comic, but there was nothing funny in the Chinese eyes. He waved the document contemptuously.

"Perhaps we should review each charge separately—"

"My answer would remain the same. Not guilty. I am not guilty of anything."

Zhou nodded at the jailer. The jailer's leg shot out, and his boot caught Stratton flush in the Adam's apple. He toppled backwards into the slop, moaning, choking, gulping air. He grabbed impotently at his throat with both hands.

After a few moments, the jailer yanked Stratton to his knees.

"Have you caught your breath?" Zhou asked.

Stratton's mouth moved, but only a dry rattle came out.

"It is a question of honor, then?" Zhou pressed. "You will not confess because your pride rebels. We know something of honor in our country, too, Mr. Stratton. I cannot tell you how many men and women have knelt before me and resisted the truth because of honor and pride—no matter what the evidence, no matter what kind of punishment awaited them. I have seen many men—some of them weaker than you—resist for days. Three, four days, even longer. It was remarkable. No food, no water. They knelt there, wetting themselves and soiling themselves and suffering . . . yet, they insisted, no matter what, that they, too, were innocent. I have to admit that I came to admire some of those comrades even after I executed them, Mr. Stratton.

"The choice is yours. Would you prefer to be admired for your valor? Or would you instead care for some warm food, and cold water. And perhaps some medical treatment for your leg? Clean clothes? A bath?"

Zhou did not smile. The jailer waited for another signal.

"One man lasted six days with me," Zhou said. "His was a political crime, truly insignificant compared to yours. I was prepared to send him to one of the far provinces for two years. Farm labor on a rural commune. It would have been a fair sentence, had he confessed. But he, too, spoke of honor. Even after three days, when we boarded the windows. It was summer, very hot and still. He was old and sick. We took away all the food, of course. By the fifth day, he was drinking his own urine. On the sixth day, I threw a live river rat into the cell and he ate it raw, tail and all. So much for honor Mr. Stratton."

Stratton could not think for the pain; each idea seemed to sting the inside of his brain. Cowering on his knees, never had he been so helpless. His captors did not have a gun, nor did they need one. Stratton was the weakest man in the cell, and all three of them knew it. All he could do was drag it out, and hope for the pain to pass.

"Do you see why you are unworthy to stand? After hearing the list of your crimes, do you now understand?"

"What if I were to confess to some of the charges?" Stratton asked in a raspy voice.

"No!" Zhou barked. "Not good enough. The crimes are related. One leads to another. It is impossible to be innocent of some and guilty of others. It is either day or night. Justice must be distinct, and clear, and indisputable. Otherwise there would be no respect for laws. So if you confess, you will confess to all of it. You *will* be truthful."

"How long have you worked for Wang Bin?"

"Shut up!"

"Are you paid well?" Stratton's tone was soft, boylike.

"I work for the state."

"Then where is your uniform?"

"Quiet!" Zhou snapped. The jailer did not understand the words, but he listened tautly, in expectation.

"Have I been convicted by the state?"

"Yes. The deputy minister pronounced—"

"No, I said by the *state*." Stratton was breathing easier, although his throat felt bruised and swollen. "If this is a state prison, then where is the PLA?"

Zhou smiled darkly. "You would feel more at home with soldiers? It would bring back old memories for you, I'm sure. That is too bad. There are no PLA here. And this is not a trial, Stratton. The trial is over. All that remains is for you to accept your conviction and acknowledge your crimes. We expect no more from you than we would from a Chinese criminal. The truth is, the deputy minister has more patience with you than I."

Zhou stood up. He spoke to the jailer, who left the cell immediately. "The smell in here is very bad. I am not certain if it is the pigs or you, Mr. Stratton. I am going outdoors for a few minutes for some fresh air, and perhaps a cold beer. In the meantime, the other comrade will give you something to think about. Then we will resume."

Zhou hitched his trousers and walked out. Stratton sagged back on his heels. He glanced longingly at the corner where he had concealed his makeshift weapon, but within seconds the jailer had returned, flinging the door open. He spoke sharply in Chinese to someone else in the corridor. Stratton rose to his knees and looked up. There, in the doorway, stood Kangmei.

Not for the first time, the old professor wondered at the futility of man. He had dedicated his life to the proposition that all mankind's creations should be appraised not just for their beauty or ingenuity, but for what they revealed about the mystery of the human mind. And now, so late in his life, to face the mystery of true evil. No Chinese artist could ever express such a horror—the betrayal of history, of art itself, of one's own brother.

It was a secret David Wang had never asked to know, but knowing, he could not let it die with him.

He was not a man of action, but he had ruminated long enough. He was certain that escape was possible. He had studied the primitive lock on the door of the Peking attic that served as his warm prison. He had even secreted a spoon that his slovenly jailers had missed, and he had bent it so that it could be prised between the door and the rusty jamb to lift the latch. David Wang was both exhilarated and frightened by the possibilities.

It had taken two days—a drugged two days—before he had come to his senses. He remembered a big dinner of roast duck, then sipping tea alone in his hotel room afterward. And then nothing—until he awoke as a captive.

For six days, David Wang had analyzed the routine of his keepers until he had identified the flaw. After his supper was delivered each day, the jailers all ate together, loudly, in a large kitchen at the end of the hallway. They never returned for the tray in less than an hour; on one occasion, they had not come again until the next morning.

An hour was plenty of time, David Wang figured, to break out, slip away from his brother's museum and lose himself in the streets of Peking. The guards had dressed him in an old-fashioned undershirt, more gray than white, baggy blue trousers and cotton shoes. In the darkness of the street, he would be indistinguishable from millions of other Pekingese.

He would walk to the American Embassy if he could. Failing that, David Wang decided, he would approach the first policeman he saw and ask for help. The policeman would not believe his story, of course, but he would take him in, just the same.

David Wang would find someone to tell: *My brother is committing a terrible crime against China, against humanity. I have seen it in Xian. He must be stopped.*

David had reached this conclusion with sadness. His important brother was a criminal. For days he had expected Wang Bin to appear at the attic to explain, to apologize, to disavow any knowledge of David's imprisonment. Then he had prayed that Wang Bin would come in repentance, denouncing his own crazed scheme, begging forgiveness. David would have given it, willingly, and returned to the United States without saying a word.

On the third day, David Wang had shouted at his jailers, demanding an audience with Wang Bin. The jailers had laughed at the old man.

By the fifth day, a new thought had occurred to David, and he came to fear that Wang Bin *would* appear. Death itself did not frighten him, but he did not want it like this, in Peking, at the hands of his own brother.

David convinced himself that the only perilous part of the escape would be finding his way out of the museum. In dim lighting, his weak vision suffered from a loss of depth and distance. He would have to move slowly, maybe too slowly.

After the jailers brought the dinner tray that night, David meticulously counted one hundred and twenty nervous seconds before he slipped the latch on the door.

The corridor was poorly lit. At one end, light seeped from a room where the jailers dined raucously. Peering intently, David Wang could make out a doorway that appeared to lead to a flight of stairs. His confidence rising, he tiptoed along the hall until he reached the door and his feet found the first flight. Cautiously, he began to descend.

The stairwell was dark. David felt his way like a blind man—one hand groped the grimy wall, the other clung to a cold metal handrail. Would it be four flights, or five? He tried to remember the size of the building from the day he had first visited the museum as his brother's honored guest.

After two flights, David Wang stopped to rest. A reassuring stillness wrapped the museum; the only sounds he heard were his own shuffling, tentative footsteps. At the third landing, David's questing hand encountered something tall and wooden.

At the same instant, his foot kicked something bulky and metallic. David dropped to all fours and used his hands to identify the objects: a ladder and a chest of tools. He found the handle of the tool chest and lifted it. Not too heavy. He would take it with him as protective coloration. It might be just the thing to get him out the back door and into the street.

Suddenly the lights in the stairwell snapped on. From above came agitated shouts, and the rumble of feet on the stairs.

For a few precious seconds David Wang was paralyzed, rooted and tremulous as the din escalated. Only when the first young cadre appeared at the top of the stairs did he act.

With a desperate jerk, David toppled the ladder. It fell in front of his pursuer. As David lunged for the door on the landing, the cadre hurdled the ladder easily. A hand clamped David by the shoulder. He spun around and breathlessly shoved—nearly threw—the tool chest into the cadre's gut. The young man staggered backwards and doubled up. When his heels hit the ladder he tumbled down the stairs in a groaning somersault.

David Wang did not wait to see his enemy stop rolling. He was already anxiously exploring the second floor of the museum. It was a large room, dominated by rows of display cases, dimly perceived, their contents a mystery. If only there were someplace to hide, and if only he could see it. Across the gallery was another doorway. David Wang did not particularly care where it would take him. He ran for it. His gait was the huffing half-waddle of an old man, no match for the athletic cadres who streamed behind him.

David was but halfway to the door when he realized that he would not make it. He meant to stop, to gather himself and surrender with dignity. Instead, he lost his balance and skidded into a glass display case housing a collection of seventh century bronzes. David Wang and the exhibit went down together with an ear-splitting crash.

When his wits returned, a circle of young men was standing over him. He expected that they would scream at him, perhaps jeer, or even beat him. But they did not. Rather, the cadres simple led David back to his attic cell with the impatience of peasants who have frustrated the ungainly escape of a commune mule.

Later, the keepers even brought the old scholar tea and

dumplings to replace the dinner he had fled. This time the spoon was plastic.

In another cell, hundreds of miles away, Tom Stratton shakily faced a contrived tribunal. The jailer returned to the chair on Zhou's left. Zhou himself sat down next, his back straight, his face unreadable. Kangmei wordlessly took the chair on Zhou's right. Her long hair had been braided in pigtails, and her Western clothes had been replaced with standard Mao blue. Stratton searched her eyes for a clue, but Kangmei looked away.

"Nice room, huh?" Stratton said. "This is what I get for taking the American plan."

"You are to remain silent," Zhou warned, "until these accusations are read. Then you will be permitted to state your confession and sign it. Then sentence will be declared. Wang Kangmei?"

"Yes, Comrade Zhou."

"Do you see the man named Thomas Stratton in this room?"

"Yes, Comrade."

"Describe him," Zhou commanded.

Kangmei studied the half-naked Stratton for several moments, up and down, and this time it was he who looked away.

"He is an American. He is tall and light-haired. With a mustache."

"And what is he doing now?"

"Kneeling, Comrade Zhou."

"And what is he wearing, Wang Kangmei?"

"A shirt, a torn shirt."

"Filthy? Unclean?"

"Yes, Comrade."

"And what else? What else is he wearing?"

"A bandage. A filthy bandage." Kangmei glared scornfully down at Stratton. "And that is all, Comrade Zhou. He has no other clothes on."

"And do you find him . . . attractive?"

"No! He is disgusting. He is a pig. A pig and a liar."

"Liar!" shouted the jailer. He propped one of his shoes on Stratton's bruised shoulder. "Liar! Liar!" Stratton pushed the foot away.

"Kangmei, what crimes did Mr. Stratton commit against you?"

"He asked me to come to his hotel room in Xian. He said he wanted to give me something that belonged to my uncle, David Wang, who had died in Peking. He said it was something of great sentimental value."

Zhou said, "Did you believe the lying pig Thomas Stratton?"

"Yes, Comrade. I believed him."

"What happened when you went to his hotel room in Xian?"

"He held me against my will. He abducted me. He beat me. He said my father, the deputy minister, represented all that was evil about the Communist Party, and that he must be destroyed."

"So," Zhou said, "he threatened to kill a Chinese deputy minister. What else did he say?"

"Thom-as Stratton admitted that he is an agent of the imperialist United States government, and that he was sent to China to encourage terrorism and disrupt the efforts of the loyal workers."

To Stratton's surprise, Kangmei did not recite her indictment in monotone. Rather, her tone was impassioned, the words seemingly spontaneous. Her eyes seemed to glisten, but whether in rage or sorrow Stratton could no longer be sure.

Zhou said, "What did you do when you heard Stratton denounce your father?"

"I argued with him, Comrade. I became angry. I told him he was not worthy to visit our country, and that I was going to report him to the Public Security Bureau. When I tried to run out of his room, he grabbed me by the arms and threw me down on the floor. Then he kicked me between the legs . . ."

"No!" Stratton bellowed. "Kangmei, please, I know what's happening, but—"

Zhou motioned to the jailer, who swiftly moved behind Stratton and dug a knee into the small of his back. Then he seized Stratton's hair and yanked back so that Stratton was forced to stare up at the roof, his neck stretched tight. Zhou scooped a handful of rancid manure from the floor and dropped it into Stratton's face. He retched.

"You will remain silent from now on," Zhou said mildly.

Stratton stared back with dead eyes. His face was chalky.

Kangmei continued her story: "Stratton gagged me so I could not scream. Then he tied me to the bed in the room."

"Then what?"

"He ripped my clothing off . . . and raped me."

"Several times?"

"Yes, Comrade Zhou. Several times . . . and once in a terrible way."

Stratton grimaced. A horsefly landed on one cheek, beneath his left eye. Even as it bit him, Stratton made no move to brush it away. His arms hung like butcher's meat.

"Finally I was rescued when two comrades came to the hotel room. They must have heard me fighting back. Stratton escaped, but at least my ordeal was over."

Stratton gazed sadly at Kangmei, and shook his head back and forth with determination. Her eyes never softened.

Zhou said, "Kangmei, do you now see the folly of your contact with foreigners, especially decadent Americans? They are a menace to the state, a threat to everything we are working for. They are not to be trusted, and never to be believed. Stratton is a model of this—a murderer . . ."

"Murderer!" Kangmei agreed.

"A thief, a corrupter . . ."

"A thief!" she yelled in a suddenly shrill voice that startled Stratton.

"A rapist," Zhou concluded.

"Rapist!" Kangmei cried. "A murderer and rapist!"

"You were deceived," Zhou said.

"Yes, Comrade, and I am truly sorry. He seemed sincere and I believed him. I was blind, like a man who suddenly loses his sight and becomes confused."

Stratton wasn't looking when she said it, but he heard Kangmei's voice crack.

"Blind, Comrade Zhou," she repeated. "Nearsighted. Clumsy. Foolish."

Stratton stiffened. He tested the muscles in his arms and legs with invisible isometrics. He hurt everywhere, but he willed himself to be ready.

"Blind," Kangmei said softly. "Blind, blind, blind!" And with that, she plucked the bottle-bottom glasses from Zhou's eyes and tossed them across Stratton's cell. They landed in the worst corner. Insects scattered.

Zhou was utterly bewildered. The jailer shouted a question in Mandarin. Stratton did not wait for the answer. He rammed a fist into the side of Zhou's head, spilling the inquisitor off the chair into a writhing heap.

Stratton grunted to his feet and stood rubber-legged, facing the jailer. The man dove for Stratton's waist and brought him down. They rolled together in the fetid slop; the jailer, clawing for Stratton's throat and eyes; Stratton, weak and nauseous, using his long arms and his weight to entangle his wiry attacker. Kangmei stood to the side, crying nervously.

"In the corner," Stratton yelled. "Dig! By the window."

The jailer hung on Stratton's back, arms clenched around his neck in a fierce choke-hold. Stratton held his breath and rolled over.

Kangmei dug feverishly. Her hands uncovered the crude three-foot spear Stratton had fashioned from the leg of the chair. In another corner, Comrade Zhou groped pathetically for his eyeglasses in the excrement.

In the middle of the small cell, only Thomas Stratton was breathing normally. The jailer, pinned beneath him, was slowly suffocating in the muck. Stratton reeled to his feet and snatched the weapon from Kangmei.

Somehow Zhou had found his precious glasses and now he was at the door, pounding loudly. His black hair was matted, his glasses stained and sodden.

"Comrade. *Tongzhi!*" he cried.

Stratton's handmade bayonet tore through the inquisitor's chest. He collapsed making noises like a leaky bicycle tire, a death wheeze.

"Thom-as, I am sorry. I am so sorry." She was sobbing. "He made me do it."

Stratton put a finger to his lips. For several moments, he listened at the door. "We must hurry," he whispered. Kangmei dabbed at her eyes. Self-consciously she turned away as Stratton slipped into Zhou's trousers. When she turned back, Stratton held her by the shoulders and said, "Your uncle is alive."

"Oh, Thom-as!"

Stratton tested the door of the cell. It was unlocked. The corridor was empty. Kangmei took his hand and together they ran.

CHAPTER 15

"IDIOTS! MY ORDERS ARE to be followed. When I say that a man must be guarded, I speak for the state and for the Party. I must be obeyed. You listen to stupid rumors like old women, and you behave as donkeys. I am still the deputy minister, and I still command here."

Wang Bin burst into the attic cell. In a pregnant moment, much was said between the two brothers, but no words were spoken. David Wang looked up at his brother quizzically.

"It is not what it seems," Wang Bin said finally. "I will explain later . . . and apologize. Now we must go quickly. Here, put on these, there is a chill."

The deputy minister handed his brother a well-cut gray Mao suit with a mourner's band pinned to the sleeve of the jacket, and a pair of vigorously polished black shoes, one-half size too small.

"Please, hurry, David. We must go."

Befuddled, unspeaking, David Wang dressed and followed his younger brother into the night. Wang Bin walked briskly. He had but thirteen hours left.

"What do you mean you can't drive?"

"I was never permitted to learn . . . it was not my job," Kangmei stammered. "In this country, we have drivers—"

"Get in," Stratton said.

The truck was a bad imitation of a bad Russian flatbed, but it was the only vehicle in the museum's parking lot with keys in the ignition. Stratton's original plan had been to hide under some lumber in the truck and let Kangmei navigate the escape, but now he had no choice. Night was on his side, but not much else. Any half-blind idiot would see that the driver of this truck was not Chinese. Stratton turned the key and urged the transmission into first gear. The clutch yelped like a dog on fire.

141

"This is terrific," Stratton muttered as they trundled down the two-lane blacktop.

Kangmei gave him a puzzled stare. Stratton laughed and reached out for her hand. "Never mind," he said. "Where to?"

"A very safe place," she answered, "but a long, long way, Thom-as. Eighty kilometers."

Stratton flicked the headlights on and tried to hunch down as low as he would go in the driver's seat. Kangmei found a dirty canvas cap under the seat, dusted it off and stuck it on Stratton's head.

"I'm worried about you," he said after a few minutes. "If we get stopped, I'm running. You tell them I kidnapped you and stole the truck. Tell them you never saw me before. I want you to promise."

"No," Kangmei said quietly. "I will not lie again. My father made me say those things at the struggle session. I am very sorry. He told me you were a spy."

"Did you believe him?"

"No." She looked at him pridefully. "It wouldn't matter if you were."

The sluggish truck picked up speed alarmingly on a long downhill stretch. A quarter-mile ahead, Stratton could make out a group of commune workers, trudging home down the middle of the road. He pressed on the horn and they parted slowly. Their ox, however, was disinclined to yield the right of way. Stratton honked again and pumped the brakes slowly. Incredibly, the barn-shouldered animal turned to face the noisy intruder.

"Oh, shit," Stratton said. As the truck bore down on the ox, Stratton leaned hard on the horn. At the last second, he cut the wheel and steered onto the shoulder, around the ox and its peasant entourage. In the rearview mirror, he saw several men shake their fists at the truck. Kangmei trembled next to him.

"Sorry," Stratton said sheepishly. "They acted like they own the road."

"They do," Kangmei said evenly.

The unlit road was newly paved in some sections, pocked and dangerous in others. The hilly countryside was lush with citrus stands, cane fields and banana groves. Here and there the night was broken by a commune's lights or the pinprick headlights of a distant truck, but mostly Kangmei and Tom

Stratton were alone. Stratton recounted his confrontation with Wang Bin in the museum cell.

"But how could my uncle be alive?" Kangmei asked.

"Because your father is planning something, and he needs his brother—at least for a while," Stratton conjectured. "When he's done, I think Wang Bin *will* kill David. We don't have much time. Kangmei, it's important that we get out of China so I can contact the State Department. Hong Kong would be the best."

"An overnight train from where we are going," she said. "But you have no papers. How will you leave China?"

"Can we go tomorrow?"

Kangmei did not answer right away.

"If I return to Peking, your father will have me arrested," Stratton said. "There is nowhere I can go but out. There's nothing I can do here for David."

"The place I'm taking you is very safe, Thom-as."

"For me, maybe. Think of your uncle. If the U.S. Embassy only knew he was alive. Kangmei, we could call them in the morning—"

She shook her head glumly. "Where we are going, there are no telephones."

"Do you believe what I'm telling you, that David is alive?"

Kangmei said, "I don't know. It is hard to accept." In the darkness, Stratton could not see the tension on her face, but he could sense it.

The boundaries of the mountain road became indistinct as it snaked through acres of tall pines. When the truck rattled past a plywood sign erected at the foot of a hill, Kangmei sat up and grabbed Stratton's elbow.

"Slow down, Thom-as. The sign says there is a police stop ahead. One half a kilometer."

Stratton quickly downshifted, pulled off the road and dimmed the lights. "We'll never slip through with me at the wheel," he said, turning to Kangmei. "How'd you like a driving lesson?"

Her eyes surveyed the simple dashboard instruments with trepidation. "I don't think so," she said.

"You've got to. Come here, sit closer and I'll show you." Stratton kept his foot on the clutch and ran through the gears one time. "Hell," he said, "my father drove one of these tanks for thirty years. How hard can it be?"

Kangmei practiced with the truck idling.

"That's good," Stratton encouraged. "Remember to watch the speedometer needle. When it gets to here, shift into second. And here, third. When we get to the checkpoint, press the clutch pedal with your left foot, and put your right foot on the brake. You'll have to use most of your weight because the drums on this truck are nearly shot. The important thing is to slow down smoothly so we don't attract attention."

"There is no one else on the road at this time of night," Kangmei remarked. "The police certainly will ask questions."

"I'll be hiding in the back. There's a bundle of wood and some old vegetable crates back there—"

"Thom-as, I don't have any identification papers. They might arrest me."

Stratton got out of the cab. Kangmei moved into the driver's seat.

"Make up a story," Stratton said, scouting the foggy highway. In both directions it was quiet, deserted. "Tell them you're on the way to get medicine for the commune. The regular driver is sick."

Kangmei's hands explored the steering wheel. "What if they don't believe me?"

"How many policemen will there be?"

"One, perhaps two at the most. It is so late . . ."

Stratton was thinking. He removed the dusty driver's cap and placed it on Kangmei's head. Gently he tucked her silken pigtails underneath it. "There! You look like a teenage boy."

She glanced down at her chest.

"Well, almost," Stratton said. He climbed into the flatbed and concealed himself in the rummage and lumber. "Okay," he called from the back. "Let's go."

The truck lunged forward, then coughed into a stall. Kangmei tried again with the same results. The third time the clutch engaged perfectly and the truck found the pavement. Stratton smiled to himself.

Kangmei drove slowly, eternally grateful that the stretch of road was straight so she could devote all concentration to mastering the transmission.

As the truck crested a small hill, Kangmei noticed a swatch of yellow light below. Half in panic, she mashed both feet on the clutch and let the truck coast. Gradually the details of the small police station became clear: a white booth, with a

Chinese flag posted on the tin roof. Three bulbs hung from a slender wire; one lit the building and the other two a zebra-striped gate that blocked the road. Inside the booth stood a man in a blue-and-white uniform. He seemed not to notice how the truck stuttered downhill, Kangmei fighting for the brakes.

She brought it to a stop with a brief screech of the tires. The policeman, who had been dozing on his feet, glanced up sharply and peered out the window of the booth.

As he approached, Kangmei shook her hair out from under the cap.

"*Ni nar?*" the policeman demanded—the universal inquiry of Marxist China.

Kangmei gave the name of a commune not far from her own birthplace. She told the policeman she was a barefoot doctor there.

"Are you a driver too?" The policeman eyed her. He did not have a flashlight so he stood very close, sticking his head through the window of the cab. In the flatbed, Tom Stratton held his breath.

"No, Comrade, I am not a driver. This truck is assigned to the commune." Kangmei made up a common name. "Children are sick, and so is the regular driver," she went on. "We have run out of medicine and I am going to get some more at the clinic in Chungzho." She fumbled in her blues for an imaginary piece of paper.

The policeman shrugged and waved her on.

"*Xie, xie, ni,*" Kangmei called in the earnest tones of a heroic worker. She pressed the accelerator, lifted her foot off the clutch—and promptly stalled the truck. Heart pounding, she wrestled with the stick shift. First gear. She could not find first gear. Again she tried to move the truck and again the engine died. *Don't flood it*, Stratton prayed from beneath the lumber and crates.

The policeman laughed and ambled back to the truck. "I hope you are a better doctor than you are a driver," he said. "Let me try."

"No, Comrade, I can do this," Kangmei said defiantly. "I must do this myself—for my commune." She turned the key, and from under the hood came a dying whine.

"Too much fuel in the carburetor," the policeman diagnosed. "Wait a few minutes and it will be fine." He opened the door to the cab. "Would you care to come in for a drink of tea?"

Kangmei reached for the door and slammed it. "No," she said sternly. "I must hurry, Comrade. I told you, the children are very sick."

Stratton had no idea what was being said. The slamming of the truck door alarmed him. Through the slats of the crate above his head, Stratton could see nothing but stars and wispy clouds. Gradually he levered himself up, turning his head slightly to gain a view of Kangmei. Suddenly the woodpile shifted and one of the vegetable crates fell, banging on the steel flatbed.

The policeman jumped at the noise. "What!" he said. "What was that?" He walked to the back of the truck and peered into the rubble of cargo. "Are you alone, driver?"

Kangmei twisted the key and jerked on the stick shift with all her strength. This time the engine responded, and the truck surged forward.

"There, I did it!" she exclaimed.

The flustered policeman dashed ahead of the truck to lift the zebra-striped gate before it could be demolished.

"*Xie xie, ni,*" Kangmei sang out as she drove past.

Stratton waited several miles before sitting up in the flatbed. Then he tapped on the rear window of the cab and signaled for Kangmei to pull over. She surrendered the driver's seat with a sigh of relief.

"Your father must be a very skilled man, to drive a truck like this," she said. "I am sure it is a most important job."

"Well, it doesn't exactly put you at the top of the social ladder in America," Stratton said. "I'm not sure what you told that cop, but you must be a wonderful actress. And your driving isn't bad for a beginner. My old man would approve."

Kangmei shyly turned away. Stratton tenderly stroked the back of her neck; her skin was warm velvet.

"Are there more road checks?"

"I don't think so," she replied distractedly. "None that I remember."

"Are you tired?"

"Just a little, Thom-as. You are the one who needs to sleep."

Stratton cruised slowly through the hillsides until he found what he was looking for. He drove the truck off the asphalt and steered it down a washboard track until it was out of sight from the road. He parked and turned off the lights. Tall trees swallowed them into shadows.

"We can nap here for an hour, but no more. We must not be on the road after the sun comes up."

"Yes, we must finish the journey tonight." Kangmei took Stratton's hand and led him through the trees until they found a clearing. They lay down together on a natural mat of pine needles, ivy and crisp cedar leaves. Stratton closed his eyes; his mind fell, spinning through the clouds toward sleep. He barely felt Kangmei's hands, gently pulling his shirt off. He heard her soft footsteps fade into the forest.

He quivered out of sleep when the cold water drenched his thigh.

"Ssshh. Lie still, Thom-as." She sponged his face with a rag and kissed him on the forehead.

"There is a brook nearby, with clean water." Kangmei washed the bullet wound in Stratton's leg. She had pulled his trousers off. In the grayness of deep night, he lay pale and limp.

"We will see a doctor tomorrow," she whispered. "He will treat the leg properly."

Stratton smiled and reached up to capture her hand. Tenderly he kissed it. She looked down at him for a long moment, a young woman of timeless wisdom.

"Yes," Stratton said at last. "Please."

In silence, Kangmei stripped. Suddenly she was astride him, a velvet presence. She moved gently at first, back and forth, until she found his lips, and then his neck. Stratton closed his eyes and held her fiercely as she sank down on him again and again.

Later, when they were in the truck again, Kangmei revealed her secret. It was as if she had saved it for Stratton, saved it for the end.

"After they dragged me from your room in Xian, I was delivered to the police," she began. "They were told I had been caught pilfering at a market. I was thrown into a cell with three other women. Each had been accused of stealing items from the Qin burial vaults. They were not mere peasants, but trusted workers on the site. Petty thieves, my father called them. Their arrests were part of a new campaign—banners, leaflets, announcements on the loudspeakers—all arranged by my father to show the ministry that he was cracking down against pilfering. It was a charade, Thom-as."

"But I saw a big article in the *People's Daily*," Stratton broke in.

Kangmei said, "Certainly there is a problem with stealing, but only a minor problem. The artifacts are worth a fortune by Chinese standards. One of the women in my cell admitted that she had stolen a bridle from one of the bronze horses. The bridle was made only of stone beads, not gold or silver. Still, she was able to sell it to a street peddler for a hundred yuan. The peddler probably sold it to a tourist for three or four times as much. Such things do happen."

"In our country, too."

"But, Thom-as, something bigger is happening at Xian. If these prisoners were telling the truth, then I know why Uncle David quarreled with my father. I know what he had found out. During the past several months, the Qin site has suffered three major thefts—the crimes are so enormous that they would create a terrible scandal in Peking. There would be a large investigation by the *Ke Ge Bo*. People would go to jail, or worse."

"What was stolen, Kangmei?"

"Soldiers. Three soldiers, Thom-as, on three different occasions. A spear carrier, an archer and a charioteer. They are among the most priceless treasures in Chinese history, buried with the Emperor Qin—and now missing."

"My God." Stratton's mind juggled the pieces of the puzzle. "David found out!"

"I think so," Kangmei said sadly. "That is why I do not think he is still alive, Thom-as, no matter what my father told you."

"No, don't you see? Wang Bin needs David more than ever now. He needs him to get out. It's only a matter of time before Peking discovers this theft, and your father knows this. There is nothing left for him to do but run."

Stratton coaxed more speed from the recalcitrant truck. Once Wang Bin learned that Stratton had escaped, he would act quickly. Quickly enough, and there was a good chance he would never be caught.

"Kangmei, what could your father have done with the clay soldiers?"

"You assume that it was he who stole them."

"I am certain," Stratton said.

Kangmei swallowed to keep back the tears. "The women prisoners said the same thing. The rumor is that he smuggled them out of the country. To America."

"How?"

"I do not know," she said wearily. "Something so large and so delicate as a statue—it would be very difficult, Thom-as, even for Wang Bin. Every box or parcel destined for your country would be subject to automatic inspection, especially if it came from a government office. The Party has been watching my father closely. Some of the old men do not approve of the way he has handled the Qin project. I'm sure they are jealous of the publicity."

"Wang Bin would never ship the artifacts directly to the United States," Stratton agreed. "The risk would be too great. Boxes like that would never clear U.S. Customs without a search." Then it struck him. "Unless . . ."

"What?" Kangmei asked.

"Oh, God." Stratton could not bring himself to say it aloud, a theory so horrible with black irony, so devious that it could be the only explanation of how a Chinese deputy minister could actually steal the storied Celestial Army, one soldier at a time.

CHAPTER 16

THE CAR WAS A SHANGHAI, requisitioned without explanation from the ministry motor pool, and it veered without grace through empty streets, a whining gray shadow. Decades before, in the army, Wang Bin had briefly driven a truck. Since then, it had been beneath him to drive at all. David Wang slumped against the passenger door with the empty gaze of a vexed old man.

"Why?" he asked again.

"I have tried to explain. It was for your own protection, brother, I promise you." The strain of driving overwhelmed Wang Bin's English. He had lapsed into the Shanghai dialect of their childhood. "The radicals . . . the madmen, they are coming back, grabbing for power. I am one of their victims."

"You caged me like an animal."

"Only to save you . . . from the madmen."

David Wang shook himself like a dog awakening. He squinted at his brother in the pale reflection of the windshield. Like watching a mirror. A mirror of lies.

"It was not the 'madmen' who drugged me and jailed me. Not the Party, or any radicals. Just you, brother. Only you."

"It was not my choice or my liking, I promise you. I had to make you disappear. They . . . they were going to arrest you."

"Nonsense. You invited me to China as a pretext. Somehow my presence was important to your conspiracy. But I still do not see—"

"A wish to see the brother that was robbed from me. That was the only conspiracy, I swear it."

"And I was so glad to see you, at first. Like seeing myself again, seeing what I might have been like, living another life in another country; the product of a totally different society, a

150

revolution. It moved me to see you, my brother, more than I can explain."

"And I, too."

Ahead, the road wound darkly toward the northern hills.

"But how fragile are our illusions, how quickly dispelled. It was in Xian. One single day of joy, discovery. And then disillusion when I saw what you had done."

"Forget Xian," Wang Bin hissed. "It is not important. It has nothing to do with you."

"At first I imagined you wanted me to help you steal. I photographed what you did not want me to see and you took my camera away. Your carefully sculpted mask slipped then and I realized that you are my brother only in name. It is well that our father is dead."

"You do not understand."

"Oh, yes, brother. I have seen it, and touched it, and tasted its majesty. What you are doing is a crime against China, against all of us. I will not allow it."

Wang Bin spared a glance from the road, expecting to see his brother's hand on the door handle, ready to bolt. It was what he feared most. But David sat with his arms folded, staring straight ahead, a self-righteous plodder chewing on a puzzle. Wang Bin despised him.

"Where are you taking me?" David Wang demanded.

"This road goes to the Great Wall and to the Ming Tombs. I am taking you somewhere you will be safe."

"I would be safe in Peking, except for you."

"You must understand," Wang Bin exclaimed with all the conviction he could muster. "They were going to arrest you . . . as a spy."

"I? A spy? Can you not invent something less transparent?"

"It's true, I swear it. Hundreds of Chinese return here each year and disappear. The government believes that once a Chinese always a Chinese. You may carry some other passport, but it doesn't matter. I heard from friends in the Public Security Bureau that you were to be arrested. Perhaps it was only their way of getting at me. But when I heard about it, I became desperate. I could not tell you. Since you have not lived in China, you cannot understand how things are. In desperation, the only thing I could think to do quickly was to hide you; to keep you safe until I could find a way to help you leave the country."

"And that is where we are going now? On an empty road to nowhere in the middle of the night? To keep me safe? To get me out of the country?"

"Yes."

"My brother, we are both old men, but neither of us is stupid. If you tell me the truth, I will try to help you. We can go to the embassy. I have important friends at home. It is not too late. Look, it is nearly dawn. Let it be the first dawn of a new life for you, my brother. I implore you. I will help."

Wang Bin never faltered. Cautiously, he directed the car across a long causeway that breasted a dry river. They entered an avenue lined with giant stone animals in pairs: camels, lions, elephants.

"This is the entrance to the Ming Tombs," Wang Bin said.

"I have seen the pictures."

"Very well, we will talk as brothers. Tell me what you think. Perhaps you are right. Perhaps it is not too late."

They were near now. Wang Bin needed only another few minutes. Of the thirteen tombs, one had been excavated and was open to tourists. The other twelve were in disrepair, their dusty grounds impromptu picnic sites for bored foreign residents of the capital. Wang Bin turned onto a narrow strip of asphalt running to a modern reservoir built in a gentle valley beneath the hillside tombs.

David Wang rambled on, but the words had become irrelevant now, like the memorial chants in the aftermath of battle. Wang Bin stopped the car on a rocky beach at the shore of the reservoir. The half light of false dawn shadowed a half-dozen wooden rowboats lying face down above the high-water mark. There was no sign of life.

Wang Bin shut off the engine. Carefully, he set the hand brake.

"Your words have great impact on me, brother," he said. "I am beginning to see my mistake, an excess of pride. Let us talk further in the fresh air. It is quite beautiful here. It is not often in China that a man can be alone like this."

Wang Bin stood with his back to the car, facing the dark, still water. He fished among the larger rocks for a flat stone and sent it skimming.

"Only two jumps. Do you remember how as boys we would skim stones in the river? Five jumps, six jumps. Anything seemed possible then."

"I remember," David's voice came from behind.

"Things are more complicated now."

"Yes, they are. Neither of us is as strong as we were once in Shanghai."

"It is true."

They fell silent, watching tiny wavelets lapping at the beach stones.

It was David who spoke at last. A voice of infinite sadness.

"I have thought it through. I understand why you invited me to China, why you held me captive. And why you have brought me here. I know now what it is that only a brother can do for you, no one else. I understand your plan for him."

"Tell me."

"He is to be your essential victim. You must murder him."

Wang Bin never turned. Unseeing, he spoke to the waters.

"Yes. I must murder him."

With a tremendous shove, David Wang pushed his brother into the shallow water. Then, clumsily, he began running along the beach toward a workman's shack that beckoned from the distance. David had not run far when he lost his footing on the loose stones and pitched forward with a groan.

It was then his brother caught him from behind.

Stratton's forearms ached from steering the hard-sprung truck over what seemed an endless series of unseen hills. The pitted road twisted, like a snake. In the tepid glint of light from the dashboard, the gauge that Stratton had decided was for gas rested on its bottom mark. The one next to it—temperature?—seemed to be rising. He nudged the girl at his side.

"Wake up, Kangmei. It will be dawn soon and the truck will not go much farther."

"I was not sleeping, Thom-as, just resting." She stretched and ran her hands through the mass of tangled black hair. "Have we passed a river?"

"On a very shaky bridge, about ten minutes ago."

"Good. We are almost there."

"Where is *there*, Kangmei?" She had been coy about that since their escape. A safe place where they would be with friends, she had said.

"It is a commune, Thom-as. We call it Bright Star. It is the home of my mother's family. I lived there during the Cultural Revolution when my father was being punished. My uncles are among the commune leaders. They will protect us."

Stratton nodded. It had to have been something like that. He riffled through the possibilities. A commune in a backward province more than a thousand miles from Peking, and probably a century in terms of control. Once they had taught him a great deal about communes, the central fact of life for eight hundred million Chinese. The instructor's voice came back to Stratton. He had been a Spec/6, dragged from a Ph.D. program to war. Shared reward for shared work, a Marxist replacement for rural villages dominated by landlords. Now there were no more landlords, only work brigades and production teams tilling common land.

What had resisted revolution was the social makeup of the communes. Almost all who lived on a commune in China were descendants of people who had lived there centuries ago. Nearly all the children born there would also die there in toothless old age. The continuity of families remained stronger than the caprice of a distant state.

Kangmei would be safe. The family would close around her, shutting out inquiries from cadres who, knowing the system, would not press too hard. She would be safe, but also empty. What kind of life would it be for an intelligent, vivacious young woman, calf-deep in paddy muck, courted by half-literate bumpkins? Whom would she talk to? Whom would she love? Kangmei deserved better than that. Stratton made himself a private promise: She would have it. Somehow. One day.

But would the commune shelter him as well? Probably, for a time, anyway.

"Kangmei, we're in Guangdong Province, right? How far from the coast?"

"No, this is Guangxi. And we are many hours from the sea, many hills and many people."

Guangxi. Memories worse than the cobra.

"Look, I think it would be better if—"

She had outthought him.

"You would never make it to the sea without help, Thom-as. And my family will be very proud to hide you, and to help you escape, especially when they see the wonderful gift you are bringing them."

"You?"

She laughed, a mountain stream.

"Oh, they will be glad to see me, too. But it is the truck they will prize most."

"The truck."

"But . . . how will they account for it?"

"They will hide it while they let all other production teams know that they have saved enough money to buy a used truck. Then one day it will appear. Imagine the celebration; the other teams will be so jealous."

"I see," Stratton said in quiet wonder.

"You will be a hero, Thom-as. My hero." She slid across the seat and kissed him with flashing tongue.

They left the truck in a copse of trees on a hillside capped by an ancient pagoda. Kangmei, bubbling with the excitement of a little girl on Christmas, led him to the hilltop. It was nearly light by the time they reached the top.

"Down there," she said, gesturing to a mist-shrouded valley. "That is Bright Star. My family lives in the houses near the school. Soon you 'will see."

With exaggerated care, she installed him on a bed of needles beneath some pine trees, about a hundred yards from the dirt path that wound into the valley.

"No one will see you here. Rest. My uncles and I will come back around lunchtime, when everyone is sleeping. It will be safe then for you to come down. It's not far." She looked at him through almond eyes without end. "You will wait for me, Thom-as. Please?"

"I will wait." He hugged her. "Here, a gift for your family." He handed her the leather-yoked keys of the truck.

When she had gone, Stratton lay with his head pillowed in his arms and watched the sky turn blue. As the tension drained from him, aches replaced adrenaline. It had been a long time since had had been this tired. Stratton surrendered to sleep.

When he awoke it was already late morning. The sun, approaching its zenith, oppressed the pine grove. It had brought sapping humidity and a winged holiday for insects of every stinging phylum. Stratton relieved himself against a tree and crawled onto an outcropping of rock that looked onto the valley, trying not to think how hungry he was.

A picturebook scene. The commune was comprised of what had apparently been four separate villages in the space of several square miles. Around each cluster of single-story wood homes well-trod dikes led to paddies of rice. In the northern quadrant lay a bright green field of what could only have been sugarcane. To the east was a well-kept citrus grove. A patchwork of small private plots lay on the fringes of the communal fields. The nearest settlement, the one to which Kangmei must have gone, was arranged around a carp pond. The only building of substance was a low, ramshackle structure with a thatched roof and a fresh coat of whitewash. Stratton decided it must be a combination school and office for the production team.

The fields and earthen streets of the village swarmed with people. Stratton watched a double file of schoolchildren, hand-in-hand, parade in a swatch of color toward a dusty soccer field where some teenagers desultorily kicked a ball. Stratton counted two trucks and a handful of three-wheeled contraptions that looked like misshapen lawn mowers. "Walking tractors," Kangmei called them.

The scene was peaceful and, by Chinese standards, an advertisement for rural prosperity. Stratton noted the slender cable of thin poles that dropped into the hamlet and spread ancillary arms toward a few of the nearest houses; by rule of thumb in China, if electricity has spilled down to individual production teams, a commune is well off.

At the base of the hillside path there appeared a supple girl and two stocky men in peasants' garb. As they began to climb, the girl waved diffidently, a fleeting, offhand movement, like shooing flies. Kangmei had found refuge.

Stratton decided to wait where he was. Idly, he began to trace the power line out from the settlement, across the fields and back toward its origin.

It was a mistake.

In almost the precise center of the valley, sheathed in trees, lay the administrative headquarters of the commune, the hub of which the four production teams were spokes. Stratton could see a dingy white water tower and, amid shadows, the perimeter walls of what once had been the landlord's house. He made out a strip of macadam and along it some shops, a vegetable market and a fair-sized building with a half-domed roof that might once have been a 1930s movie theater.

Stratton saw without seeing the red-starred flag that hung limply from the building. He saw a chimney thrusting unnaturally from among the trees and knew without knowing that it belonged to a homespun woodworking factory that made grapefruit crates and slatted folding chairs. He saw a glint of water through the trees and knew that, except in the rainy season, the river that flowed there could be safely forded by men five feet ten or taller.

Stratton groaned aloud. In an instant of black despair, he cursed the luck that had forsaken him in rags among Chinese pines.

He rose to run.

Before him stood Kangmei. Smiling at her side were two erect, honey-colored men of late middle age with the same subtle, alluring facial structure that Kangmei had inherited.

"Thom-as," Kangmei said gravely, "these are my uncles. They will help us."

They were Zhuang, members of a race more Thai than Chinese that had settled in the southern hills in the mists of time. The Zhuang survived in modern China as the country's largest minority. Kangmei's mother was Zhuang, her father, Wang Bin, a member of the majority Han. The combination was what made her so striking. Stratton should have realized it before.

I know all about the Zhuang. They taught me that, too, Stratton wanted to yell, and wondered about his sanity.

Kangmei stared in open-mouthed concern.

"Thom-as! What is the matter? There is no danger. These are my uncles. They—"

"What is the name of this fucking place?"

"Thom-as!"

"Goddamn it. Tell me." He took an involuntary step toward the girl and the two peasants closed around her.

"I told you. We live in Bright Star."

"That's not the right name. I know. Tell me in Chinese."

The two peasants began talking angrily. Kangmei interrupted them with a stream of local dialect that seemed to mollify them.

"Thom-as, I have told them that you are feverish and hungry and very tired. But you must be polite to them, please."

"I'm sorry." Stratton grappled for composure. "Tell me the real name, please. I want to hear it."

"We live in Bright Star," she said slowly, as though instructing a slow child. "Over there is Sweet Water, and there, Good Harvest, and there, Evergreen. Why is it so important?"

"And the place in the middle? Where the factory is, and the water tower?"

"That is where the cadres live, and some soldiers. It is not important. Our people go there only when they must—for Party discussions, to buy shoes and bicycle tires."

"What is it *called*?"

"It is called Man-ling."

"Man-ling, yes, Man-ling. Oh, sweet Jesus."

Stratton sank to his knees and buried his head in his hands. The peasants' hostility surrendered to concern. Kangmei sprang to his side.

"Thom-as, do not weep. Come, you will be safe. My aunts will cook special food. There is a warm bed and a doctor for your leg. Yes, a doctor . . . you can trust him. He is a friend of my uncles'. Come, please. It is not far to walk."

"I can't. I must not."

"Please, Thom-as. Please. Soon there will be too many people. Already there are rumors about things that happened last night. . . . Please."

"No. No. No," Stratton muttered in an anguished litany that was a warrior's penance.

He was too weak to resist when Kangmei and her uncles levered him to his feet and led him blindly down the gentle hillside into yesterday.

The general came late.

He had lunched too long—a farewell banquet for a retiring colleague: sea cucumbers, suckling pig, whitefish, pigeon, shark's fin soup, tree fungus for dessert, and torrents of *mao tai*. The colleague, eighty-four years old, a Party militant for nearly half a century, had never cracked a smile.

The general rebuffed chastising glances from the two civilian members of the tribunal with a short nod and settled noisily into his padded chair. He spared hardly a glance for the gray-haired man disintegrating before the prosecutor's tongue-lashing. He thumbed briefly through the docket on the polished wood desk before him. The man was a musician of some sort.

The general did not know him. He ignored the stream of accusation and thought of his own son. The surveillance reports were quite concrete: The boy had been meeting foreign journalists, hanging out at the International Club, perfuming his hair, reading Western magazines. He had even, apparently, bedded a diplomat. The general would not have minded that, but the omission of the diplomat's name, nationality and sex—certainly a calculated omission—could mean only the worst.

The young fool had been a mistake from the beginning, a winter child by the general's third wife when he was already fifty-seven. The boy had inherited his mother's looks, but not a scrap of common sense. He wanted to study in the United States. In the dawning Chinese political winter he might as well declare his intention of walking on the moon. The general dozed off, deciding that the boy would have to go into the army. If he let the Public Security Bureau have him, the boy's mother—another mistake, she cackled like a chicken—would make the general's life impossible.

". . . compose and play unauthorized, bourgeois, decadent and immoral music.

"Twenty-six. You are accused, during the visit of foreign guests, to wit, the Berlin Philharmonic Orchestra, of playing foreigners' instruments without authorization and of demeaning the prestige and honor of the People's Republic by publicly suggesting that they were of a quality superior to those made in the People's Republic . . ."

The general roused himself for the climax. When the prosecutor asked for life imprisonment, the musician fainted. The general watched expressionless. He had seen that before, and stronger men wet their pants. When guards had roused the musician and the president offered to commute the sentence to self-criticism and twenty years at a state farm in Qinghai Province, the idiot actually seemed grateful.

Qinghai, on the unforgiving Tibetan plateau. One of the loneliest, coldest, most savage places on earth. If he was still alive in six months, it would be a miracle. Soft-handed wretch.

When the president intoned "Qinghai" he looked over at the general with arched eyebrow, as though inviting an objection, a local joke. The prosecutor smothered a smile.

Silently, the general assented. He had never liked musicians.

After the last of that afternoon's accused had been dismissed, the prosecutor summarized the results of the day before.

Normally, while the tribunal members smoked and sipped fresh tea, the prosecutor would report that all of the senior comrades given twenty-four hours to mull their fate had volunteered to accept lesser sentence rather than to contest the charges.

That afternoon was different. Head down, voice muted, almost embarrassed, the prosecutor began reading:

"The following comrades who appeared before the Tribunal

yesterday have agreed to self-criticism and reform through labor: Wu Ping, Sun Liu . . ."

Surprised, the president riffled through the papers before him.

"Wait until I find the list, Comrade," he demanded with raised hand. "Very well, proceed."

When the prosecutor had finished—after repeating some of the names as many as three times to accommodate the president, whose hearing was not what it had once been—he remained standing.

Slowly, lips moving, the president read through the list of names he had checked.

"The list is complete except for Comrade Wang Bin," the president said at last.

"Yes, Comrade President."

"He demands a trial?" The president was incredulous.

"No, Comrade President."

"What then?"

"I do not know, Comrade President."

"What are you saying?"

"Comrade Wang Bin has not reported to the Tribunal within the time afforded him, Comrade President."

The prosecutor was frantic. Such a thing had never happened before.

"Why has he not reported?"

"I do not know, Comrade President."

"Where is Wang Bin, Comrade Prosecutor?"

"I do not know."

"It is your job to know."

"It is the job of the Public Security Bureau. I have asked them."

"What do they say, idiot? What do they say?"

"Comrade Wang Bin is missing. He has not been seen anywhere since last night. There is no trace of him. The Public Security Bureau—"

The president surged to his feet with the sudden furious energy of a man fifty years younger. He slammed his fist on the desk, scattering papers and upsetting his tea.

"Find him!" the president roared. "Find him and bring him to me, Comrade Prosecutor. Do it now!"

The general belched.

CHAPTER 17

THEY WALKED BY THE RIVER, a nurse and her patient.

Stratton's confidence was returning with his strength. He had slept for nearly twenty-four hours, a half-life in which he had grayly drifted around reality without ever reaching it: sober-miened women scrubbing him; a middle-aged man probing gently at his leg; wondrous soup, piping hot, that tasted of the earth and scissored through the pain. And the beautiful woman who sat by him, whispering reassurance. That, he would never forget.

When Stratton had at last surfaced, tears of relief belied Kangmei's fixed smile.

He had reached out for her clenched fist and gently pried open the fingers.

"I'm all right. Really I am," he had comforted.

"I was afraid, Thom-as. So afraid."

Later, watching him wolf down a mound of rice with scraps of chicken, she had seemed like a little girl again.

"You must listen, Thom-as. To my mother's brothers I have said that you are a good man who is being pursued by evil men; nothing more. They are simple peasants, but good, and strong. They will not betray you. To the rest of the people in Bright Star my uncles are saying that you are a foreign expert from Peking who has come to show us new ways to grow better rice. I am your guide."

"I don't know anything about rice." Except what paddy mud feels like, wet, consuming.

"That is not important. When the people of Bright Star learn that you are *our* rice expert, they will not speak of you to members of the other production teams, or to the cadres at Man-ling. You will be safe then, do you not see?"

"I must not stay here, Kangmei," Stratton had insisted weakly. "I must try to help David."

161

"Yes, Thom-as. My uncles have cousins who work on the railroad. They think it would be possible to get you to Guangzhou."

Guangzhou in Chinese. In English, Canton, China's sprawling southern metropolis across the border from Hong Kong. Canton was still China, but from all he had read of it, the city was also a curious East-West hybrid infinitely more relaxed than Peking. In a teeming and sophisticated city where foreigners were no novelty, he had a fighting chance.

"Guangzhou would be fine."

He slept again, and when he awoke it was midafternoon. Kangmei laughed when he tried on clothes smelling of strong soap that had been neatly stacked alongside the bed. The trousers bottomed out four inches too soon. The shirt went across his shoulders, but only the bottom two buttons would fasten.

"These are the biggest we could find, Thom-as. But you will never be a peasant. Come, let the people see their new rice expert."

Along the river there was a kind of promenade, a path of beaten earth flanked by shade trees. Stratton smiled at the peasants they met and tried to look knowledgeable.

"This is the end of Bright Star," said Kangmei. "Over there is Evergreen."

She gestured to the far side of the brown river, flanked on both sides by steep banks. The water flowed swiftly and looked deep.

"And beyond Evergreen is Man-ling, right?"

"Yes." She led Stratton to a spot where the promenade had been widened to include a graceful copse of palms. He sat beside her.

"This looks to me like Bright Star's lovers' lane," Stratton remarked.

"I do not understand."

When he had explained she smiled.

"It is true that many young people come here at night and that they do not always discuss politics."

They kissed.

And then she asked the question that Stratton had dreaded.

"Why are you afraid of Man-ling, Thom-as?"

It was not so much that she deserved to know. To his surprise, Stratton discovered that he wanted to tell her.

"I was there once. In a war. While you were a child."

She sat quiet for a time, tracing circles in the dirt with a stick. Stratton stared down at the river.

"Was it very sad, Thom-as?"

"Yes."

"I would like to know." She spoke to the stick.

He told her.

March 18, 1971

A black sergeant in plainclothes had brought the summons to the Saigon villa Stratton shared with Bobby Ho. An hour later, they were in a briefing room protected by concentric circles of invisible guards.

A squat, sweat-stained colonel abandoned an uneven struggle with a balky room air conditioner.

"Captain Black," the colonel said, shaking hands with Stratton.

"Captain White. Congratulations." The colonel gave Bobby Ho's hand an extra pump. He had been a captain only for six days, but no one outside the room was even supposed to know that Bobby Ho was in the army. Deniability, they called it. Officially, Stratton and Ho were civilian psychologists on contract to the government: studying stress.

"Rested up? Everybody's talkin' about it."

On the last one they had been close enough to see the lights of Hanoi.

"This one should be even more fun." He passed across aerial photos. "The Chinks are involved in this little old war, up to their slanty assholes."

"Who is that, Colonel?" Bobby Ho asked quietly. Stratton stifled a grin. Bobby Ho's parents ran a pawnshop in San Francisco. They had raised their son to be an American, but there was no way you could tell by looking at him. Vietnam had intercepted Bobby Ho between Stanford and medical school. He wanted to be a pediatrician, and he spent a lot of his time and most of his money with some French nuns who ran a clinic near the village. When the army made him White for missions that didn't exist to places that were never named, Bobby Ho hunted with uncommon skill.

The colonel had the grace to color.

"The Chinese. The Chinese are teachin' the Viets how to

brainwash our boys. Remember what they did in Korea? I was there, man. The last thing you wanted to happen was to get captured by the Chin—Chinese. They turned people inside out; tell you Ike was a faggot and make you believe it."

The colonel poked a pudgy finger at the aerial photos.

"What we hear is that the Chinese are trainin' Vet interrogators in that building there in the middle of the picture. They got about a dozen of our POWs up there as guinea pigs."

"Where is it—the village?" Stratton asked.

"Jesus, I just told you. It's in China."

"Shit," said Bobby Ho.

"We supposed to go in and get them?" Stratton asked.

The colonel nodded. "Yeah, go get 'em out and fuck Chairman Mao. Does that offend you, Captain White?"

"Not a bit, Colonel," said Bobby Ho.

"What's the name of this place?" Stratton asked.

"Man-ling it's called. You guys see Joe and the boys. They got it all worked out, pictures, models, the whole shootin' match, just like usual." The colonel's eyes assumed a faraway cast. "If it was me, I'd take about four gunships and hit 'em so hard and so fast they wouldn't have time even to find their little red books. That's the only way to win this war, hard and fast. That's how I'd do it, if it was me."

Hot air. Stratton would write the operational orders and the colonel knew it.

"If it was you, I'd stay home," said Bobby Ho.

They took one chopper off a quiet carrier high up in the Gulf of Tonkin. Stratton, Ho and four sergeants. Captain Black was traveling light. If he needed help, it was only minutes away in the air behind them.

For a landing zone, Stratton had chosen a paddy about three miles east of the village. He had wanted the farmland and the village between the chopper and the PLA camp that lay a few miles to the west. Intelligence said a regular infantry company used the camp. Intelligence had not said why it believed the nowhere village called Man-ling had been chosen to brainwash POWs.

They landed in driving rain and gusting wind, ankle-deep in water—killers dressed for the country in dark, rough civilian clothes without nationality. In the distance, at night, they might pass for peasants. Close up it would be harder. Stratton's peasants bore a Russian AK-47, Chinese grenades, a silenced

East German pistol, a Thai killing knife and a cyanide capsule. On his back, each man carried a folding bicycle. They looked superficially like Chinese machines, but were half as heavy and twice as fast. Stratton had insisted. A question of image: See a man on a bicycle and you assume he lives nearby and knows where he is going. He belongs.

The same reasoning had ordained the timing. It was midnight, and the helicopter would return one hour before dawn unless Stratton called earlier. They might have come later, but anything moving in the Chinese countryside between midnight and dawn would alarm sentinels accustomed to seeing nothing move at all. Even midnight was cutting it fine, Stratton knew, but he had not dared come until the village was asleep.

They watched in silence as the chopper clawed for the clouds on muffled engines. It was the seventh time Stratton had endured that particular parting. The seven loneliest moments of his life.

Even in the mud, the bicycles worked like a charm.

They were the only thing.

A sentry materialized, wraithlike, from the shelter of a tree about a mile from the village. PLA.

The sentry hollered something that was lost in the wind. Bobby Ho, riding point, head down, waited until he was within ten yards of the man, until the pistol would bear. He answered in Chinese.

Maybe the man had heard the helicopter. Maybe Bobby Ho said the wrong thing. The sentry coiled, unslinging his rifle. From the shelter by the tree, two more wet soldiers emerged. The six American slithered off their bikes into the mud like a satanic rank of marionettes.

It ended quickly, but one of the sentries managed a shot. It ricocheted like flat doom through the blackness.

For five breathless, unbearable minutes, Stratton's team crouched by the road, safeties off, ears aching, praying. No one came. The sentry had died in vain.

Bobby Ho tried to break the tension.

"These Chinks ain't even tryin'," he whispered in jocose mimicry of the fat colonel. It didn't sound funny.

The single guard at the head of the village main street died in silence for his sloth. He must have felt the blade administered by a saturnine Puerto Rican named Gomez, but he never saw it. Stratton left Gomez and a fireplug Tennessean named Harkness to watch their back door.

They met the boy a few minutes later, creeping through such stillness and total absence of color it gave Stratton the eerie sensation that the entire village was a two-dimensional fantasy.

Bobby Ho flushed the boy from a pile of rags in the imperfect shelter of a shop doorway. Panofsky grabbed him, roughly clamping his jaw. The boy wriggled, a minnow in the maw of a shark. Stratton saw the knife come up and winced.

"Wait!" Bobby Ho hissed. "He can't be more than twelve, all skin and bones."

The knife wavered. Panofsky looked over at Stratton. Everybody knew the rules. It wasn't even a judgment call. Stratton made it one. It was Bobby Ho's play.

Panofsky's eyes flashed with anger.

In a sibilant, harsh undertone, Bobby Ho tongue-lashed the boy in Chinese. Stratton watched the boy's eyes: flat, emotionless. They showed intelligence, but no surprise, no curiosity. And most of all, no fear.

At length, the boy nodded. Bobby Ho stepped back.

"It's all right."

Again Panofsky looked at Stratton.

"Let him go," Stratton said. Sometimes you break the rules.

The rag boy massaged his neck. With arrogance that could only have been inherited, he turned his back and stalked away, vanishing within seconds up an alley on pencil legs that seemed unequal to their sixty-pound burden.

"I told him we are on a secret training exercise with foreign friends, and that if he ever interrupts the PLA again, I will personally shoot him and everybody in his family."

"I hoped he believed you."

"He believed me."

Panofsky snorted. Bloomfield grunted. Stratton sent them up to the far end of the main street to share their scorn.

Lights burned inside an old movie house that now featured Mao slogans on its sagging marquee. Bobby Ho prised open a side door. They cached the Kalashnikovs in the shadow outside; assault rifles are useless for close work.

Inside, the building smelled of molding concrete, stale tobacco and rancid bodies. Wooden chairs, neatly arranged, filled the pit of the theater. Empty, every one of them. The stage had been divided into four separate rooms, each with double doors facing the audience. All the doors were closed. From behind one set rose a high-pitched monotone that gave Stratton goose bumps.

" . . . Delano Roosevelt . . . Harry S. Truman . . . Dwight David Eisenhower . . . John Fitzgerald Kennedy . . . Lyndon Brains Johnson . . . Richard—"

"Baines," a deeper voice interrupted. "Lyndon Baines Johnson."

The first voice resumed, a record returned to its groove: "Lyndon Baines Johnson . . . Richard Milhous Nixon . . ."

The voices were Chinese. Stratton looked at Bobby Ho, who gave an elaborate shrug. A teacher and his student. What else could they be?

Stratton gestured and Bobby Ho nodded. He would check the area around the stage and watch Stratton's back.

The basement, intelligence had said. The prisoners are held in the basement. They are paraded upstairs for onstage interrogation classes.

Stratton found the stairs without trouble. He went down with a gentle rush until he came to a stout wooden door. He nudged it open with his boot and let the pistol precede him.

Blackness. Absolute. And a terrible smell: fresh soap thinly overlaying the smell of fear and anger. Stratton let a cone of light from his Czech torch play around the room, and came within a heartbeat of firing at a sound in the far corner. Two rats, red-eyed and territorial.

In took Stratton fifteen minutes to explore the basement thoroughly. Six cells. Stratton toured them, one at a time. In the fourth, scratched into the cheap concrete, a lover's testament had survived its author: "Rick & Connie Houston '70." With the leaden movements of an old man, Stratton visited the remaining two cells. In the last one, he found traces of blood the cleaners had missed. They had come too late. How long? A day? Two? Stratton would never know and never forget. He ran the back of his hand across his lips to moisten them and tasted ashes. He had only another instant to mull his disappointment.

From above came the unmistakable sound of boots hammering the tired floorboards. Not furtive. Authoritative boots.

Stratton listened from the head of the stairs. Two men, speaking Chinese. Plus the student and his professor. At least four. He and Bobby Ho had played against worse odds than that.

From the back of the theater came Bobby Ho's voice. Stratton understood none of the words. He understood too well what they meant. The tone was enough: arrogant, strong, with a touch of exasperation. An officer's voice, informing more than explaining.

Bobby Ho was playing the cover story, singing loudly enough to alert Stratton.

The cover was pretty much what Bobby Ho had told the ragged boy: He was a PLA officer down from Peking on a training mission with East Germans en route to North Vietnam to help the heroic struggle there. It was not a bad story. There were plenty of Caucasian instructors with the Viets, even some Germans. In the jacket of his pocket, Bobby Ho had a set of orders that looked like the real thing.

It might have worked. But it didn't. Three or four voices speaking at once drowned out Bobby Ho. The shouts grew louder. Wood smashed. Bodies fell. Stratton didn't hear Bobby Ho again until he screamed.

Stratton rammed through the door with the pistol ready. The neatly ordered folding chairs lay in matchstick piles. In their chaos stood four Chinese, two uniformed, the other two in bureaucrats' white short-sleeved shirts, their red books of quotations clutched protectively. As Stratton's eye recorded, his brain raced to establish target priority. The student and his professor were unarmed. Shoot last. The other two both had pistols. One was pressed against the head of a kneeling Bobby Ho. Its owner was screaming at Stratton.

Stratton let his gun arm come down, slowly, with emphasis. He reversed his grip on the pistol. Holding it by the butt, he walked toward the Chinese.

"Vas is los?" Stratton demanded in his own officer's voice.

The man with Bobby Ho barked something that brought the student and professor to life like wind-up dolls.

"Comrade Commissar Wu . . ." they began together.

" . . . instructs you to put down the gun and to raise your hands," concluded the professor.

Stratton forced a rictus grin.

"English. *Nein. Deutsch.*" He tapped his chest. "*Kamerad.*"

After a cursory search, they tossed Stratton into one of the rooms on the stage. He was alone for twenty-seven minutes by his watch. An important eternity. He listened to them working on Bobby Ho. The shouts became one-sided, the screams dwindled to pathetic groans.

When they came for Stratton, they brought Bobby Ho unconscious. Stratton tried not to look at him.

There were still four of them. No one had left, so without phones, they had made no attempt to spread the alarm. Stratton asked himself why. Were they swayed by the cover story? Or were they simply in a hurry, trying for good information before seeking help?

The commissar was a lean, gray-haired man in PLA green with red tabs and a four-pocket tunic reserved for officers. The other uniformed man, balding and pot-bellied, wore the blue and white of the police. Stratton marked him as a local.

The policeman did the heavy work. He jabbed Stratton in the belly with a truncheon. When Stratton involuntarily clammed forward, the policeman struck him on the head.

The professor screamed: "How many men in your unit? Where are they? What is your mission? Talk or die, imperialist running dog!"

"*Deutsch.*"

It lasted about ten minutes. The policeman enjoyed his work. An expert, a fat man with bad breath, who stung without maiming. Stratton rolled with the blows and calculated his chances. The student, nearest the door, held a Chinese carbine with familiarity. The professor was unarmed. The policeman had his club and a holstered pistol. The commissar held a heavy Chinese military pistol.

Stratton, fighting the pain, babbling in the few words of German he knew, realized that Captain Black was finished. Sooner or later they would alert the PLA garrison outside of town and that would be that.

Then the Chinese made their mistake.

From the night came the sound of small arms fire. Stratton heard the pop of Chinese weapons and the crack of AK-47s. The PLA already knew. The shooting flustered the Chinese. The commissar spoke in English for the first time.

"There is no time for this. Pick up your friend."

Stratton stared dumbly. Only when they all began to shout and wave did he allow himself to understand.

He picked up Bobby Ho the way a mother bundles an injured

child. Blood from Bobby's mouth ran off the shoulder of
Stratton's jacket. There was a jagged hole where his teeth had
been. Stratton held his head gently and pressed him close.
Bobby Ho rasped a final sentence into Stratton's neck.

"It was the kid . . . sorry, Tom . . ."

Bobby Ho spun from Stratton's arms and lunged for the
student. The carbine, shockingly loud in the small room, cut
him in half. Impelled by momentum that the bullets did not
reverse, the corpse of Bobby Ho collided with his killer.

The commissar was too slow. A bullet from his pistol
plucked at Stratton's ribs. Stratton's open palm drove the
commissar's nose into his brain.

Then Stratton had the pistol. He shot the policeman twice,
and then the student as he writhed to free himself from Bobby
Ho's last embrace. The professor burst from the room, vaulted
off the stage and darted among the chairs, a frenzied hurdler.
Stratton shot him in the back.

Outside was a holocaust. Two trucks burned at the far end of
the street, and along either side civilians spilled from single-
story hutches whose thatched roofs burned with a hungry
crackle. The PLA had arrived in force. Stratton counted eight
or nine rag doll figures in army khaki sprawled around the
trucks. Stratton saw Panofsky go down hurling a grenade.
Bloomfield dove after him. He didn't make it.

Screaming, waving his assault rifle to scatter peasants who
seemed more curious then frightened, Stratton headed back up
the street the way he had come. Two knock-kneed soldiers
emerged from an alley. Stratton took them with a short burst.
He ran back to where he had left Gomez and Harkness. An old
man brandishing a cane appeared from nowhere. Stratton
clubbed him with the rifle.

He found Harkness's body propped against a tree, and then
Gomez, firing methodically at dancing shadows from behind a
low concrete wall.

Together they broke away from the village and into the
black, beckoning fields. Stratton's wound bled freely. Every
step was a fresh souvenir of defeat. After about fifteen minutes
he could go no farther. He huddled in an irrigation ditch,
Gomez beside him. The Chinese had paused at the edge of the
village. To regroup, to await orders, or simply to separate
soldiers from civilians. It made no difference. They would
come soon enough.

"What a fuck-up," Gomez growled.

Stratton gasped for breath, wincing with pain.

"Did you call for help, for the chopper?"

"Bloomfield had the radio," Stratton whispered.

"Shit. I got no ammo left."

Stratton checked his own rifle. One magazine remained.

"They're all around us, Captain. I can feel it. And the civilians are worse than the fucking soldiers. Crazy bastards. One guy came at us with a cleaver."

Stratton knew what the next question would be, and he dreaded it.

"How are we gonna get out of here, Captain?"

"Pickup is in about thirty-five minutes," Stratton gasped. "Do you think you can find where we left the beacon? It can't be more than a mile or so."

"I can find it."

"Go. I'll stay here and keep them busy till the last minute. When the chopper comes I'll be right behind you."

"Sure," Gomez muttered in a way that meant it would never happen. "Adios."

"Good luck," Stratton called, and waited alone to die.

The bugs were bad. He ignored them. Every time he shifted, his jungle boots squished in the mud. He held perfectly still. The second hand crawled around the face of his watch like a turtle with palsy. He willed himself not to look at it.

The flames were dying now, but enough light remained to make the village a perfect target. The Chinese recognized that. They could not know how large was the force opposing them, and they were in no hurry to find out. Stratton blessed their fear.

Stratton heard officers hollering and the whine of new trucks arriving, but it was nearly twenty minutes before the first infantrymen burst from the closest buildings and dove for cover. They were in range, but Strtton did not fire. To fire was to die.

He waited another agonizing five minutes. Then he crouched and with all his strength hurled the last grenade as far as he could off to the left, away from the route of escape. The night ignited once more: the grenade, followed by Chinese carbines, firing blind. Tracer bullets streaked along the treeline like orange meteors.

Stratton slithered from the ditch and trotted for the landing zone.

He had nearly made it when he heard a grunt and the thrashing of a desperate struggle about thirty yards ahead. In the moonlight he saw a figure wielding a pole, a ghostly jouster.

A scream pierced the night, and then a terrible, expiring "*Madre . . .*"

Stratton crashed forward like a murderous boar, the Kalashnikov on full automatic. Before him, squat gray shapes rustled away. Peasant killers. Systematically, Stratton cut them down. One. Two. Three. Four.

It had not been a pole, but a pitchfork, and it had impaled Gomez as he lay on the moist earth beside the homing beacon that would bring the rescue helicopter. Gomez was dead when Stratton reached him, the pitchfork deep in his chest.

Mindlessly Stratton knelt by his friend's body and activated the ultrasonic beacon. Already he could hear the invisible helicopter, waiting for the signal. From behind he heard whispers from approaching Chinese soldiers as they skittered between clumps of cover.

Stratton glanced down at Gomez and smothered a moan. He passed a grimy hand across parched lips. All he could do was wait; it would be a very near thing. Wait in silence for deliverance, for the sight of the rope ladder peeling out of the chopper's belly. Pray that the chopper came before the Chinese found him.

Stratton heard a noise and knew instantly that the helicopter would come too late, an eternity too late.

It was a squelch in the mud, and he whirled to face it. Another gray shape, only a few yards away. It had been watching him; he should have sensed it.

Stratton sprang forward, his hand working on the Thai blade at his belt. The shape had no gun or he would already be dead. But it could scream, and if it screamed, he would be discovered.

In three frantic bounds he reached the peasant. It was a young woman. She cried out and backed away, her eyes wild. The distant throb of the chopper blades grew louder. A minute or two, maybe more.

The woman turned to flee.

Let her go?

But she would scream. He knew she would scream. She ran in awkward steps, her arms around her belly. Stratton swiftly caught her, sobbing. Not this time, Bobby Ho. Not again.

With his left hand Stratton jerked back the girl's head, and the fire's glow shone on the flesh of her neck. He killed her with a single savage thrust.

Still she screamed, a thin, piteous wail lost in the clatter of the descending helicopter and the confused shouts of the Chinese soldiers. She screamed for her life, and that of the child who lay heavy within her. Two senseless deaths.

Thomas Stratton did not care.

CHAPTER 18

STRATTON'S THROAT WAS DRY, his voice rough. He felt himself winding down like a cheap clock.

"Like it was yesterday," he said. "I still dream about it. It still hurts. I murdered them. The woman, the baby . . ."

Kangmei worried a deep furrow with her stick.

"It is a very sad story, Thom-as," she murmured at last.

"I'm sorry."

"Men should not fight, Thom-as. they should live in peace and build beautiful things. Man is for good, not for killing."

"I wish I could believe that."

"Oh, but it is true. For every evil old man like my father, there are hundreds—many thousand—who are true and loving. Leave your unlocked bicycle at their door and it will be there tomorrow, and the day after. Those are the Chinese people, Thom-as. Not my father, not commissars who play with people's minds."

"Your Uncle David is a good man."

"Yes, I could see that."

"Until today he was the only person who had ever heard my story."

"Thank you."

"I wanted you to know. It was important . . ."

"I understand. I am not a witch, like one of the old women in Bright Star, but I have seen the sadness inside of you."

"Kangmei, I . . ."

Stratton let the thought drift away. He watched the swift river, as muddy as his own thoughts. He felt light-headed and empty. And yet purged, as though retelling the horror would at last allow him to file it in some dusty mind bin, where it belonged.

On the far side of the river a young woman led a file of nursery-school children toward an old wooden footbridge. A flock of pigeons alighted in the trees around them. The palm leaves glinted with fleeting gold in the brief tropical dusk. Soon it would be dark, and a few hours after that he would be gone. Kangmei's family had found a friend of a friend who was a conductor on the overnight train to Canton. Tomorrow the vestige of Captain Black would take over. Canton would be no problem. It was tonight that hurt. Stratton wanted the ghost of Man-ling banished as quickly as the Chinese railroads would allow. He wanted to get to Hong Kong, and from there to save David Wang. But he did not want to leave the strong and idealistic woman at his side.

He was assembling the question when Kangmei spoke. Again, she had anticipated him.

"Have you ever loved, Thom-as?"

"Yes, sure," he said, but he could not separate the images of a clichéd decade: blondes and Titians, quiche and Perrier, trim-cut ski jackets, designer sheets. Carol, who had proved a more devoted doctor than wife, more brittle than beautiful, a better diagnostician than mother.

"No," he said. Not like this.

"I loved once," she said, so far away, so fragile he wanted to gather her into his arms, but dared not molest her privacy.

"A gentle boy, not tall and strong and handsome, but short and plain. One leg was shorter than the other and he limped. His face was so round you thought it was the moon, and he could not see well, so he wore heavy glasses that always slid off his nose and broke. There was no place he could hide: People would point and say, 'Oh, how ugly.' But when they saw what he wrote, no one laughed anymore. His poems were beautiful, like the morning sun creeping along an open field. His poems were as simple as the birds in these trees and as pure as those children across the river.

"He was a happy boy who did not mind being ugly. He laughed at his bad luck and lived for the hours when he could write his poetry. During the days he worked as an electrician in a big factory. At night he would compose in a workers' dormitory. At first he showed his poems only to his friends. That was when he was happiest. He gave poems to his friends as gifts and then showed them to other friends until finally other writers saw them, writers who work without Party control. He gave poems in secret to his friends at the factory and finally the top cadres of the factories saw them, too. The writers went to him and said, 'Write of life. Be freer.' The cadres of his unit went to him and said, 'You have great talent. You must write of the workers' heroic struggle.'

"My friend was a happy man who wanted everyone to share his joy. So he wrote for the writers about larks and joy, and he wrote for the cadres about the beauties of blast furnaces and socialist progress. At first both were very pleased. 'More,' they said. 'Write more.' So my friend wrote more, and more, until he could hardly remember whether the next poem was supposed to be about the glorious fulfillment of factory quotas, or every man's right to find his own truth.

"Then one day my friend said, 'No more.' He went to the writers and to the cadres and told them, 'I must write for me, not for you. What I write for you is not me, and it is not good.' They both became very angry, the writers and the cadres. They felt my friend had betrayed them. They yelled and screamed at him. The factory gave him the most dirty and dangerous jobs. The writers no longer invited him to tea or to walk in the park. My friend became very unhappy. Soon he could not write at all—not even for himself. He would limp around the city looking for inspiration, his great moon face empty, like a man whose father has died. He wrote nothing. All this happened the year that I loved him."

Kangmei smiled through tears. "That is my sad story, Thom-as."

"I'm sorry, Kangmei. Is your friend still in Peking?"

"He is beyond Peking."

"What happened?"

"One day at the factory he picked up two heavy cables in his hands and rubbed them together. They were full of electricity. Perhaps it was an accident. . . ."

"I'm sorry." A temporizing banality.

"I love you, Thom-as."

"I was trying to say the same thing. Come with me, please. We'll find a way to Hong Kong. America is a strange country, I know, but you will like it. If you don't, we can come back to Asia. Anywhere you want . . ."

"No, Thom-as, no. This is my country. China is where I belong."

"But you will be hunted here. You have sacrificed everything for me. Your school, your family . . ."

"I have done what is right."

"That will not protect you."

"My relatives here will protect me now. Later, I will find my protection in the millions of young people who believe as I do. I have talked to you about them and I have seen how you looked at me—like an uncle looks at a young girl who says she can walk to the moon. I am right. You will see."

Damned if she wasn't mad, twin points of color blazing from her cheeks.

Stratton tried not to sound patronizing.

"Kangmei, let's not argue. I believe in your vision, but I want to be with you. If a man and a woman can find love—isn't that enough?"

"I, too, have thought about that. I am . . . confused. A part of me wants to go with you, but another part insists that I stay. So I will stay and I will think. I—"

"Look!" Stratton was on his feet, pointing. On the far side of the river, bellowing in fear, blind with pain, ran a pig. In the failing light, Stratton could see the stream of blood that marked the pig's passage and, in distant pursuit, a peasant with a knife. Running pig of Chinese commune-ism. A weak joke.

There was nothing funny about the running pig.

It veered onto the narrow dirt promenade that paralleled the one Stratton and Kangmei had walked on their side of the river. Striking from behind, the dying pig tore through the line of schoolchildren like a berserk bowling ball. The youngsters flew to the left and right. Most were simply shuffled. Stratton saw one trampled. A peasant woman in black dumped a load of laundry from her head and kicked viciously at the pig. It staggered off the path. The young teacher who had been leading the children screamed. Around her frightened, crying children needed immediate attention and reassurance. But that was not the worst of it. Two of the children—they could not have been more than three years old—tumbled down the steep bank and into the river. First the boy, then the girl. They made twin ripples.

"Aiyee!" Kangmei screamed.

Across the river, Stratton could see men running. Behind him, too, there came the sound of feet. They were all too far away. And in minutes, the rescuers would need flashlights if they were to be of any use at all.

Tom Stratton threw himself down the bank with a rush that

left his leg yelping in protest. He entered the water in a long, flat dive.

The river tasted of mud. Stratton angled upstream, fighting the current. It was his only chance. Wait until the water brought the children to him.

Stratton had three enemies in the warm, pungent river. First was the current, stronger than it had seemed. It tugged and caressed, unyielding, eternal. Treading water, trying to ride as high as possible, Stratton knew he was barely holding his own. If he was pushed downstream he would travel roughly at the same speed as the children who even now should be, must be—God, where were they?—approaching him. They would certainly drown then.

Second was the light. Precious little remained. If he did not find the children while he could still see, he would never find them.

Third was his strength. His leg, he felt sure, was bleeding again. The bicycling motion in the water reminded him how badly his body had been abused by Wang Bin's thugs. He hadn't much stamina.

People dotted both banks now. He saw one man running up with a ladder and another setting a match to a kerosene lamp. On the Evergreen side a middle-aged man with a coil of rope was purposefully making his way down the embankment. Stratton wondered how long the rope was. He would know when the man reached the water's edge.

But where were the children? He couldn't see . . .

"Thom-as! Swim to the right." A banshee's command. Kangmei. Smart girl. She had stayed up on the embankment where the elevation expanded her vision. She had never taken her eyes off the children from the moment they hit the water. For the first time Stratton felt a surge of hope. Obediently, he swam right, challenging the current.

"Four meters . . . three meters . . . two meters . . . now! Now! Now!"

Still, he almost missed it, a bundle of color that was on him before he saw it. Stratton grabbed. Missed. Grabbed again. He pulled the child by the hair until its face came clear of the water. He could not tell if it was the girl or the boy, but it was alive, feebly fighting his grasp.

"Right again. Now! You must hurry!"

Stratton windmilled right with one arm, clutching the child

tightly with the other. Within seconds the arm felt as though it would wrench from his socket. He seemed rooted.

"Faster! Faster!"

Stratton swallowed a mouthful of water. He gagged. He wanted to scream. *I'm swimming as fast as I can.* He wanted to rest. *I never said I was Superman.* He wanted to tell her, *I love you.* Stratton swallowed more water.

The little boy whimpered as he swept past, a chick peeping. Got ya, you little bastard. Gotcha. He grabbed the boy by the collar of his shirt. His strength failing, the children clutched to his chest. Stratton pumped his legs ruthlessly, fighting off extinction for three flickering candles. It was dark now. And he was so tired. He must rest. Tomorrow he would finish. . . .

Talons that felt like steel yanked Stratton's hair. He cried out.

The stocky man had not thrown the rope. He had tied one end to the trunk of a dead tree and the other around his waist. Mercilessly, the stocky man pulled again at Stratton's hair, gasping in Chinese.

"All right, all right," Stratton protested. "You win, take one."

Clumsily, a splashing *pas de deux* for the blind, they transferred one of the children from Stratton to the man on the rope. His arm free, a fiery, tremendous, unbearable weight suddenly lifted, Stratton grasped the man's shirt. Willing hands reeled them in. Tom Stratton felt as if he were flying.

CHAPTER 19

HAROLD BROOM PUT ON his most expensive tailored suit—navy, with a fine ash-gray stripe—and plunged into the muggy Washington afternoon. He flagged a taxi at 14th Street. Six blocks was too damn far to walk on a hot day in your best suit.

The curator was waiting in a private office. It was a Monday, and the museum was closed to the public.

"Hello, Dr. Lambert."

The curator nodded. "You have the photograph?"

Broom gave it to him.

"I asked for an infantryman," Lambert remarked with a scowl.

"Not available," Broom said curtly. He didn't like Lambert at all; he didn't like experts in general.

"When was it dusted?"

"Two, three months ago," Broom answered. "I'm not sure."

Lambert grunted.

Broom said, "If it's the quality you're worried about, don't bother. It's been stored in a dry place, safe from the elements."

The curator unfolded a schematic of the Qin tombs. The drawing illustrated each of the eleven columns under excavation. The location of the archers, the chariots, the spearmen and the armored infantry was noted in pencil.

"Which vault did this one come from?"

"I have no idea," Broom said. "That's my partner's end of things. And what the hell difference does it make? You know exactly what you're getting, friend. There's seven thousand of these buggers underground in China, but this is your only chance to get your hands on one."

"It's history," Lambert said stiffly.

"History, my ass. It's an investment."

"You're revolting," the curator said in a hoarse voice.

"I'm also late for a plane. I want the down payment right now—that is, if you're still interested."

"Oh, I'm interested, Mr. Broom. But first: How many of these have you and your *partner* smuggled in?"

"This is the only one."

Lambert's eyes turned to ice. He stood up. "Good day, Mr. Broom. You're welcome to come back when you've sobered up."

Broom sighed. Lying to the crazy Texan was one thing; he should have known better with Lambert. He signaled the curator to sit down.

"There's three of them," Broom said, his voice low.

"And the other buyers?"

"Some junior oil tycoon in Texas who doesn't know Qin Dynasty from Corningware."

"Who else?"

"An Oriental restaurant guy down in Florida. I think he's going to put the soldier next to his salad bar."

"That's it?"

"Yes, I swear."

"I'll find out if you're lying," Lambert promised. "How much?"

"Seven fifty."

"Six hundred," Lambert said. "Three hundred now, the rest on delivery. If it's damaged when I open the crate, you won't see another penny—so I suggest you wrap it in heavy quilts and pack it in styrofoam. So . . . we have a deal?"

"Shit." Broom grimaced.

Lambert smiled. "Good. Now, when can I expect delivery?"

"A week, maybe more. You're number three on my list."

"But why?" Lambert cried.

"Because the others already paid us," Broom said, rising, "and their checks cleared."

Lao Fu had lived more than eighty years amid the monuments to dead Ming emperors. As a boy, he had witnessed the fall of China's last dynasty. For Lao Fu, the Communists were newcomers; when he thought about them at all, it was as emperors with different names. What difference did it make? A man lived and worked and, if he was lucky, his children cared for him until he died. At Sunrise Commune, Lao Fu was a man

of distinction. There was nothing he had not known about
ducks, and little he had forgotten. Had he not three times
personally traveled more than fifty li to Peking to hear
successive generations of chefs praise his ducks? Didn't the
young men of the commune still come to him for advice when
their foolish practice of force-feeding the ducks made the birds
sick? Lao Fu was a man who possessed wisdom. So it was that
the commune leaders chose not to know of the pastime that
had, once a week, occupied Lao Fu for nearly half a century.
Who would invoke bureaucratic injunction to an old man who
could not read?

On a summer's afternoon, Lao Fu walked to the reservoir
that nestles among the Ming Tombs. He borrowed a rowboat
from the caretaker. With a small net, each perfect knot tied by
patient hands, Lao Fu went fishing for carp. He fished in secret
places.

When he returned that day, Lao Fu left a plump brown fish in
the boat where the caretaker would find it and carried two
others home to his family. At dinner, everyone praised his skill.
They devoured tender white flesh. Lao Fu did not eat, refusing
even the eyes and the maw, the most succulent and honored
pieces that were his right.

Afterward, his eldest son asked Lao Fu if he was sick.

"I will die soon," the old man said.

"You are healthy and strong. You will not die for many
years."

"My time is gone. There is too much I cannot understand."

The eldest son thought of the new commune television set,
of the noisy diesel tractors, of the experiment to produce more
ducks by keeping the lights burning in their roost. Each of
these things he had carefully explained to his father. But it was
difficult.

"What troubles you, Father? I will try to help."

"What lives in the water?"

"Fish."

"What lives on the land?"

"Man and the other animals."

"Is it still so?"

"Yes, my father."

"You are wrong."

"How am I wrong?"

"Today I fished a man."

* * *

They brought Stratton tea, and a hair-curling local moonshine. They wrapped him in a blanket. A doctor came and, clucking, dressed his leg and gave him a shot of antibiotic with a needle meant for horses. They produced clothes that almost fit, and a pair of rope-soled sandals. People pressed around, all talking at once. They smiled and bowed. They shook his hand and pounded his back. Stratton let it happen.

He had been bundled onto the back of a truck, he and the waterlogged stocky man, peasant women cuddling the two little bodies and, it seemed, half the commune, a tight-pressed gesticulating horde.

Where else would they go but to the seat of power, the headquarters of the commune, the site of the local dispensary?

They had come to Man-ling.

Shivering in the humid tropic night, Stratton viewed himself as though from another dimension. Could it have been inevitable? All this time, all these years? Karma? Fate? What else could account for it? Of all the villages on the planet, he had been returned to the one that had seared him and stained him and left him a man of palpable sadness.

To that village was he led back, bearer of two tiny corpses. Fresh bodies for Man-ling. I am your plague, don't you see? I have only to come and people die. Forgive me. I am sorry. This time I did my best. I tried. Now, please leave me alone. There are ghosts here who frighten me and of which I shall not speak. I want to leave.

Someone handed him a bowl and a pair of chopsticks. Eat, they gestured. He ate. Face buried in the bowl, he could not see. It was better not to see.

The dispensary was new, single story and freshly whitewashed. It contained six beds, some rudimentary medical equipment and windows that opened onto the village main street. The view was of an old movie house across the street. Weary and sagging. In passing headlights, Stratton could see where bullets had marched up the facade. The movie house was as quiet, as dingy and as terrifying as it had been the first night he saw it. They had not even painted it.

Imagine.

After all these years they had not even painted it. His mind had seen the building thousands of times. And always he had imagined that it was white again, that someone had come, orders had been given, workers had arrived, and paint had covered the scars. White paint.

But his nightmare had deceived him. No paint. No clean-up, fix-up, paper-it-over. It was the wrong country for that. China. Let the scars be seen. The people's struggle. Stratton wondered if Bobby Ho's body still lay on the stage.

Kangmei arrived at last and, with her, a measure of sanity.

She hurled herself at him, burying her head in his chest. Stratton's rice bowl went flying. From the spectators came laughter, nervous and polite. Women in the New China did not embrace foreigners, in private or public.

"Oh, Thom-as, you are so brave. So brave."

He kissed the top of her head.

"The children?" he asked, dreading the answer.

"The boy is well, Thom-as. The girl . . . the doctors are still working."

One for two. It could have been worse.

"Kangmei, can we go now? We have to talk." She felt so good in his arms.

"No, we cannot. There are very many people. Now you are *everyone's* rice expert. They want to express their thanks."

"I just want to be alone with you."

"The train will be here in less than one hour."

He had forgotten.

"An hour?" He had so much to say to her.

The Chinese seized on Kangmei as their link to Stratton. They pushed and shoved and jostled for her attention. She yelled something in her struggle-session voice, and the crowd quieted. The semblance of a line formed.

"They will come individually to greet you. They want to take you across to the old theater where there is more room, but I said you were too weak. Also, I have told them to say only a few words and leave you to rest. Once they have left, so can we, not before."

"Let's get it over with." Stratton fixed a smile on his face.

A ruddy-faced man with iron gray hair appeared, speaking forcefully.

"This is the boy's grandfather," said Kangmei. "On behalf of his family, he extends his most grateful thanks and wishes you a speedy recovery. It is his wish that you will be guest of honor for a banquet once you are well."

"Tell grandfather that I am pleased to have been of

assistance and that I would be honored to meet his entire family—when I am recovered."

An uncle replaced the grandfather. Then cousins and aunts, the boy's mother, fighting back tears, even neighbors. Stratton thought it would never end.

"Kangmei, let's get out of here."

"This is a Zhuang tradition and, for you, a great honor. We cannot offend these people."

A few minutes later, while a portly man whose relationship to anyone seemed only dimly established spoke at length in a politician's growl, Kangmei said suddenly:

"You are very handsome."

"Did *he* say that?"

"He says all the usual things. *I* say that."

"Come with me, please, to America."

"I cannot."

"I love you."

"This man is the best friend of the boy's mother's second sister and he wishes to convey to you . . ."

Stratton noticed a commotion at the door. Three men came in. Peasants made way for them.

"The leaders of the commune," Kangmei whispered.

Stratton nodded. Their bearing alone made that clear.

The commune president wore an impeccable white shirt outside his belt. His were the first clean fingernails Stratton had seen all day. The vice-president was a me-tooer, handsome and suave. They were both Han Chinese, their lighter skin and sharper features distinguishing them immediately in the room of Thai-like Zhuang. They came forward smiling, hands outstretched.

"Comrade president explains that he was at a regional meeting and has only just returned. He has heard of your bravery and would like . . ."

The third man in the delegation was old and fat. He had a cruel saucer face that made smiling a parody. He walked with a cane. The sleeve of his jacket was pinned neatly to his right shoulder. The absence of the arm, and the limp, gave him a sinister, off-balance appearance.

". . . regrets that the comrades in Peking had not informed him of the arrival of such a distinguished guest or he would have come personally to Bright Star to welcome you," Kangmei translated. "Don't worry about that, Thom-as. After tonight no one will ever ask for your papers and he will be afraid to ask Peking why they did not tell him.''

The saucer-faced man's smile had vanished. He rocked back and forth on his cane. He shuffled to the left and right to measure Stratton from different angles. Stratton's eyes never left him.

". . . will offer a banquet of welcome and thanksgiving within the next few days and pledges full cooperation of all of the commune work brigades and production teams in your work. You have only to ask—".

"*Kuei!*" The word can mean either ghost or devil. In this case, it was doubly apt.

Screaming, the old man lunged with the cane, jabbing with it as more than a decade before he had jabbed Stratton with his truncheon.

Time had not been kind to the old man. Stratton easily parried the blow. He wrenched away from the cane, sent it spinning to the far corner of the room, and tried to look aggrieved.

The old man's voice cracked with fury. His eyes bulged. The muscles in his neck corded. He threw himself on Stratton, splintering the chair. They rolled to the floor, the old man striking repeatedly with the only fist Stratton had left him.

Stratton covered up protectively. He did not fight back. It would not last long. It didn't. The peasants pulled the old man off and built a human fence between him and Stratton. Stratton didn't even bother getting to his feet. Instead, he scrambled over to the wall and leaned against it, waiting for what he knew must come.

Quivering, weeping, the old man shouted in a high, reedy voice. Within seconds a hush had fallen over the dispensary waiting room.

Kangmei translated. She needn't have bothered.

"The old man was the head of the Public Security Bureau in Man-ling for many years—the top policeman. He knows you. He says you are an American spy who came to spy and to kill. Everybody will remember the night, he says. The night of the heroic people's victory. The old man says he saw you then. He talked to you. You killed cadres. You shot him twice, once in the leg, once in the arm." Kangmei's voice jumped an octave, almost falsetto. "He says—"

Stratton had heard enough. He dug his nails into Kangmei's arm.

"That's enough, Kangmei. Tell the comrade that I understand his distress, but that he is mistaken. I have never been in China before this month. I have never been in Man-ling before. I have never been in a war. I am a rice expert. Say it calmly. Make it sound true."

When she had finished, the old policeman began again, but the president of the commune silenced him. The president's apparent perplexity mirrored expressions around the room. Whom to believe? What to do? The Zhuang, Stratton sensed, were with him. The Han cadres would probably side with the policeman. They were vastly outnumbered, but they had what counted most: authority.

The commune president ran a hand across his brow and seemed on the verge of speaking when a tall man appeared wiping his hands on a towel—the doctor who had bandaged Stratton. The doctor spoke quietly to one of the Zhuang near the door. The man's face lit up, and he began chattering loudly. In an instant, the entire room was abuzz. Stratton watched the one-armed policeman say something to a slender young man who nodded and hurriedly left the room.

A new crop of smiles blossomed among the peasants, and fresh tears. One woman fainted. In the hubbub, Stratton had to yell to make himself heard.

"What is going on?"

Kangmei squeezed his hand. She was smiling and crying.

"It's the little girl. They thought they had lost her, but now she is breathing well and seems to be out of danger."

"Thank God." For the nameless little girl, and for Thomas Stratton.

One of the peasants who had ridden on the truck with Stratton addressed the commune president.

"He says your goodwill and good intentions are plain for anyone to see and, while he does not dispute Comrade Ma's word, he believes the comrade is mistaken. He says you should be allowed to return to Bright Star now with the thanks of the commune for your heroism."

Kangmei finished her translation amid an assenting chorus from the Zhuang peasants. The commune president chose not—or dared not—to affront the majority. He nodded slowly and Stratton could almost see him thinking: to hold Stratton on the unsupported word of an overwrought old man would anger the peasants. To release him cost nothing. Tomorrow they could always bring him back in. Stratton sensed that the man was the kind of political bureaucrat who would most of all prefer to make no decision at all. If Stratton were to disappear from the face of the earth, so much the better.

Favoring his leg, Stratton used the wall as a crutch to gain his feet. Kangmei stood at his side.

"Say something graceful and let's go."

Before she could speak, the old policeman fired a fresh stacatto burst.

"He says he knows how people are tired of the memories and the obsessions of an old man who will not forget. But he begs for patience. There is another witness, he says, one who will say positively that you're a murderer and a spy. The witness will come soon."

The commune president sighed resignedly. He would humor a trusted old colleague.

The president spoke briefly and courteously to Kangmei.

"He asks if you would please remain for another few minutes, even though you are tired, so that this matter may be finally resolved without further affecting our friendship."

Stratton shrugged. It was a sugar-coated command, but the worst was over. Mentally, he ticked off the witnesses who had seen his face that other night in Man-ling. Besides the policeman, only the commissar, the professor and the student. All dead. The policeman should have been, too. There had been no other witnesses.

They left Stratton and Kangmei alone then, side by side on wooden chairs in a corner of the room.

"The train will be leaving soon," said Stratton.

"There is still a little time. Would you like some tea?"

"Yes, please."

She was back in a minute with gossip and two steaming mugs.

"The witness is a schoolteacher, a young man who is very bright, but is of poor family background."

"What does that mean?"

"His father, or perhaps his grandfather, was a landlord or a capitalist. That means he cannot go to the university or join the army or belong to the Party. So he is a schoolteacher."

A lovely system, Stratton mused. Convict a man for his

ancestors' crimes. For how many generations? He sipped his tea and watched shadows from an overhead lamp play across Kangmei's lovely features.

And then Stratton knew who the witness would be. His cup fell, set free by stricken fingers.

"Thom-as, your tea!" Kangmei exclaimed in alarm. "You are shaking. What is wrong? Shall I get the doctor?"

"No, no," he said. And thought for the second time that night of Bobby Ho.

The young man entered the room with quiet poise. The policeman limped over and spoke urgently with him, gesturing at Stratton, the hatred unmasked. The president said something to the young man and so did one of the peasants. Lobbying, Stratton supposed.

The young man dragged up a chair and sat directly in front of Stratton—mute reviewer of a one-man play. They stared at one another across three feet and eleven years.

The rag boy had added weight to the skin and bones, but not much. The face had filled, but still it spoke of suffering. The body had remained as insubstantial as it had looked the night Bobby Ho's quixotic, absurd, fatal gesture had spared one life and cost many more. The inborn pride had not changed, or the cold, calculating intelligence in the masked obsidian eyes.

Stratton knew he was finished.

There was eloquence in the poker gaze of the grown-up rag boy. His identification was as certain as Stratton's. He, too, like the tormented old policeman, like Stratton, still dwelt in the debris of horror.

Did he also weep, alone at night, for friends so brave? Did he dream terrible dreams of acrid tracers and bullet-stitched buildings that should have been white? Did he still gnaw at desolation? And what had he suffered for a preasant woman and her unborn child? He hadn't felt the knife go through her neck.

Stratton waited for the denouement. Captain Black riffled methodically through escape scenarios. The dice roll, man. Nobody lives forever.

But at least make him work for it.

You bastard. Stratton stared at the rag boy. You chicken-shit son of a bitch. We let you go. I could have ended your pitiful knitting-needle existence with a nod, but instead I let you go. In return you killed my friends.

"It was the kid . . . Sorry, Tom. . . ."

Stratton plumbed the Chinese, seeking the man behind the intelligent eyes. He found nothing. And then he made a decision. We both of us should have been dead these eleven years, son of a bitch. Call in the cards. It was a simple decision. It refreshed Stratton and gave him strength. The instant the rag boy raised his voice in accusation, Captain Black would kill him. One dead man kills another. Justice in Man-ling. To finish what had been neglected that night in the rain. I'm sorry, Bobby Ho.

Stratton was sizing the blow when he saw what he had not dared hope to see.

The Chinese eyes spoke plainly. I know you. I have you. You are mine.

And then, the final message:

A life for a life.

"Bushi," the man spat in an unexpectedly deep voice.

He stalked from the room.

"Thom-as, he says it was not you," Kangmei cried.

"Of course not."

Babbling peasants erased the tension. Minutes later, Stratton and Kangmei were alone in the back of a jeep. Stratton had departed without pity for the old policeman, agape, blubbering alone in a corner of the room.

Rest in peace, Bobby Ho. You were right and I was wrong, all this time, all these years.

CHAPTER 20

"OPEN YOUR SUITCASE, PLEASE."

"It's locked."

"Find the key and open it," said the U.S. Customs Inspector Lance P. Dooley, Jr. He strained to be polite. His boss was working the next aisle.

"But the key is in the suitcase," whined the young man in Dooley's line. "I packed it by accident. I'm sorry, officer." The man had just debarked from Pan American Airways Flight 7, Peking-to-Tokyo-to-San Francisco. He wore blue jeans and a Van Halen concert T-shirt, with Day-Glo lettering. His black hair was long and straight, tied in a ponytail. Dooley studied the face. Malaysian, he decided. The passport confirmed it.

"Sir, I want to take a look in your suitcase. Either you find a way to open it, or I will. We have special tools," Dooley said. "Hardly put a scratch on it, you watch."

"But it's a brand-new Samsonite," the young man objected.

"So it is."

Behind the young man a haggard procession of travelers stretched and sighed and muttered their annoyance at the delay. Second in line was a stocky, handsome Chinese man in his sixties. His hair was neatly combed, and he wore gold-rimmed eyeglasses that gave his features an intent, scholarly cast. His clothes fit somewhat loosely: beige slacks slightly wrinkled from the long flight, a knit canary-colored sports shirt buttoned all the way to the neck, and a dark brown sweater with a monogram on the left breast.

The Chinese man carried only one piece of luggage, a cumbersome old suitcase exhibiting thirty years' worth of scuffs and dents. The man did not hoist the suitcase to the conveyor belt, but kept it at his feet, one hand firmly on the grip, as if it were a Doberman on a leash. He seemed transfixed by the argument in front of him.

"You can't just break into my suitcase," the young Malaysian insisted.

"Sir," Dooley said, "if you decline to have your luggage searched here, we will escort you to a private inspection room where we will not only search the suitcase, we'll ask you to take off your clothes—and we'll search some more. Which do your prefer?"

Dooley's supervisor glanced disapprovingly at the long line at Dooley's aisle. Dooley got the message and tried to step it up.

"The key, sir?"

The young man figeted. Dooley nodded to a couple of other customs agents, who had been leaning against a square pillar. They stepped eagerly to the front of Dooley's line.

"Okay, okay. I'm not hiding anything. Let me see if I can get this open." The Malaysian played with the latches on the Samsonite and it popped open. "Go ahead, see for yourself. Just clothes and some junk I brought back from Singapore."

"Do you live in Singapore?" Dooley asked as he picked through underwear, socks, snapshots, toothpaste, a packet of condoms.

"No, I live here in Frisco," said the young man. "Lived here since I was ten. My father still lives in Singapore. I got two brothers there, too. I go back five or six times a year."

This was the talking phase. Dooley smiled to himself. He took his time. It was here somewhere.

"I'm a chef," the young man volunteered. His eyes were glued to Dooley's hands, sifting and exploring. "It's a Chinese joint off Market Street. Li-Siu's. Have you been there? I make good money. And I send half of it home every month—"

"What's this?"

"Film. Kodak film."

Dooley studied the two yellow packages. The end flaps of one were creased, and off square from the carton.

"I bought those here, before I left."

"Really?"

"I didn't take as many pictures as I thought I would." The Malaysian grinned nervously.

Dooley opened one of the film cartons and removed the black plastic containers. He snapped one of the caps and looked inside. The two agents behind him edged closer. The

Chinese man, waiting in the customs line, craned his neck to get a glimpse.

Dooley showed the inside of the canister to the two agents. Gingerly he probed with his pinky finger; it came out covered with what looked like flour. Dooley tasted it with the tip of his tongue. Then he popped the top back on the container.

"Heroin," he said.

"No!" exclaimed the young Malaysian. "You're kidding."

"High-speed film, all right," one of the agents growled.

The Malaysian was led away, squirming. A third agent appeared and confiscated the Samsonite and the film packages.

"Sorry for the delay, folks," Lance Dooley said to the rest of the passengers. "We'll move right along now. Next?"

The Chinese man wrestled his huge suitcase to the conveyor belt. Quickly, almost frantically, he opened the latches.

Dooley looked at the passport. "You are returning from the People's Republic of China. Is that right, Dr. Wang?"

"Yes, sir."

"Says here you've got some scrolls and some pottery." Dooley was reading from the customs declaration form.

"That's right."

"Worth about?"

"One hundred dollars. Approximately."

Dooley opened the suitcase. The scrolls were on top— inexpensive but delicately painted wall hangings. You could find them all over the place on Fisherman's Wharf.

The pottery had been carefully wrapped in several layers of Chinese newspaper. Each piece was packed for protection between stacks of clothing. Dooley unearthed two large parcels.

"Vases."

"I'll be careful with them, Dr. Wang." Dooley peeled the newspaper away, making a lame effort not to rip it.

Cobalt dragons writhed on the body of each vase, beneath a crest of ornate blue scrolling, a field of peonies and, nesting there, a mallard. The vases were identical.

"Very nice," remarked Lance Dooley.

"Imitations, I'm afraid, but lovely bookends. For my office at the university."

"How much did these cost?" Dooley asked.

"Sixty-five dollars. A tourist shop in Peking."

Dooley set the vases on the conveyor belt, next to the suitcase. "Dr. Wang, could I see the sales receipt for these?"

"Certainly, it should be right here." He sorted through a billfold. "That's odd. I can't find it. See here—the receipt for the scrolls—"

Dooley gave it a cursory glance and handed it back.

"I keep all the receipts in the same place. It must be here . . ."

"Do you recall the name of the store?"

"No . . . no, I don't. But it was printed on the receipt."

Dooley's boss shot him another glare from the next aisle. "Lance you got another one?"

"No, sir." Dooley could take a hint. Quickly he rewrapped the vases in their paper cocoons and placed them back in the suitcase.

"Where is your final destination, Dr. Wang?"

"Ohio. Pittsville. My flight doesn't leave until tomorrow. I can search for the receipts this evening . . ."

"That won't be necessary," Dooley said. "How long were you in China?"

"Three weeks, approximately. Eighteen days, I think."

"Have a good trip home, Dr. Wang. Next, please."

Later, on his lunch break, Dooley sat down at a video display terminal in a small gray office and typed the name and passport number of David Wang into a U.S. government computer. He also typed the port of entry, the date of entry and his own identification number. On the single line alloted for general remarks, Dooley typed: "Queried China pottery/blue-and-white vases (2)."

Dooley pressed the "store" button, and turned his attention—and the remainder of his lunch hour—to the mountain of paperwork generated by the capture of the Malaysian scag mule.

Danny Bodine stuffed his hands in his pockets as he stood in the doorway of the Dong Fang Hotel. Outside a hard gray rain pelted the city of Canton. Things could be worse, he told himself. It was the typhoon season. Traffic crawled on the slick streets and bicycle riders pedaled at double speed, their heads wrapped in newspaper or crinkly plastic rain hats. Everywhere people clustered in doorways, waiting for a break in the downpour.

Maureen and Pam had scheduled an excursion to White Cloud Mountain. Danny had hired a cab for the trip—but there would be no sightseeing today.

A cargo ship docking on the Pearl River sounded its horn, piercing the shroud of rain. Danny was afraid his wife was about to suggest a trip to another museum.

"Let's go to a teahouse," he said, a preemptory strike.

"For lunch? I'm hungry, Danny."

"Me, too." It was Pam, Maureen's sister, fresh from her morning makeup marathon. She looked pretty damn good, Danny had to admit.

From somewhere out in the rain, a bedraggled American came bounding up the steps of the Dong Fang. He excused himself as he passed Danny, Maureen and Pam in the doorway. Pam watched him in the lobby, his blond hair matted and dripping. He wore thin, ill-fitting cotton clothes.

"Wonder where *he's* been," she said.

"One of those swell tailor shops near the river," Danny said.

"Be nice," said Maureen. "Maybe he's with a church group."

As Danny had feared, the three of them wound up at the Guangdong Provincial Museum.

When they returned to the Dong Fang three hours later, the American stranger was still in the lobby. Danny and Maureen paid no attention and went up to the room, but Pam sat down next to him in a high-backed leather chair. "What are you reading?"

"Oh, just travel brochures," said Tom Stratton, smiling. "It's all I could find."

"Are you a tourist, too?"

"Sort of."

"We came from Denver—me, my sister and her husband. He works for an oil company that's got an office in Hong Kong. He'll be there a couple of months, I guess. Maureen and I are going back to the States day after tomorrow."

"Oh? I am too," Stratton said. "Are you at this hotel?"

Pam nodded. She liked his smile, but he looked—well, like he'd come off a three-day bender. In Denver she'd never approach a man who looked quite so worn out, but this wasn't Denver.

"I'm on the eighth floor," Stratton lied. "Eight twelve."

"We're in seven eighteen," Pam said, then added, for clarification, "It's quite a big suite."

Stratton told her that he taught art history. Predictably, she had never heard of the college. "It's a small place," Stratton explained, "but very peaceful."

"It sounds nice," Pam said. She was thinking about the flight home; maybe they could sit together, she and her new friend, if Maureen wouldn't mind.

"What oil company does your brother-in-law work for?"

"Rocky Mountain Energy Corporation," Pam said. "Danny's a vice-president. I don't think he's too crazy about Asia, though. He's heavy into domestic shale."

"Oh."

"What are you doing for dinner?"

Stratton shrugged. "Nothing special."

"Why don't you join us, Tom? We're all going to the Ban Xi. Have your ever tried quail eggs?"

Stratton shook his head.

"It's supposed to be a beautiful restaurant. You can eat on a houseboat. Danny won't mind if you come—he'd kill for some male company."

"That's very nice. I could use some company, too." Stratton caught her glance after he said it. "What time?"

"We'll meet your here at about seven, okay?"

"How about if I meet you at the restaurant? I'm waiting for a telex. Besides, it'll take me a while to clean up."

"Fine, we'll see you there about seven-thirty." Pam stood up and said brightly. "Maybe the rain'll stop by then."

"Let's hope so," said Stratton, hating himself.

He snuck into the People's Republic's only hotel sauna and baked for ninety minutes. The heat was luxurious, soporific; wisps of steam curled off the tiles. The grit and dust of Manling washed away. Stratton closed his eyes; as exhausted as he was, he could not even doze. Training—that's where the feeling came from. Pack your gun and put your conscience in a drawer.

And love? Where do you put that? No training needed. It just happened. It can even happen when you are fighting for your life.

The ache in Stratton's belly was more than simply hunger.

In the unsprung jeep, they had embraced clumsily, kissing, chattering toward calm after the dispensary confrontation.

"But why, Thom-as? Why? If the young man knew who you were, why did he not say so?"

"*I'll* never ask him, but I can guess."

"Tell me."

"I'd rather kiss you. I think you are wonderful."

"No more kisses until you tell me."

"Let's say the rag boy—now the young teacher—has given a lot of careful consideration to what happened that night, like I have, and the policeman. I think he came to realize over the years that he was a dead man who had been reprieved by one of the evil invaders he had denounced."

"So he lied."

"I think he was trying to apologize."

"And the fat old policeman. He—"

Stratton stopped her with a kiss.

"Kangmei, I don't want to talk about it anymore. I want to talk about you, and about me. About us. I love you. Please come with me."

She ran cat's paw fingertips across his jaw.

"I must try to do what I believe is right, my brave Thom-as. Would you respect me if I did not?"

"Respect! I'm talking about love. I want you with me. I need you."

"And I you. But I must try. And I must think. Perhaps one day I will see that you are right; that, as you say, harmony between a man and a woman is really what is most important."

"And then?"

She smiled.

"And then I will confess to you what I feel now, but must resist: that I, too, am empty without you."

"If that happens, will you tell me, please?"

"Yes, I will tell you. I promise."

"I will come back to get you."

"No, Thom-as."

"Why not, damn it?"

"Because." She squeezed him tight enough to hurt and bit playfully at his ear. "Because," she murmured, "I do not wish to witness a war between our two countries."

The train was waiting. At the station, like a schoolboy

fighting a curfew, he had scribbled his address on the back of a yellowed old timetable.

"Write to me, please."

"I love you, Thom-as."

A smiling conductor who spoke only with a warning finger at his lips led Stratton to a darkened soft-class compartment and locked the door.

All the way to Canton the rails whispered her name.

Stratton lay aside his reverie and the sauna precisely at seven thirty-five. Dressed again in the strange-fitting commune clothes, he took the elevator to the seventh floor and padded the carpeted hallway until he found 718. He knocked sharply. No one answered.

Stratton found one of the floor attendants sorting cakes of soap.

"Excuse me, but I seem to have locked myself out of our suite. Seven-one-eight. The name is Bodine. My wife is down at the hairdresser."

"I help," the attendant said. The master key hung from a chain on his cloth belt. The attendant unlocked the door to the darkened suite and Stratton went to work.

He shed his clothes and concealed them beneath a mattress on one of the beds. From Danny Bodine's closet he selected a navy blue necktie, a pin-striped business shirt and a pair of dark trousers. The clothes fit almost perfectly; Stratton had guessed as much when he had first noticed the American oilman in the hotel lobby. Even Bodine's black wingtips felt snug.

Stratton removed a blue suitcase from the closet and opened it on the bed. Haphazardly, he tossed in a suit, a couple of shirts, another pair of slacks. One could not very well leave China without some luggage.

In the bathroom he borrowed Bodine's cordless Remington.

Danny Bodine was a second-drawer man—that is, the kind of traveler who hides his most precious valuables in the second drawer of the bureau, instead of the top, in the belief that this will outfox the burglars of the world. A jet-setter's illusion.

Stratton triumphantly located Bodine's passport under a stack of jockey shorts. Next he guessed that the oilman's emergency cash would be either carefully taped on the underside of the drawer, rolled into his socks, or divided in equal sums between the two hiding places.

Again, Stratton silently congratulated himself. A pair of black nylon knee socks yielded three hundred dollars and two hundred yuan. Stratton took only the dollars. Traveling expenses—he had lost everything in Xian.

Before he left Bodine's room, Stratton checked his watch. It was barely eight o'clock. He picked up the telephone and asked the switchboard operator to ring the Ban Xi restaurant. It took five full minutes for a waiter to locate "the American woman named Pam" and lead her to the phone.

"Hi," said Stratton. "I've got some bad news: I don't think I'm going to make it to dinner. I'm sorry for all of the trouble."

Pam was disappointed and curious.

"Did you get your cable?"

"Yes, and that's the bad news. I've got to go back to the States tomorrow," Stratton said. "For a funeral."

"I'm so sorry."

"I'm the one who's sorry—for all the inconvenience. Could I have your address? I'd like to write after we get back." This time he was telling the truth. Stratton wrote down her address in Denver.

"I'm going to send you something," he said. Something the size of a man's suitcase, he thought. Bodine would be thrilled to get his wingtips back, not to mention the three hundred bucks.

"You're missing a great dinner," Pam said. "I skipped the quail eggs and ordered something called 'fragrant meat.' It's very tasty, Tom."

"Dog meat," Stratton muttered.

"What did you say?"

"Never mind. Good night, Pam."

The rain had stopped. Stratton left the Dong Fang Hotel by foot, carrying Bodine's suitcase as nonchalantly as if it were a briefcase. He strolled past a city park, lushly landscaped, its circular ponds ringed by orchids. A young Chinese couple sat together on a bench, whispering in the twilight, touching each other's hands. On a downhill sidewalk, slick from the rain, Stratton was startled by a throng of teenagers who flew by on roller skates, giddy with speed.

At the Guangzhou Railway Station he had only an hour to wait for the train to Hong Kong. Bored immigration inspectors barely glanced at the passport.

CHAPTER 21

THE TAXI CLIMBED HALTINGLY toward Victoria Peak through the morning rush-hour snarl. On all sides, Hong Kong howled at Tom Stratton; a glitzy, avaricious, sequined city, a century from Peking, light-years from Kangmei's bucolic Bright Star. It seemed impossible that they shared the same continent, let alone the same blood. Below, the famous harbor, tickled by the prows of a thousand boats, glinted gold in the early light.

The driver braked to a stop at the foot of a steep hill. Behind the taxi, a long line of cars bunched up, honking—gleaming Subarus, BMWs and Jaguar sedans, all seemingly driven by serious, thin-lipped businessmen. Stratton scrambled out of the cab, dutifully toting Bodine's suitcase. On the hillside sat the United States Consulate, square-windowed, flat and uninviting. It reminded Stratton of a cut-down version of the Boston City Hall except for the forest of antennae prickling from the roof.

Stratton lugged the suitcase up a winding flight of steps. By the time he reached the black iron gate, his injured leg throbbed in misery. He was intercepted by a young Marine in a white hat and a starched blue-and-khaki uniform. Stratton asked to meet the station chief.

"Sir?"

"The head spook, Sergeant. It's an emergency."

"Wait here, please, sir."

Stratton sat down in a waiting room, paneled with fine honey-colored wood. The sound of typing chattered from behind a closed door. Stratton's shirt clung to his back, and the cool breath of the air conditioner brought goose bumps. With one foot Stratton slid the suitcase across the waxed floor into an empty corner.

"Sir!" The Marine was back. "Mr. Darymple."

Mr. Darymple was a young man with perfectly sculpted

black hair that looked to Stratton like it had been parted with a laser beam. Stratton pegged him as an idle subordinate.

Darymple held out a slender hand and introduced himself as the assistant administrative officer.

Stratton said. "I need to see the CIA station chief."

"I'm not really sure whom you mean." Darymple smiled officiously. "Perhaps I could help."

"Very doubtful," Stratton said. "I've just spent the last week or so getting the shit kicked out of me in China."

Darymple expressed concern. "You'd like to report an incident?"

Stratton sighed. "An incident, yes. Go get your boss and I'll tell him about it."

"Could I have your name?"

"Stratton, Thomas. Tell him I was classified Phoenix."

Darymple stiffened. "Here?"

"No, Saigon. 1971. Go ahead and check, but hurry. Then go tell your boss I need a line out, right away."

Darymple said. "He'll want to see your passport."

"It was taken from me in Xian."

"Then how did you . . . excuse me, Mr. Stratton." Darymple walked out of the office in long, hurried strides.

The trick was to give them enough to chew on so that they would help, but not too much. Stratton knew what it meant to get the agency involved; he also remembered the not-so-friendly competition between stations. The boys in Hong Kong would want to claim him as their own. Peking could tag along for the ride, of course. Hong Kong probably would want to make an actual *case* of the whole thing. This, Stratton knew, he could not afford, nor could David Wang. There was no time for tedious little filemakers like Mr. Darymple.

When Darymple returned, he was accompanied by a beet-faced man in his early forties. "This is our chief political officer."

"Whatever you say."

The beef-faced man turned to Darymple and said, "That'll be all, Clay."

When they were alone, the CIA man said, "Tell me what's going on."

"I need to speak with your counterparts in Peking," Stratton said. "An American citizen is about to be murdered."

* * *

Linda Greer was clipping an article about rice production from the *People's Daily* when the buzzer went off. She snatched a notebook from the top of her desk and hurried to the station chief's private office. He was on the phone. He motioned her to a chair.

"She's here now," the station chief was saying. "I'm going to put you on the speaker box."

"Linda?" Stratton's voice cracked and fuzzed on the Hong Kong line. "Linda, can you hear me?"

"Tom!" She could not mask her elation or astonishment. When Stratton had vanished without explanation, Linda was certain he had been killed. She had blamed herself; after all, Wang Bin had been her target. The station chief had sent a curt note: *No record to be kept of your contact with Stratton.*

Yes, Linda had agreed, no record. But now Stratton had surfaced, and for the moment she didn't give a damn about her precious case file or all the cables to Langley.

"Are you all right?" she asked.

"Torn and frayed," he said. "Nothing serious."

"We had people out looking," Linda Greer said. The station chief shook his head disapprovingly. The message was: Don't say too much.

"Well, I appreciate the concern," Stratton said drily, "but I imagine the trail got pretty cold at Xian. You've probably figured out that this wasn't a government operation."

"What do you mean?" asked the station chief.

"It was Wang Bin's personal project. No army, no *Ke Ge Bo*, just his own private goons. He did it that way for good reason, the same reason he wanted me out of the picture."

"Tom, haven't you heard—"

"Let him finish!" the station chief barked. Linda Greer opened the notebook on her lap, mocking the pose of an obedient secretary. The station chief scowled.

"Start with what happened to you at Xian," he instructed Stratton.

"Forget what happened to me," Stratton said impatiently. "You need to get to Wang Bin as soon as possible. Call the ministry and leave a message. Tell him I'm alive. Tell him I know about David—"

"What about David?" the station chief asked.

"If you folks have any decent sources at all, you probably

know what's been happening at the Qin tombs in Xian. During the past few months several large artifacts have been stolen."

"What kind of artifacts?" Linda said.

"Soldiers."

"*The* soldiers?"

"The emperor's death army," Stratton said. "Didn't you know?"

The pause on the Peking end gave Stratton his answer.

"How many did you say, Tom?"

"I didn't say how many. I said several."

"The ministry mentioned pilfering," the station chief said. "Pottery, jewelry, trinkets—small stuff. Didn't say anything about the soldiers. How would you do it, Stratton? And what in the world would you do with them?"

Stratton laughed harshly. "You guys ought to try to get out of Peking once in a while. It'd open your eyes."

Linda Greer was thinking ahead of her boss. "For money," she said. "Wang Bin was getting out."

"Exactly," Stratton said excitedly. "He's a smart man, like his brother, and the future was plain: all his old comrades dropping like ducks in a shooting gallery. Wang Bin knew it wouldn't be long before they took away his limousine and made him the number-three tractor mechanic at some commune in the sticks. That's a long fall from deputy minister, and Bin didn't want to take it. Linda, he's your pet project. It fits, doesn't it?"

"There were rumors," she acknowledged, "rumors that he was in trouble."

"But were there rumors of defection?" the station chief asked.

"I'm not talking about defection," Stratton snapped. "I'm talking about disappearance. Remember that Wang Bin is a wealthy man from his smuggling enterprise. The clay soldiers are worth . . . who knows? A fortune, certainly. The best market is the United States, and I'll bet that's where the bank accounts are—a fabulous nest egg. But how does Bin get to it? How does such a well-know official escape from China? By boat, or plane . . . or scaling the fence at Kowloon? No. All too risky. And think of all the noise and hoopla if the spooks this side of the border get hold of him." Stratton winked amiably at the beet-faced man across the rosewood table.

"No, Wang Bin would want to go quietly. Wouldn't you, if

you had a couple hundred thousand U.S. dollars squirreled away?"

"Getting out would be nearly impossible," Linda Greer said.

"Suppose he had a passport," Stratton ventured. "A legitimate U.S. passport—with a photograph that seemed to match."

"How?" the station chief demanded.

"Oh, God," Linda sighed. "His own brother."

"I've heard enough," the station chief said. "Stratton, you're out of your mind."

"Tom, go on," Linda said.

"Check your files. I had Steve Powell try to run down David's passport a few days after he supposedly died. Oddly enough, no one could find it—but it was Wang Bin who provided the explanation, remember? He said David's passport was destroyed accidentally at the hospital."

Linda Greer recalled Powell's memo about the incident, a two-paragraph brush-off.

Stratton said, "What happened to David's belongings, the stuff in the vault at the embassy?"

"I assumed it went home with the body," Linda replied.

"Who picked it up?"

"A driver. From the Ministry of Art and Culture."

"Don't you see?" Stratton exclaimed.

"It was simple protocol, Tom. Wang Bin was David's brother and he wanted to handle things. We could hardly argue, especially after you welched out of the funeral flight. We aren't in the business of insulting foreign governments."

"I understand, Linda, but think . . . think! Instant wardrobe, instant identity, a ticket to the States—it adds up. Picture the deputy minister in David's eyeglasses—could you tell them apart? Would immigration ever question the passport photo? No. It's one goddamn perfect plan." Stratton's voice cracked.

"Yes, perfect, thought Linda Greer, except for one thing. She spoke soothingly. "It's a good theory, Tom."

Stratton was in a fury. She was patronizing him.

The station chief said, "I think it's a crazy goddamn theory and it's time to cut the shit. Whatever Wang Bin was up to, it doesn't matter anymore."

"Listen to me," Stratton insisted. "David Wang is alive! His brother intends to murder him any day, any second."

"No, Tom," Linda said, shooting a glance at the station chief. "Maybe the deputy minister *was* planning something big . . . but it doesn't really matter anymore—"

"You keep saying that . . . "

"—because Wang Bin is dead."

From Hong Kong came only static. Linda Greer glanced anxiously at her boss. She leaned closer to the phone speaker. "Tom? Did you hear what I said?"

Stratton battled waves of nausea. His head sagged to the rosewood table; sweat beaded on the back of his neck. He raged silently, the private agony of a terrible failure. Now he knew; it was too late.

"Tom?"

"How?" came a hoarse voice from Hong Kong.

"Drowned," the station chief reported. "An old fisherman snagged the body in the Ming reservoir. The Public Security Bureau found a capsized rowboat near the shore. We got wind of it yesterday afternoon. Today the government newspapers say it was an accident. We hear differently."

"Oh." Head bowed, Stratton mumbled through clenched hands.

"We hear it was a suicide."

Stratton laughed sadly. "What?"

"Suicide," the station chief repeated, with emphasis. "Wang Bin was due to appear before the Disciplinary Commission earlier this week. Obviously his number was up, and he knew it. So he cashed all his chips. No fancy stuff— phony passports, secret Swiss accounts, all that Hollywood bullshit—just good old-fashion Chinese honor. In this country, anything beats total disgrace, and that's what Wang Bin was facing. So he chose to die an honorable man. That way, at least, all the brass show up at your funeral."

"Will there be a state service?" Stratton wondered.

"Yeah, and you're not invited. Party types only, mid-level flag wavers, we're told. Courtesy, but no fanfare. And, Stratton, no flowers."

"Have you seen the body?" Stratton demanded.

"The coffin is *closed*. For God's sake, he'd been in the water a couple of days. Do I have to spell it out to you, Stratton? The man looked like a bloated carp."

"Please, that's enough," Linda Greer implored. "Tom, are

you all right? I know you've been through hell—maybe I ought
to fly down."

"No, thanks, I'm fine. If the nice folks here will just get me
a new passport, I'll be on my way." The beet-faced man at the
oblong table nodded helpfully; it would be a relief to book this
yo-yo on the next Pan Am. "Phoenix" indeed.

Sitting in Peking with the station chief, talking into a
squawk box to an unseen face across the continent, Linda
Greer could say none of the things she wanted to say, and none
of the things that mattered now. Stratton was safe, somehow
returned from the files of the dead, and for that she could be
happy. But there was something else, something troubling
about his theory . . .

"It's over now, Tom," she said softly. "Whatever hppened
between your friend and his brother is finished. I'm sorry about
everything."

It was only after Stratton hung up that Linda Greer realized
what the loose end was: the soldiers. Stratton had never
explained about the clay soldiers. He'd never told her how
Deputy Minister Wang Bin had done it.

As night shrouded Victoria Peak, a galaxy of bare-bulb
lights sprinkled the hillsides of Hong Kong. Jim McCarthy sat
in the Foreign Correspondents' Club, sipping gin, imagining a
shanty-porch view of the ravenous blast furnace of a city. The
poor looking up on the rich; the rich too busy to look down.
Once McCarthy had written a feature story about three Hong
Kong families who shared a tiny attic in the heart of the city—
ten adults, six children, no running water, not even a ceiling
fan to stir the air. After he filed the piece, an editor called to ask
how many Hong Kong Chinese actually lived like that.
Hundreds of thousands, McCarthy had told him; it was right
there in the story. The editor told him they were looking for
something a little more offbeat, a little sexier. And so the next
day the newspaper sent McCarthy off to do a feature on the
manufacture of counterfeit Rubik's cubes. That story made the
front page.

McCarthy ordered up another gin-and-tonic. Cursing the
idiots—that's what R-and-R is for. Get it out of your system,
Jimbo.

The club was bustling and noisy with journalists hell-bent on
a night of sloppy decadence—British, Australians, New

Zealanders, a Frenchman, even two American network guys. Behind the huge padded bar, stone-faced Cantonese bartenders poured quickly and expertly. As the night wore on, McCarthy knew, the ratio of water to booze would escalate in proportion to the patron's inability to tell the difference. McCarthy, who could hold his liquor and appear to when he couldn't, kept a close eye on the Tanqueray bottle behind the counter. The instant the bartender made a secret move for an off brand, McCarthy would lunge for this throat.

At the big table in the center of the club, one of the American network guys was screaming at the French magazine free-lancer. Vietnam again, McCarthy thought. Every time he was in the place there was a fight about Nam. Almost everybody in the club had covered the war, some of them with a fanaticism otherwise reserved for the World Series or slot machines. Everybody had a story, everybody had a theory, everybody had a pain. The walls of the club had become a Nam shrine: headlines, photographs, tributes to fallen colleagues like Larry Burroughs and Sean Flynn. When Nam had been hot, Hong Kong had been the jump-off point for journalists. The club had been electric then, swirling with stories of war; the war had been the story, and even besotted Fleet Street could focus on it. Now the story was China, McCarthy reflected, huge, ungainly, enigmatic, unsexy China. There was only so much you could write, so many telescopic shots of the Great Wall, before the guys on the desk started hollering for more Rubik's cubes.

McCarthy guided himself to the men's room. Standing at a urinal, he observed that in the eight months since his last visit, there had been only one addition to the wall graffiti: a strikingly accurate likeness of Lady Diana, reclining languorously. The Aussies, McCarthy decided, it had to be. As he was admiring the steady hand of the artist, the door swung open and McCarthy was joined by another man.

"Remember me?"

McCarthy studied the face in the mirror. "Stratton, baby! Gimme a second here and I'll be right with you."

"Take your time," Stratton said.

"Hey," McCarthy said, zipping up, "you don't suppose the princess is really double-jointed?"

"Not like that, Jim."

To make room for Stratton at the bar, McCarthy gently

shooed a buxom prostitute who had costumed herself like Marilyn Monroe in *Some Like It Hot*. Stratton immediately claimed the barstool and ordered a Budweiser.

"Heresy!" McCarthy exclaimed. "Every time I see you you're ordering the wrong beer. What brings you to this seedy place?"

"You do," Stratton said. "I need your help."

After leaving the consulate, he had walked for hours through Hong Kong, dazzled and disoriented, distracted from the city's raucous vitality by his own despair. Stratton mourned for David, and for Kangmei. Once, in an alley market where old crones cooled their feet in vats of live shrimp, he had spotted her, swaying through the crush of people, an ebony trail of silken hair. He had run, hurdling racks and side-stepping vendors, until he had caught her, taken her by the elbows, turned her and seen a stranger's face. The young woman had smiled shyly and backed away, but Stratton had been too sad to apologize.

He had taken a tram to the Peak, and from a windy platform imagined china unfolding beyond Kowloon. Somewhere, David's body. Somewhere, Kangmei. As the sun set, the grand harbor had shimmered and then in darkness evaporated to a vast black hole. The famous floating restaurants sparkled like stars, bobbing on a windy night. For an hour Stratton had clung to the solitude of the Peak until ghosts had caught up with him, and he had gone looking for Jim McCarthy.

"I called the bureau in Peking. They said you'd be here for a couple of weeks."

"Sheila and the kids fly in tomorrow," McCarthy said. "I can't wait to see 'em. Hell, another night or two alone in this town and a hard-drinking Irishman might buy himself some serious trouble. Like Peroxide Lucy over there. You ever see a Chinese with a wig like that? This club is a regular Mardi Gras, just what you need when you're fresh out of China."

"Your clerk had a pretty good idea you'd be here."

"She's a doll. I'd trust her with my life." McCarthy suspiciously eyed the bartender, who was pouring another gin. "Tom, I was just thinking about you yesterday. Your friend, the old professor who died, wasn't his name Wang? Well, his brother, the honcho deputy minister of whatever, died this week, too. Did you hear about it?"

"Yes. Supposedly drowned."

"Dressed in full uniform, resplendent Mao gray, according to some of our embassy boys. Ironic, isn't it? The old guy had a black mourning band pinned to his sleeve. The big whisper is suicide."

Stratton started to say something, but reined himself. "Are you doing a story about it?" he asked McCarthy.

"Naw, I don't think so." McCarthy looked up from his drink. "You think it's worth a story? I dunno, you might be right. The death of two brothers—one American, one Chinese. The ultimate reunion! The desk might go for it. They're slobbering for human interest stuff."

A screech came from the big table in the middle of the club. McCarthy and Stratton looked over just in time to see one of the American network correspondents punch the French free-lancer in the nose.

"Bravo, baby!" McCarthy called out. "Hoist the flag right up his ass!" He turned back to Stratton. "I'm not so sure about this Wang story after all . . . maybe I'm just not in the mood to write." McCarthy sighed. "I'll feel a hell of a lot better when Sheila's here."

They drank together for half an hour, eavesdropping on the slurred debates and laconic come-ons, watching the fog turn to cotton over the harbor. Finally McCarthy said, "What was it you needed from me?"

"A list."

"Of what?"

"Remember the story you wrote on 'Death by Duck'? You told me about it—about all the American tourists who die over here . . ."

"I did the story two years ago, Tom. You want a list of all of them?" McCarthy could not mask his curiosity.

"Not all of them. I want a list from the last four months, a list of every American who died in China. Can you get it?"

McCarthy shrugged. "No sweat. All it takes is a phone call."

"What else is available?"

"Ages, hometowns, occupations. That's about it."

Stratton leaned forward. "Hometowns are all I need. How big a list are we talking about?"

McCarthy shifted on the barstool. He was not accustomed to being grilled. "A small list, Tom. A half-dozen names, at the most. I'm just guessing. I really haven't been following the death-by-duck box score since I wrote that one story."

"But you *can* get the list?"

"Sure, Tom." McCarthy fingered his fiery beard. "But I've got to ask why. I'm not too drunk to listen."

Stratton stood up. "I can't tell you, not now."

McCarthy smiled. "Someday?"

"Maybe," Stratton said. "It's possible."

"That's good enough for me."

Stratton slapped a Bodine twenty-dollar bill on the counter and motioned to the flinty-eyed bartender. "Good God, don't be a fool and leave the whole thing," McCarthy hissed. "He's been pissin' in the drinks all night."

Stratton laughed and shook the newsman's hand. "I'm at the Hilton. My flight leaves at about noon tomorrow."

"Hey, you're talking to an ace foreign correspondent." McCarthy roared. "You'll have your list by ten sharp."

Stratton walked back to the hotel room and stood under a steaming shower for twenty minutes. The melancholy and bitterness gradually receded to a remote corner of his mind; he began to feel galvanized, perversely exhilarated by what lay ahead. One race was finished, and he had lost. Another was beginning. This time the track was his.

CHAPTER 22

STEVE POWELL CAUGHT UP with Linda Greer in the hall outside the embassy conference room.

"Did you win today?" she asked amiably.

His hair slick from an after-tennis shower, Powell nodded with an air that said no contest. "The dust was murder out there. Took some top spin off my serve." He propped his briefcase on one knee and opened it. The yellow cable was on top of a stack of files.

"Here," Powell said, handing it to Linda. "It arrived this morning from San Francisco."

Linda read the cable twice and went cold.

"Whatever it means," Powell said, "I don't think I ought to mention it at the staff meeting."

It means Tom Stratton was right, Linda thought.

Powell said, "Some guy with two Ming vases makes it past customs and immigration using David Wang's passport. Strange. Didn't the late, great deputy minister tell us that the passport was destroyed?" Powell snapped the briefcase shut. "The question now is, Who was this guy? And how the hell did he get the passport?"

The passport. *No*, Linda told herself, it *can't* be true.

"Maybe the deputy minister swiped it, then turned around and sold it," Powell theorized, "like he was selling everything else. There's quite a few Chinese who'd give anything for a U.S. passport. Your old buddy Bin could have found himself a rich customer."

Powell watched Linda's expression carefully. She was ashen.

"I guess you'll have to cable customs," she said finally. "They'll want some kind of report."

"I've got to let them know the guy was illegal, and screw the damn vases."

Linda lowered her voice. "Steve, can you wait on it? Two or three days, tops. I need a little time, a head start."

"For what?"

Powell could never know, nor cou'd anyone else at the embassy. It would remain her secret because it had been her mistake. Angrily she flashed back to that night at the foreigners' morgue. She had not recognized the welder who had bent over David Wang's coffin, nor had she protested when the odd Mr. Hu had declined to open it for the requisite inspection. *I am required to see it first*, she had said. *You were late*, he had replied.

Now she knew why Mr. Hu had sealed the coffin so swiftly: it must have been empty. David Wang had been alive. Then.

"Steve, I can't say much. Maybe when the boss gets back from Singapore. All I can tell you is that this"—Linda waved the cable—"is very serious. Extremely serious. Can I count on you?"

Powell smiled. " 'Course you can. Took customs three days to get us a wire from Frisco . . . might just take another three days for them to get an answer. Fair is fair."

Linda squeezed Powell's arm and whispered a thank-you.

The staff meeting was soporific and Powell droned through the agenda—new guidelines for visa requests, an upcoming visit by an undersecretary of state, still more travel restrictions for American tourists leaving Peking. . . .

Linda drifted in a rough sea. Stratton was right: she had lost the deputy minister. Not merely lost him, but let him slip away like an eel. He was cunning, but was he the murderer that Stratton claimed? It added up, all right. The mystery coffin at the foreigners' morgue, the "official" drowning at the Ming reservoir, the hasty Party cremation—and now San Francisco.

The sonofabitch had done it, bought his way out of China with the blood of his own brother.

Now Wang Bin was free. Stratton knew. And he would find out where to look. And when Stratton caught up with Wang Bin it would all explode. There was no avoiding it. My secret, Linda thought, my failure. "One case is all it takes, right?" Stratton had said at that long-ago dinner. Yes, one case was all it took for glory—or for demotion down to some backwater, shuffling papers for the rest of her life. All those years fighting those stupid patronizing male smiles just to get somewhere— and now this. There'd be nothing left to save.

". . . and finally," Powell was saying, "I got a call yesterday from one of our friends in the fourth estate. He wanted another update on our deaths-by-duck, so I presume we'll be reading about it in the next week or so. I'm sure the travel agents back in the States will be thrilled to tears."

"Excuse me, Steve, who—" Linda began.

"Jesus, what else can they write?" piped one of the preppy junior officers. "Didn't the Chicago *Tribune* and the Boston *Globe* do big take-outs year before last?"

"Yeah. So did AP," Powell grumbled. "But I had to give out the list, it's a public record."

"Steve!"

Powell was startled. "Yes, Linda."

"Excuse me, I was just wondering who it was who called." Her tongue was chalky; her heart pounded.

"McCarthy. Jim McCarthy from the *Globe*."

"He's the one who did the first story," interjected one of the junior officers, hoping that someone would remark on his keen memory.

But it was Linda Greer's memory that stabbed at her, jolted her back to the first day Tom Stratton had walked into the embassy. Jim McCarthy had been the one who had sent him; Stratton had said so.

She was sure it was no coincidence. McCarthy wouldn't be updating his story, not so soon. Oh, he wanted information, all right, but not for a newspaper story. For a friend.

"Linda, is there a problem?" Powell asked. "We gave Jim a full list the first time around. Interviews, too. No one said there was a problem."

Linda smiled. "Oh, no problem. I was just curious." She thought her voice sounded tremulous.

Powell seemed not to notice. "It's really nothing," he said. "McCarthy just wanted to know how many Americans had died here over the last couple months. I gave him the names. No big deal."

"Sure," Linda said agreeably. No big deal. Jesus, if Powell only knew. "Is that all for today?"

In the hallway, she could scarcely keep from running toward her office. Now she knew everything. She knew that Stratton's plan was already in motion, and it spelled disaster for her.

In a bleak way, it was funny, she reflected. It all came back to the goddamn morgue—*her* job, too. An awful little job—

late at night. A simple detail, really. Or one would think. But Linda had botched that, too.

She would have to leave immediately for the United States. Sick leave, Linda would call it, or an illness in the family. There was no time to fight the bureaucracy.

Tom Stratton would have to be stopped.

Wang Bin would have to be caught.

She had to get to one of them before they got to each other. And she had to do it alone.

Wang Bin, Stratton—her responsibilities, both of them. That's what you're here for, the station chief had told her. That's what you're good at. Do what you have to, he had said—not warmly—but get them where we want them. Keep them there.

Gone was not where she wanted them.

Getting them back was the only thing that would save her career.

There was no time to worry about breaking a few laws.

A warm breeze from Tampa Bay ruffled Stratton's hair and stood him up as he walked across a broad, green lawn that seemed to ramble all the way to the water. Wheeling gulls bickered high above and a dour pelican plunged into a school of mullet. The splash startled the old man who had been pushing a lawn mower around the tombstones.

"Hello!" Stratton called.

The old man cocked his head. He glanced up to the sky, wondering if one of the noisy birds had actually shouted to him.

"Here! Hello!" Stratton yelled over the mower's engine.

The old man spotted Stratton and muttered a grumpy acknowledgment. He turned off the mower and pulled a handkerchief from the belt of his trousers.

"I'm looking for the grave of Sarah Steinway," Stratton said.

The old man noticed that Stratton carried a modest spray of flowers.

"Are you a relative?" he asked.

Stratton said he was a nephew. "I came all the way from New York."

"Jesus H. Christ," the old man said, shaking his head. "I'm sorry to hear that."

He led Stratton along the water to a footpath that took them up a gentle man-made hill. On the other side was a stand of young pine trees that formed the boundary of the cemetery's newest lot.

"If you'd have come tomorrow most of it would have been cleaned up," the old caretaker said apologetically.

"What are you talking about?"

"Come on."

Stratton followed him to the gravesite. Many of the plots were recently turned; others remained untouched, the gravestones bare—prepurchased, Florida-style.

They walked to the end of a long row before Stratton saw what the old man meant. The caretaker stopped and pointed up and down the column of graves. "Look what they did!"

"They" had gone amok, toppling the headstones, shredding the flowers, trampling and thrashing the soil. On one grave sat a mound of rotting garbage, with bright blue flies buzzing obscenely. Another was peppered with broken whiskey bottles. Still another grave had been defaced with bright crayons. Stratton bent over the granite slab and read:

> There was an old geezer named Saul
> Who dropped dead in the Hillsborough Mall
> His wife called a cop
> Then went back to the shop
> So she wouldn't miss the sale, after all

"Cute," Stratton muttered.

"It's sick," the old caretaker said. "Teenagers, that's all."

One double headstone read: "Eva and Bernard Melman." Beneath the names, smeared in burgundy, was a Nazi swastika. In dripping letters at the base of the tombstone, someone had painted the words MORE DEAD JEWS.

Stratton stepped closer to study the vandalism. After a few moments he turned to the caretaker and asked, "Did you call the police?"

"Of course. They sent a man. So what? What can they do?"

The old man moved forward and pointed with his foot to an area around the Melmans' granite slab. The dirt was dark and moist and loose, as if a shovel had been plunged into the ground and withdrawn.

"I figure they were interrupted by a car," the old man speculated.

"What about Aunt Sarah?" Stratton asked.

The caretaker pointed to the next headstone on the row:

Sarah Rose Steinway
1919–1983

The only mark of vandalism was another swastika, this one drawn in orange crayon between the "Sarah" and the "Rose."

"Look at that," Stratton said disgustedly.

"That'll come right off, mister. I can get it with some turpentine, or some real strong acetate. Won't harm the marble, either. I'll clean it off this afternoon."

Stratton set the flowers on the grave and stepped back to the footpath. The caretaker took a deep breath. "It's impossible to guard a place like this twenty-four hours a day. You understand, don't you? We're just a small cemetery—I mean, we've got a watchman, but he's old and he doesn't hear so well."

Stratton was only half listening. He concentrated on the Steinway grave. The sod around the marker was puckered in several places, and badly gashed near the headstone.

"When did all this happen?"

"Either last night or the night before. See, I don't get around to this side every day. I mow it three times a week, though, and if there's a visitor like yourself, or the men who came a couple of days ago, then I'll bring 'em here to show the way."

"What men?"

"They brought flowers for your Aunt Sarah there . . ." the caretaker began.

A lovely touch, Stratton thought.

"How many men?"

"Two. Said they were good friends of the deceased."

The old man dabbed at his neck with the handkerchief. "I'm trying to remember their names. One of them was a thin fellow, about forty-five, fifty maybe. Had black hair. Dressed kind of bright for the cemetery. The other guy looked Japanese. He didn't say much. Last time I saw them they were just sitting on the bench, talking quietly. I'm glad they weren't here to see what happened to their flowers."

* * *

Stratton found two motels within a half mile of the small cemetery. He went first to the Holiday Inn. The young junior-college student at the registration desk was helpful. He allowd Stratton to study the check-in cards going back for seven days; there were no Oriental names registered. Stratton asked the young desk clerk if he remembered an American and a Chinese staying there. The clerk shook his head no.

"And I probably would have noticed them," the clerk said. "This is the slow time of the year. A lot of our business is lunch hour." He winked.

Across the street at the Bay Vista Court Stratton was greeted by an attractive, middle-aged woman with frosted hair and a warm smile.

"Carl Jurgens," he said, holding out his hand. "Apex Car Rentals."

"I'm Mrs. Singer," the woman said. "How can I help you?"

"Well, a few days ago we rented a car to two fellows. A red Oldsmobile, brand-new. When they picked it up at Tampa Airport, they wrote on the rental agreement that they'd be staying here at your place. I've got a copy of the rental papers in the car."

Mrs. Singer nodded. Stratton could tell that she was curious.

"Anyway," he said, "they stiffed us. Dumped the car at a Grand Union over on Dale Mabrey."

"I still don't see how I can possibly help."

"Simple, Mrs. Singer. Just tell me if they were here, and maybe let me have a look at the registration cards—to see if they left an address, or a phone number. The ones they gave our people were phony, of course. Maybe they paid you with a credit card. Now that would be great."

Mrs. Singer stood up and smoothed her dress. "How much did they get you for?"

"A hundred and ninety-four," Stratton replied. "It's not Fort Knox or anything, I know . . ."

Mrs. Singer smiled. "It's a lot of money. I understand, believe me. We've been burned a few times ourselves." She pulled a Rolodex wheel across the counter and thumbed through the cards. "What were their names?"

"One was an Oriental man, a Chinese. His name is Wang. W-A-N-G. Like the computers."

Mrs. Singer nodded vigorously. "Yes, I remember him. Here." She unfastened a three-by-four card from the Rolodex.

"They stayed one night. Room forty-one, no phone calls. Paid with a Mastercard. Here's a copy of the charge slip."

Stratton read the name: Harold Broom.

Broom ... . Broom? Then he had it: the overbearing art broker he had met at the consular office in Peking. What was it he had said: *This is new territory, and I don't know whose back needs scratching. Maybe we could help each other out.* Hey, pal, wanna buy some artifacts?—it was almost that blatant. Broom was a soulless cretin, the perfect confederate for the deputy minister of art and culture.

"Are these the men?" Mrs. Singer inquired.

"Yes. This is very good."

"But they weren't driving an Oldsmobile, Mr. Jurgens. They drove a white van—like a U-Haul, only white. Mr. Broom did all the driving."

A van, of course. Prosaic but practical—a modern hearse for an eternal warrior.

Mrs. Singer asked, "Do you rent vans like that?"

"No, only cars. Perhaps they got the van after they ditched our Oldsmobile. Well, the important thing is that these are the fellows I'm looking for."

She gave Stratton a coy look. "I might be able to help. Mr. Broom asked to borrow a phone book—we don't keep them in the rooms anymore. They just get stolen. Anyway, I let him borrow the telephone book. Then he walked over to that pay phone and called Delta Airlines. He made reservations for today to New York. La Guardia, I think."

Stratton wanted to hug her.

He drove to a Holiday Inn on the other side of St. Petersburg and checked in. It was almost dusk. He turned on every light in his room, slipped out of his shoes and sat down at a wobbly desk. From another pocket in his suit jacket, Stratton took the piece of paper that Jim McCarthy had delivered to him in Hong Kong. The list was typed under the letterhead of the Boston *Globe.* It said:

U.S. citizen deaths May–August 1983:

Steinway, Sarah	5-10-83	Canton	St. Petersburg, Fl.
Mitchell, Kevin P.	6-22-83	Xian	Baltimore, Md.
Bertecelli, John	7-4-83	Xian	Queens, N.Y.
Friedman, Molly	8-14-83	Peking	Fort Lauderdale, Fl.
Wang, David	8-16-83	Peking	Pittsville, Ohio

With a blue felt-tip pen, Stratton circled the name of John Bertecelli, who had died on the Fourth of July in Xian. Bertecelli's body now lay somewhere in New York. Probably Broom and Wang Bin were already there, and maybe already at work.

Stratton thought: I ought to leave right now. There is no time to do what I had planned. Catching them will not be easy, even with the right grave.

The right grave.

Stratton contemplated his macabre odyssey. Chasing the coffins was a shell game. Five caskets, three Chinese soldiers. Scratch off McCarthy's list the name of David Wang, whose "death" at the Heping Hotel had been staged after the theft of the warriors. That left four possible caskets.

Stratton had arrived in San Francisco with a simple strategy: geography. He could think of no other logical way to go at it. He had booked a flight to Miami where he had planned to begin the search, moving north, following his death list.

Molly Friedman had been first. A death noticed published in the Fort Lauderdale *News* had announced that Molly was at rest at the Temple of David Mausoleum in Hallandale. A brief memorial service had been held four days after her sudden death in Peking. Rabbi Goren had kindly presided.

Stratton had found his way from the newspaper offices to the Temple of David. Bearing a small parcel of flowers from a Moonie working the stoplights on Federal Highway, he had been greeted at the door by a small balding man dressed in a dark wool suit. "Molly Friedman, please," Stratton had whispered, and the greeter had led him down a chilly hallway with high granite walls. They had entered a huge vault bathed in purplish light that filtered from stained-glass panels set high in a rectangular ceiling.

The balding man had consulted a small, leatherbound directory. Then he had taken ten steps forward and pointed high up the wall. "There," he had whispered, "G-one-two-oh."

Stratton had squinted to see the name. Molly Friedman's remains lay seven rows up, on a granite ledge—in an urn. A Chinese urn.

"Your flowers," the greeter had whispered. "We can arrange them."

"That will be just fine," Stratton had said. Two hours later he had been on a plane to St. Petersburg.

And now the trail was red hot. Stratton rocked the chair, gripping the cheap desk by its corners. He was jittery, restive. How easily all the old hunting instincts had returned. He envisioned the icy-eyed old Chinese prowling a foreign graveyard, a remorseless night bandit. Why not go to New York tonight? Stratton thought. The grave of John Bertecelli waited. He could end it there.

Stratton thought of the old caretaker with the lawn mower at the St. Petersburg cemetery. He thought of the stinking garbage on the graves, the bloody swastikas, the vulgar poem—all doubtlessly the work of Harold Broom, relishing his role as a teenage vandal. If Wang Bin was a man to be feared, Broom clearly was a man to be hated. And not to be taken for granted. What if the despoliation was a double-blind, a misdirection on the off chance someone was following them? Unlikely, but . . .

Stratton resolved not to leave St. Petersburg without seeing the evidence with his own eyes, erasing what little doubt remained. He would do the work swiftly and neatly, leaving no clues.

He changed into jeans and a black T-shirt, and tied on a pair of Puma jogging shoes. At an Army-Navy store a few blocks from the motel, Stratton purchased a heavy-duty flashlight and a portable screw-down shovel. At midnight, he headed for the graveyard near the bay.

Stratton parked in a municipal lot not far from the gate. Carrying a shovel under one arm, he melted into a stand of pines and scouted the cemetery on foot. The caretaker had mentioned a security guard; Stratton found him in a matter of minutes. He was sitting in a compact car, reading a magazine by the dome light—a silver-haired black man, wearing the usual rent-a-cop uniform.

Stratton crossed behind the guard's car, running low to the ground. He chose a path through the trees and scrub and purposely stayed clear of the water, which shimmered revealingly with the lights of Tampa. After about a hundred yards, Stratton flicked on the flashlight.

The caretaker had worked earnestly to clean up Broom's foul mess. The trash was gone, and most of the glass had been swept up. The old man had scrubbed the Melmans' grave marker until only a shadow of the swastika was visible. He had obviously devoted equal energy to the stone of Sarah Rose

Steinway, although the orange crayon had proved stubborn. The Nazi emblem had become a permanent greasy smudge between the "Sarah" and the "Rose."

Stratton unfolded the shovel and tightened a bolt at the neck. He began to dig with short, powerful strokes. There was no slab on the grave, only a layer of new sod. Below the grass, the earth was moist and soft. It gave way easily—too easily for a three-month-old grave.

For ninety minutes Stratton dug. He expected that the coffin had not actually been interred six feet deep, and he was right. He was only up to his armpits in the hole when the shovel bit struck metal. He dropped to his knees and cleared the rest of the dirt by hand. At the foot of the coffin, Stratton carved out a trench for himself. He stepped down and bent over so far that his chin nearly met the lid. In the darkness he fished like a raccoon for the corners of the coffin.

Stratton got a good grip and stood up with an involuntary grunt. The coffin came loose of the earth. Stratton backstepped out of the grave, dragging the thing half out of its cool pocket until it rested at a peculiar angle—head down, feet toward the sky.

Stratton was panting. He scoured the pines and the cart paths for headlights. His hands trembled and he wiped them on his jeans. He thought it obscene to use dirty hands for this. Obscene, but not inappropriate. With the point of the cheap shovel he gouged the seal of the coffin, and the lid flopped open with a cold click.

Stratton took a deep breath and aimed the flashlight.

The coffin of Sarah Rose Steinway was empty.

The cheap cotton lining bore the indentation of a rigid human form. Something sparkled microscopically against the fabric. Stratton ran a finger lightly along the inside of the casket, as if tracing the spine of the invisible dead.

In the beam of the flashlight, Stratton examined his fingertip and noticed a powdery film of red-brown clay. The ancient dust of another grave, another violated tomb.

CHAPTER 23

THE CAB RIDE FROM La Guardia was no more harrowing than a spin through downtown Peking, and Wang Bin rode in unperturbed silence. He grunted once when a sleek black limousine cut sharply in front of the taxi, and jumped slightly in his seat at the sudden blast of a trucker's horn. But it was the vista of Manhattan, seen from the Triborough Bridge, that left him breathless. At first glimpse Wang Bin leaned close to the window and stared at the vast skyline marching along the river, molten in the pink light of the late afternoon. The city was like nothing the deputy minister had ever seen.

Harold Broom glanced over and smiled with a superior air. "Hey, Pop, the cabbie is Russian. How about that?"

Broom had taken to calling Wang Bin "Pop," an annoying term that the deputy minister did not understand.

"Didya ever think you'd be riding with a Russian through the streets of America?" Broom roared at some dim irony while Wang Bin watched out the window in fascination as the skyline swallowed them.

The two men checked into a small, comfortable hotel on Central Park South. Broom did all the talking—to the cabbie, to the doormen, to the desk clerk, to the rental agent. Wang Bin had nothing to say; New York was richer and more bewildering than he had ever imagined. Compared to that of Peking, even the air was a tonic. The crowds of walkers were garish, and certainly less orderly than the Chinese, but the Americans were equally hurried and wore the same expressions of determination. And the automobiles were boggling—more cars than Wang Bin believed existed in all of China, stacked on every street, inching forward with horns blaring. The noise jarred his nerves.

Wang Bin stood at the window of the fifth-floor hotel room and watched a hansom cab clop down the street toward the

Plaza Hotel. On the sidewalk at Columbus Circle, a ragged group of men and women waved placards and shook their fists. Two policemen stood at the corner, chatting calmly. Wang Bin did not understand why they did not hurry to arrest the demonstrators. He decided that the officers must be waiting for reinforcements.

Broom groomed himself in the mirror. "So what's it gonna be tonight, Pop? Studio 54?"

Wang Bin scowled at the joke. "I am tired."

"Okay, no disco. But we gotta eat," the art broker said.

"I want to rest before we work."

"Look out there, old man. That's the greatest city in the world. Don't you want to have a good time?"

"I am tired."

"Hey, Pop, let's celebrate a little. We're rich, remember? You and me, we're on a roll now. Packed our little pal off to our Florida buyer yesterday—that's one down, two to go, and money in the bank." Broom rubbed his hands together hungrily and gave the deputy minister another one of his winks. "Let's see the sights!"

"You go ahead," Wang Bin said, stepping away from the window. "I want to sleep."

The deputy minister was dressed for the graveyard when Harold Broom returned at one in the morning.

"Hey there, Pops, you missed a good time." Broom weaved across the room and eased down on the sofa. He kicked off his shoes and scratched at his feet.

"You are drunk," Wang Bin said angrily.

"Don't worry, partner." Broom struggled out of his clothes without assistance, but Wang Bin had to guide the art broker's arms and legs into the dark gray coveralls that they had selected as their grave robbers' uniform.

"Didya see the *Post* tonight?" Broom babbled. "It made the headline on one of the back pages: VANDALS DESECRATE JEWISH GRAVES AT FLORIDA CEMETERY. Just a little story, no big deal, but they printed part of my poem. Even had a photo of one of the headstones."

Broom stretched out on the sofa and groaned feebly.

"It's time to go now," Wang Bin said, standing over him.

"In a minute."

"Now!" said the deputy minister, grabbing Broom's arm.

The art dealer easily shook himself free and pushed the old man away. "Don't fuck with me, Pop! I got a tiny headache right at the moment so I'm gonna rest. I'm the driver, 'member? We go when I say."

Wang Bin sat down only when he heard Broom start to snore.

Tom Stratton slouched glumly in the Eastern Airlines lounge that overlooked the main runways at the Tampa-St. Petersburg Airport. A long line of jets sat in the slashing rain, the wing lights flicking red and white and red again, the pilots waiting for the weather to clear. Stratton's flight to New York had already been delayed thirty minutes.

Stratton was on his second beer when he got the idea for a modest head start. He found a nest of deserted pay phones in the main lobby near the gift shops.

In a neat brownstone in one of the better neighborhoods of Queens, Violet Bertecelli cracked her shin on a coffee table as she fumbled in the dark for the telephone. When she finally found it, she was in too much pain to say a gracious hello.

"Do you know what the hell time it is?"

"Is this Mrs. Bertecelli? Mrs. John Bertecelli?" asked a fuzzy voice.

"Yes. Yes, it is. Is this long distance?"

"Yes, ma'am," Tom Stratton said. "I apologize for calling at such an hour, but it's morning here in China—"

"What? You're calling from China?"

"Yes, ma'am. Peking. I'm Steve Powell, with the United States Embassy. I handled the arrangements after your husband's unfortunate . . ."

"Death," Violet said helpfully.

"Yes, of course, back in July. That's the reason I'm calling, Mrs. Bertecelli. I'm not exactly sure how to go about telling you this, but in recent months there have been reports of irregularities in the shipment of human remains from China back to the United States."

Violet said, "Johnny died of a coronary."

"Yes, I know. But we've had complaints from a couple of families about the quality of the metal on the coffins. In the case of one poor fellow, the hinges snapped off and the lid came loose."

"The coffin was just fine. It was actually very nice. Did you pick it out yourself, Mr. Powell?"

"No, ma'am."

"Well, it was lovely. Everything was just fine with Johnny. They sent him to Riordan's Funeral Parlor and he was buried out at St. Francis with his ma."

"That's excellent," Stratton said. "And our files show he was laid to rest in plot E-seventy-seven."

"No, sir, that's wrong," Violet said. "It's plot number one-sixty-six. I remember 'cause one-sixty-six was Johnny's best-ever score in the bowling league. That's how I remember the plot number."

"I'm sorry, Mrs. Bertecelli, you're absolutely right. I see it here now, right in the file. Plot one hundred sixty-six."

"Thank you, Mrs. Bertecelli. That was St. Francis Cemetery?"

"That's right. Grand Central Parkway, Queens."

Tom Stratton hung up the phone and hurried to the nearest Eastern ticket counter. The video monitor now showed that his flight to Kennedy Airport would not depart until two in the morning. Dejectedly Stratton walked back to the lounge and ordered another beer and stared out the window to the runways, where the jets still waited in the rain. He prayed that it was storming like hell in Queens.

Wang Bin sat down in a heap on the ground. His chest heaved, and he could feel drops of sweat trickling into his eyebrows. He watched furiously while Harold Broom grappled with the coffin, muttering obscenities from the dank hole where he worked. The sky was cloudy. Cars and trucks raced by on the parkway, drowning out the other night noises. Headlights from the scattered traffic would suddenly turn the tombstones yellow, and cause an eerie dance of shadows across the hillside.

"We need assistance," Wang Bin declared.

"We need a backhoe," Broom growled. "The dirt down here is like concrete." He tossed down the shovel and tried swinging the pick. The musty earth around the coffin crumbled away in hard clods, but the box itself held fast where it had been buried under a chorus of Hail Marys. "Get down here and help me lift," Broom said.

But the two of them—Broom, nauseous and half-drunk; the

deputy minister, exhausted, his thin arms cramped from the shoveling—could budge the coffin only a few inches and no more.

Broom glanced at his watch. Four in the morning. Time was running out. Wang Bin was right: They needed help.

"Stay here," he said, fishing for the keys to the rental car.

Wang Bin was too tired to object to being left alone, but after Broom had been gone half an hour, he began to worry. What if the fool never came back? What if he got scared and abandoned him? Enough money had been collected already to finance a very comfortable life for a man like Broom . . . and where would that leave Wang Bin?

He stood up and stretched his aching arms and legs. The headlights from the highway caught him square in the eyes and he turned away grimacing. In the opposite direction the sky was tinged orange by the incredible lights of Manhattan. Wang Bin doubted if he could ever grow accustomed to life in this city; he understood now why David had chosen a rural place, a small and orderly place. A manageable place.

Not far away, a dog barked excitedly.

Where was Broom?

The deputy minister regarded his American partner as a truly despicable man. He had not understood the vagaries of Broom's behavior at the graveyard in Florida, only that the desecrations had been meant as a ruse to confuse the police. The art broker had assured him that no one would check the coffin after they had buried it again, and he had been right. But it was the way Broom reveled in the vandalism that Wang Bin found so utterly repulsive. He would shed himself of the man as soon as possible, and now . . . now he was stranded in a cemetery, desperately hoping that Broom was greedy enough to come back. Wang Bin needed Broom and this, too, was a foreign emotion. In China, he had been provided everything he needed; here, without his title, absent of his authority, he felt helpless and common. To defer to a man like Broom was disgraceful, but, for now, quite necessary.

Wang Bin's heart raced at the sound of an automobile winding up the road toward St. Francis Cemetery. An involuntary smile came to his lips when he saw Harold Broom, flanked by two tall, slender figures, trudging down the hill.

"Pop, say hello to Tyrone and Charles."

Wang Bin nodded but caught himself before he bowed.

Tyrone and Charles were both angular black teenagers, but they appeared very strong. Tyrone sported a red ski cap and Charles was dressed in a white-and-green sports jersey of some sort. It occurred instantly to Wang Bin that the two strangers could handily overpower him and Harold Broom and steal the treasure themselves.

"These gentlemen were testing the back door of a liquor store down the street," Broom was saying. "Good thing I happened to see 'em before they got into real trouble. They said they'd be happy to help."

"For how much?" the deputy minister inquired.

"Hundred bucks apiece," Broom said.

Wang Bin said nothing. Broom shrugged. "Whaddya want at four in the morning, Pop? I didn't have time to take out an ad in the goddamn *Times*. They look like good workers to me. Right, boys?"

Tyrone shrugged and Charles said, "What the hell is this deal?" He gestured at the open grave. "What's the fuckin' story? I ain't messin' with no stiffs."

"Me neither," Tyrone said.

"I'm not asking you to *mess* with a stiff, pal. I'm asking you to help us get the coffin out of the ground. A little manual labor, that's all. Won't kill you, take my word for it."

"Don't seem right," Charles said, peering into the hole.

Broom said, "Fine! You don't like it? Then beat it. Get the hell out of here!"

Wang Bin looked at him sharply.

"I didn't know you guys were a couple of pussies," Broom said. "Shit. For two hundred bucks I'll go find a couple of *men* to help with this."

As Broom waved his arms theatrically, Charles calmly seized him by the back of the neck and said, "Shut up, you greasy jive mo'fucker. Give us the bread and we'll dig."

The art broker huddled with Wang Bin as the two teenagers wrestled with the coffin. "You got to know how to talk to these people," Broom explained.

"I don't like them," Wang Bin whispered.

"Of course you don't."

"I don't trust them."

"Relax, Pop."

Broom hopped into the grave. Within minutes, he and the two teenagers had hoisted the coffin of John Bertecelli from the hole and laid it on the ground. Tyrone sat down on a headstone and said, "So who's in it, Dracula?"

"I don't want to know," Charles said. "Let's split."

"No, man, I want the dudes to open it."

"You can go now," Broom said. "Thanks for the help, fellas."

"Open it, man!"

"No."

"Okay. I'll open it." Tyrone lifted the pick and windmilled it at the coffin. The lid skewed from the hinges. Tyrone kicked it off with one of his basketball shoes.

"Shit," he said. "It's a mummy!"

Swaddled in plastic, a Chinese spearman stared through wise eyes into the firmament.

Broom stepped forward and said, "That's enough. You've seen it, now get the hell out of here."

"What's it worth?" Charles asked, leaning over the coffin, hands on his knees.

"Let's haul it out of there," Tyrone suggested. "You get that end—"

"No!" Wang Bin said.

The black teenagers looked up to see the old man pointing a chrome-plated pistol at them. They noticed that his arm was rigid. Charles chuckled and fumbled with the statue.

"Why you so uptight?" Tyrone said to Wang Bin. "This mummy must be somebody special for you, that right? Is this your old man?"

"Tell your friend to let go of the artifact," Wang Bin instructed.

"He ain't gonna break it."

The crack of the pistol got the dog barking again. Charles wriggled on the damp ground, clawing at his right arm. Tyrone was speechless.

"Oh shit, Pop," Broom said in a husky voice. "We've got to get out of here."

"I agree," the deputy minister said. "Mr. Tyrone, would you please help Mr. Broom carry the artifact to our car? If you make trouble, I will shoot your friend again and again until he is dead."

By this time Charles was sobbing, and his New York Jets jersey was sticky with fresh blood. Tyrone gingerly lifted the Chinese spear carrier by the head while Broom—suddenly

sober—carried the other end. The two unlikely pallbearers
tenuously made their way up the hillside, weaving among the
tombstones. Wang Bin held the pistol steadily on his captive
and wondered sourly if this was going to be the only way to
gain people's obedience.

The first cop on the scene was a patrolman named Sanderson, who borrowed a spool of kite string from one of the
neighborhood kids and cordoned off the gravesite using four
other tombstones as corner posts. The total effect, Sanderson
noted with self-satisfaction, was to convey the impression of
an actual crime scene. All that was missing was the chalk
silhouette.

Tom Stratton arrived by cab at 7:15 A.M., a haggard
presence among the rabid, coffee-hopped reporters. Because
he was carrying a fresh spray of flowers, Stratton was
immediately marked as a grief-stricken relative and besieged
with questions. Who would want to steal Mr. Bertecelli's body?
Had a ransom note been received? Did Mr. Bertecelli practice
satanism? How was the widow holding up?

Stratton deflected his interrogators and was relieved when a
plump brunette woman identified herself as Violet Bertecelli
and began to tell her sad story to the mothlike newsmen. The
moment also offered a breather for Officer Sanderson, so
Stratton walked up and asked what had happened.

"Some assholes ripped off a corpse here, which is grand
theft, presuming the item taken has a value in excess of one
hundred dollars. We're looking for two or three perpetrators, at
least one of them armed with a pistol." Sanderson shrugged.
"Who knows what to think? You want my opinion? Kids.
Maybe it's some kind of sick fraternity ritual. Else it could be
'Ricans. They're all into that witchcraft shit. Voodoo, eatin'
chicken heads. Could be that. Hey you! Get out of the fuckin'
hole!" Sanderson waved his nightstick at a photographer. "Get
out of the goddamn grave. What are ya, some kinda sick
hump?"

"Somebody said there was an ambulance here," Stratton
remarked.

"Yeah, that's the odd thing." Sanderson took out his
notebook and read from the top page. "Victim's name was
Charles Robinson, aged seventeen. Long juvenile record for b-
and-e, shoplifting, boosting bicycles. Nothing like this."

"Was he hurt badly?"

"Naw, you know them people. You got to shoot 'em in the asshole to do any real damage." The cop laughed. "You a relative of Mr. Bertecelli or what?"

"No, I brought some flowers for my grandmother's grave. It's up the hill a ways. I was just curious, that's all."

"Well, the little shit was shot in the arm. He'll live. I'm pretty sure he was involved in the whole thing. He's not talkin', naturally. Says he was walkin' by the graveyard on his way to church when some crazy Chinaman shot him." Sanderson shook his head admiringly. "You got to give these douche bags credit for imagination. Fuckin' weird, even for Queens."

The retinue clinging to Violet Bertecelli suddenly moved with her to the edge of the damaged grave. She stared at the broken casket and began to wail, accompanied by the sibilance of a dozen motordrive Nikons.

CHAPTER 24

THEY DROVE SOUTH. Broom was careful to stay at fifty-five, and even so he could not keep his eyes off the rearview mirror. He was ragged and nervous. A shooting had been the last thing he had expected. The Chinaman had balls, that was for sure—how the hell had he gotten that gun?

As always, Wang Bin rode in silence. In contrast to Broom, the deputy minister was placid, almost serene. He seemed to pay particular attention to other cars. The brighter and newer they were, the more he stared. One time, when a black Porsche flew past them, Broom thought he noticed Wang Bin smiling.

He's like a little kid, the art dealer thought. A little kid with a chrome-plated .38.

"I am hungry," Wang Bin said.

Broom found a Burger King. He used the drive-in lane, braking as they pulled abreast of a plastic menu board.

"What do you want?" he asked the deputy minister.

Wang Bin squinted at the colorful menu sign for a long time. A young girl's voice cracked on a speaker box and said, "Good morning, can I help you?"

Wang Bin sat back, startled.

"Tell her what you want," Broom commanded.

"Tell who?"

"The girl! Tell her what you want to eat!"

"I see no one." Wang Bin looked above and beneath the sign. "Who is speaking?"

"Welcome to Burger King, can I help you?"

"It's a bloody microphone, Pop!" Broom leaned out the window and shouted: "Two Whoppers, two fries and two coffees!"

After Broom paid for the food, he parked the car in the shade of a maple tree. He tore open his hamburger carton, took two bites and said, "It's a good thing I'm your partner. Otherwise you'd fucking starve in this country."

Wang Bin meticulously unwrapped his hamburger. He lifted the bun and examined the meat. He was overpowered briefly by the hot smell.

"Go on, eat," Broom said. "We've got a long ride."

Wang Bin forced himself to take a bite, and chased it down hastily with black coffee. "I would have preferred to wash myself before—"

"Sorry if I offended your Oriental hygiene, Pop. After all this is over, I'll take you to Hong Fat's for real won ton soup."

Wang Bin said, "I would like an accounting of the moneys."

"Finish your lunch. We'll talk about it later."

Wang Bin sipped at the coffee, but found himself longing for tea. Broom was impudent, and shamefully greedy; this the deputy minister had known from the first day. Now, in the final stages, it came down to trust. Wang Bin studied his oily partner as Broom gnawed on a french fry. In a cold rush it struck him how foolish he had been. Broom was his chauffer, his travel guide, his interpreter, his caretaker; Wang Bin needed him. There was no doubt.

Yet Broom did not need *him*. Not anymore. The soldiers had arrived. The buyers were in place.

Coldly, Wang Bin began to see himself as excess baggage.

"What of the money?" he asked again.

"We've been through this."

"Once more, please."

"All the accounts are in the name Henry Lee. That's both of us. We're both Mr. Lee. Both signatures are good at all the banks. As of today we got money in Texas and Florida. Lots."

"You said the spearman is for a Washington museum."

"The curator of an important museum. An expert," Broom muttered. "He would only agree to three hundred thousand, C.O.D. No money down."

That extinguished Wang Bin's faint hope that Harold Broom might be an honorable man. Broom was a liar. Wang Bin knew there had been a substantial down payment on the Chinese spear carrier. He had found the deposit slip in Broom's wallet, three hundred thousand dollars at the Riggs National Bank in Washington. The date on the deposit matched the date Broom had met the curator.

Wang Bin sighed. If only David had been cooperative, there would have been no need for an alliance with Harold Broom. If only David had agreed.

Now he was dead, and Broom was on his way to being a millionaire.

"Three hundred thousand for the spear carrier is an insult," Wang Bin declared.

"I agree, Pop. But the buyer has me over a real barrel. He heard about the other soldiers—don't ask me how—and accused me of cheating him. See, I'd promised him an exclusive. I *had* to. Anyway, when he heard about the other two soldiers he almost threw me out of the museum. I had to do some fast talking to jack him back up to three hundred, believe me."

"Find another buyer."

"It's too late."

"Why?"

"Because we're hot now," Broom said urgently. "The papers will have fun with our noisy escapade last night at St. Francis'. And if that little spade you plugged decides to talk, we could be in trouble." Broom jerked his thumb toward the trunk of the car. "I'm going to unload Charlie Chan on a train to Texas this afternoon. After that, just one more. Then we split the money and disappear, the sooner the better. By the way, where did you get that gun?"

"I purchased it last night, while you were sleeping off the liquor."

"Where?"

"In a place where people speak in my language."

Broom grinned, a yellow half-moon. "Chinatown! You old son of a bitch."

Wang Bin turned away.

"Eat your french fries, Pop. I've got a couple important calls to make, then we'll be on our way. Can't keep the customers waiting."

Broom sauntered down the street to a corner telephone booth. Wang Bin collected the lunch debris and placed it in a trash can outside the Burger King. He stretched his legs and breathed deeply of the summer day. He felt the butt of the pistol dig into his midriff, and he adjusted the gun a fraction in his waistband. From the highway overpass came the now familiar din of speeding traffic. Wang Bin thought how pleasant it would be to find a place untouched by the big road and all its relentless noise. A city of bicycles had certain advantages.

Harold Broom returned to the car with a pinched look on his face. He refolded the spiral notepad in which he had scribbled the vital phone numbers and slipped it into his pocket.

"I've got bad news, Pop," he grumbled. "Real bad news."

For nine hours Tom Stratton kept his place in the amphitheater. In throngs the tourists came and went, cameras dangling, children bounding up and down the marble steps. Twice an hour one audience replaced another, yet Stratton held his place, watching the lean young men in their dark blue uniforms. He glanced now and then down the gentle hill where Kevin Mitchell was supposed to be buried.

Eighteen times Stratton watched the guards change at the Tomb of the Unknowns. The cameras clicked most often when the guards faced each other and presented arms. There were three or four different Marines, working in shifts. Despite the heat and humidity, each man looked crisp and fresh as he strode to the marble crypt. For Stratton, the drill was his clock. From the amphitheater he had a clear view of grave 445-H, third row, fourth from the end, a small white cross in a sea of crosses, geometrically perfect.

Perfect, Stratton mused. Perfect was always the way the military wanted its men, but in war that was impossible. In death it was easy; dead soldiers can march precisely as desired.

Stratton thought of Bobby Ho, and wondered morbidly what had become of his friend's body after the massacre at Manling. Had the Chinese buried it? Burned it? Displayed it as a trophy? Perhaps they had fed Bobby's flesh to the starving dogs and cats of the village.

Arlington was for heroes.

Bobby ought to have a place here, Stratton thought. If not his body, at least his name. Wouldn't take much space, and God knows he was more of a hero than most of the men planted in the sea of crosses that rolled toward the Potomac.

The last tram of the day sounded its horn, and the tourists thundered from the amphitheater. Stratton rose from his spot, as if to follow, but instead took a different path downhill, and melted into the trees to wait for nightfall. He sat down at the base of an old oak and took out a pair of small Nikon field glasses. From his new vantage, Stratton could read the name on the cross:

Lt. Kevin P. Mitchell, USAF
B. 11-22-29
D. 6-22-83

A fighter pilot, World War II and Korea. Medal of Honor. After the wars Mitchell had joined Boeing as a test pilot and later became a captain with Pan Am. He'd died on a vacation to China—a heart attack, the U.S. Embassy had reported, while riding a bus to the Qin tombs at Xian. Death by duck.

Baltimore was where the family had wanted the coffin sent—a family plot, Stratton had learned, where one of Mitchell's brothers was buried.

Arlington had been an afterthought, Mrs. Mitchell's idea. A real honor, the family agreed. The Medal of Honor ought to count for something.

But Baltimore was where the embassy had sent the coffin, and Baltimore was where Broom and Wang Bin would go first, Stratton reasoned. He would wait for them at Arlington—days, weeks, whatever it took. How they could dream of ever trying it here . . .

Someone was walking among the graves.

Stratton panned with the binoculars along the crosses until he froze on the figure of a woman, dressed in black. Dusk was cheating him of the finer details. She was tall and wore a veil. Chestnut hair spilled down her back. She walked slowly, elegantly, stopping every few steps to study the names on the crosses.

She was young, Stratton decided, younger than the soldiers who lay buried in Section H. Too young to be a widow.

The woman in black stopped walking when she came to grave 445. She stopped to read the inscription. Then she reached out and touched the cross with her right hand. It began as a light and sentimental gesture, and from a distance would seem nothing more than a sad moment. But through the field glasses Stratton could see that the woman was not merely touching Kevin Mitchell's cross, but *testing* it, pushing on it with discernible force. Then she stood up straight and with a quickened pace made her way out of the rows of graves to a footpath. There was something familiar . . .

Stratton followed at a distance. He was careful to stay in the grass so his steps would not echo. Arlington was nearly empty now. The trams had stopped running and the tourists had gone back to the city. The woman in black walked alone, no longer in the gait of a mourner. Her heels clicked sharply on the pavement, and the sound dominoed along the tombstones.

"Hey there!" Stratton called.

Self-consciously she slowed, then turned as Stratton ran up. She looked at him and smiled. "So *there* you are!"

"Linda!" Stratton said.

"How'd I do?"

"I like the dress. Black becomes you. What are you doing here?"

It was a pointless question. She knew. He knew.

She kicked out of her high heels and said, "These things are killing me. Come on, walk me to the car."

"I can't."

She took his arm. "Come on, Tom, they won't come at night. They'll never find it at night."

"You're wrong, Linda. How did you know—"

"The same way you did. I had to play catch-up, that's all. I should've listened to you before, Tom, and I'm sorry. I didn't see what was happening—but even if I had, I'm not sure it would have made a difference."

"Nobody would have believed it, least of all your boss."

"Wang Bin was my case. The last couple of days I've had a lot of time to think about how I could have caught on sooner." She did not tell Stratton about the foreigners' morgue in Peking. She was afraid he had already figured it out.

"Are you here alone?" he asked.

"For now," she said.

"Me, too. And I'm staying."

He started back up the hill and she followed. "Tom!" she called. "I'm ruining my goddamn stockings. Slow down. Listen to me, they aren't coming tonight. They think the coffin is in Baltimore—"

"They've beaten me twice already. This is my last chance."

"Tom, be serious. I'll have some people here tomorrow. When the bad guys show up at the gate, we'll arrest them."

"What makes you so sure they'll use the gate?"

"Once they realize where the coffin is buried, they'll give up on it. They'll never try to dig this one up. Christ, it's *Arlington*, Tom. They can't possibly get away with it."

"This way," Stratton said, leaving the asphalt path and winding through a stand of tall trees. "I've got a good view from up here."

Linda Greer sat next to him under the oak, tugging the black dress down to cover her knees. She had hoped he would notice, but he didn't. He offered her a thermos of coffee.

"This is like summer camp," she teased. "Are you really going to stay here all night?"

"Why not?"

Linda edged closer until her cheek touched his shoulder. "Might as well make the best of it," she whispered. "It's a soft night, isn't it?" Stratton nodded but did not look at her. "Tom, relax—it's like I'm snuggling up to one of those damn gravestones."

"I'm sorry."

Stratton trained his eyes on Kevin Mitchell's plot. A lemon moon, nearly full, was rising behind the capital across the river. The silent cemetery became a sprawling theater of shadows; the crosses turned into tiny soldiers with arms extended, whole battalions frozen on the hillsides in calisthenic precision.

"I stopped at the Kennedy grave this morning," Stratton said.

"Which one?"

"Both of them. That's where all the tourists go. I'd never seen them before, only pictures."

Linda said, "I took my little sister a couple of years ago. She cried."

"Last year some guy fell into the flame and died," Stratton said. "He got drunk and pitched face down into the Eternal Flame. They found him the next day, burned to death. When I saw the story in the paper, I had to wonder about that guy. What was he thinking about that night? Why did he come here, of all places? I could just see him standing there in front of the President's grave, after all the goddamn tourists were gone. I could see him crying. Sloppy drunk tears. Staring at the flame and crying like a baby. Then it made sense: If you want to be sad, this is the place. Look out there, Linda. Look at them all. So many you can't even count them. I think this must be the saddest place of all. I think the guy knew exactly what he was doing."

Linda kissed him gently on the neck. Nothing. Stratton was loaded like a spring. She wondered sadly if their night in Peking had left any tender echo. It would make her job so much easier if it had.

"Can I ask you something?" Stratton said softly. "Are you here to stop them—or me?"

Harold Broom had had about all he could take from the snotty Chinaman. Being cursed in Mandarin was not so bad, but now Wang Bin had begun to call him "fool" to his face, as if it were part of his name. Broom was not a violent fellow, but now he shook his fist at the man in the passenger seat and said, "Shut up before I punch you in the nose!"

Wang Bin merely grunted.

"It's not my fault," Broom said for the tenth time. How could he have foreseen that Mrs. Kevin Mitchell would change her mind about the funeral? How could Broom have known that her husband's coffin would wind up at Arlington instead of the old Mitchell family plot in Baltimore, which would have been just as lovely. It would have been a cinch.

"Son of a turtle!" Wang Bin snapped.

"These things happen."

"How are we to find Mitchell's grave?"

"Simple," Broom said. "We aren't. There's acres of soldiers at Arlington and not all of them are dead, Pop. They've got crack Marines with very nasty rifles—not pea-shooters like yours. No way we're going to try to dig up that coffin."

"But this cannot be!"

"Oh, but it is. Your precious Chinese warrior can rest forever. He'll be right at home, believe me. I'm not risking a trip to jail."

The deputy minister snorted. "I must have the third soldier."

"Pop, don't be greedy. There is no way we can pull it off. You want to get shot in the back? Those Marines are genuine marksmen, Pop, and you're old and slow."

Wang Bin stared straight ahead at the highway. "It can be done," he said. "And if it cannot, at least I want to see for myself."

Broom surrendered. They stopped at a camera store in

Crystal City and purchased a couple of cheap 35-mms. This way, the art broker explained, they'd look like everybody else on the blue-and-white trams that chugged through the cemetery. Broom also bought a large canvas shoulder bag to conceal the collapsible shovel and two hand picks. "This is insane," he grumbled. "And if anything goes wrong, you're on your own."

"Meaning what?" Wang Bin asked.

"Meaning I never saw you before in my life."

It was mid-afternoon when Broom drove down the Jefferson Davis Highway toward the national cemetery. He turned left past Fort Myer, then right again on Arlington Ridge Road. He drove half a mile and pulled the car up on a curb. "Get out now," he ordered Wang Bin. "Try to be useful."

The deputy minister silently followed the art dealer on a long sidewalk up a slope, through the gates of Arlington and onto a motor tram. The Chinese and his canvas shoulder bag sat down with a conspicuous clatter. The tram wound slowly up the hills. Wang Bin gazed in wonderment at the burial markers that seemed to march on forever.

"All soldiers?" he whispered to Broom.

"Yes. The Fields of the Dead, they call it."

"How many?" Wang Bin asked.

"Thousands," Broom said. "I checked with a guide back at the office and our friend is supposed to be resting in Section H. Grave number four-four-five. I got a map, but I'm not sure it'll help."

"We have nothing like this in China," Wang Bin marveled. "There is no land for such a place. All our dead are cremated."

"You build temples, we make graveyards. Each to his own."

Wang Bin took a deep breath. "Like Xian, in a way. This is your Imperial Army, is it not, Mr. Broom?"

Stratton spotted them without the field glasses.

They emerged from a copse at the foot of a hill, perhaps one hundred meters from Lt. Kevin P. Mitchell's white cross. They found the footpath and walked side by side, Mutt-and-Jeff silhouettes. Once they stopped to confer, and Stratton noticed the beam of a small flashlight as they bent over together, pointing. A map, probably. They resumed walking, with Broom leading the way.

Stratton slipped away from the oak tree where Linda Greer slept, curled on a damp bed of leaves. He moved in a familiar half-crouch, using the trees and the dappled shadows to hide his advance. He stopped only to watch them, pace them, and anticipate their path up the hill to Section H.

Stratton got there first. He chose a spot slightly downhill, across the footpath from Mitchell's grave, in an older section of the cemetery. Here a six-foot granite marker paid homage to a four-star general and one of his three wives, and it was here that Stratton easily concealed himself.

He had already decided against a confrontation among the tombstones. The park police would arrive swiftly, to be sure, but what would they have—a couple of prowlers? No, it was better to let Harold Broom and Wang Bin finish their task. The evidence would be obvious, and afterwards the ghouls would be pegged as criminals.

Part of Stratton's decision owed to logic, and part to curiosity. He wanted to see if they would really try it.

Whispering, Broom and Wang Bin passed above him. The two men shuffled off the footpath and began probing grave markers in Section H. Stratton rose from his knees—dampened by the grass—and peered over the general's headstone.

He heard a voice counting: "Four-fifty, four forty-eight . . ."

And another: "It is here."

The flashlight threw a skittish beam from the ground to the trees to the crosses. Stratton crept out of the tombstones, sliding caterpillar-style along the earth until he reached the paved footpath. From there, braced on his elbows, he studied the grave robbers.

Wang Bin struggled out of the canvas shoulder bag and turned it upside down. The shovel and picks landed with a sharp clink against one of the white crosses.

"This is fucking insanity," Broom muttered.

"Where are your Marines?" Wang Bin chided. "It appears we are alone. You dig first."

"We're going to wind up in Leavenworth!" Broom said.

"There is a fortune beneath your feet. Now dig."

Grudgingly, Broom assembled the portable shovel. He removed his knit golf shirt and draped it across the arms of Kevin Mitchell's cross. As Broom poised at the edge of the grave, Wang Bin took one step back and folded his hands at his waist.

"Keep your eyes open!" Broom instructed. He planted his shoe on the shovel and rammed it into the moist green sod.

The exhumation went on for two hours. Stratton watched the shadows trade places, and measured their progress by the muffled grunts and curses, some in Chinese, some in English. Otherwise Arlington was perfectly still, save for the changing of the guard at the Tomb of the Unknown.

Stratton felt himself dozing when the sound of muffled voices arose in Section H. The flashlight snapped on, and he was able to see both of them: Broom, shirtless, sweaty, up to his waist in the pit; and Wang Bin, toweling his own forehead, exhorting Broom from the edge of the grave.

Then the flashlight went black.

Stratton squinted, waiting for his eyes to readjust. When he focused again, the two shadows were moving with belabored haste, a blur of pick and shovel, flinging dirt back into the grave. Then Wang Bin himself dropped to his knees and pressed ragged squares of green sod back into place, like so much carpeting.

"Let's get out of here," Broom said.

Wang Bin took the feet of the ancient soldier while Broom cradled its head. They walked without light, an odd and halting procession made easier by the perfect geometry that ruled the Fields of the Dead.

Fascinated, Tom Stratton did not move at first, but merely watched them recede among the graves.

Then he was on his feet, padding quietly behind them at a distance of fifty meters. When they reached an iron fence, Stratton dropped to one knee and raised the field glasses. Broom went over first, ripping his golf shirt. Wang Bin followed, grimacing with the exertion. The soldier was brought over on a precarious makeshift pulley, fashioned from two long ropes. Through the binoculars, Stratton noticed that the artifact had been carefully wrapped in a canvas bag.

Stratton scaled the fence easily, and followed the men along a deserted road. Fearful that they might wheel around and spot him, Stratton clung to the trees and hedges.

"Faster!" he heard Broom say. "We're almost there."

Ahead, parked on a curb, was a car. Stratton ducked into a

grove of young trees. He did not move again until he heard the sound of the car doors.

Then Stratton stepped to the middle of the road, twenty meters from the car. The trunk was open. Beside it stood Harold Broom and the smaller figure of Wang Bin, their backs toward him. Stratton drew a .45-caliber pistol from his belt and took aim at the base of Wang Bin's skull.

It was an easy shot. Even in the dark he'd never miss. David Wang's murderer would die instantly—die without knowing who had claimed revenge.

Behind Stratton, something rustled in the trees.

Wang Bin whirled, his face a fright mask. At the sight of Stratton the fear vanished in a portrait of pure hate.

Another noise. Wang Bin slowly raised a finger, as if to point. Broom's arms fell to his side.

Footsteps. Stratton's pulse hammered. He held the gun steady. Someone was there, beside him. He turned to see.

The pain hit Stratton high in one leg. It seared like a snakebite, racing up his thighs, burning through his lungs until it choked him. The gun dropped from his hand. Stratton spun down like a top, clawing at his leg, his throat, mashing the heels of his hands into his eye sockets.

Even as he lay there rasping, the galaxy exploding in his skull, he was aware of someone standing over him.

The last thing Stratton heard was the faraway voice of the deputy minister.

"Miss Greer, it is very good to see you again."

CHAPTER 25

ALL THE NEXT MORNING, Dr. Neal Lambert waited.

Harold Broom phoned at eleven. "All set," he had said. "Be ready at noon."

But noon came and went, and Lambert's excitement soon dissolved into panic. He paced the halls of the museum. He told himself not to worry; people like Broom were *always* late. They were incapable of common courtesy.

At six the museum closed. Lambert sank into the chair behind his polished desk and ranted out loud. Every few minutes he would dial the number that Broom had given him, only to be reminded by a very bored answering service that, no, Mr. Broom had not called in. Would he care to leave a number?

Lambert grew despondent. Broom was a greasy twit, but would he dare sell the Chinese soldier out from under him? And was he resourceful enough to locate a new buyer on such short notice? Doubtful, Lambert assured himself.

He wrung his hands and stood at the window of his office, gazing down the mall toward the Washington Monument. Gravely he thought of his three-hundred-thousand-dollar down payment. Then he thought of something worse: someday, years from now, walking into another museum, maybe Renner's in Atlanta or that bastard Scavello's in New York, and discovering his own Chinese warrior on grand display in the main room.

No, not even Broom—his minimal reputation at stake— would stoop so low, Lambert concluded. Something else must have gone wrong. The possibilites were numbingly depressing. He picked up the telephone and tried again.

Tom Stratton awoke in the back of a taxi. He was dizzy, queasy, babbling.

243

"Easy, bud," the cabbie said. He led Stratton up the steps of the Hotel Washington and into the arms of a doorman.

"I took a twenty off you, okay?"

Stratton nodded foggily.

"What happened?" the doorman asked.

"Some broad called. Told us to go get this drunk out by the cemetery." The cabbie glanced down at Stratton. "That's where I found him, crawling around on all fours like a mut."

Stratton groaned.

"Better get him up to his room," the cabbie advised, "before he urps on your nice carpet."

Stratton lay alone, dreaming of coffins. Slowly the pain drained from his limbs, but cotton clung to his mind. He could hear the sound of a city outside his window. A police siren. Screeching tires. A jet roaring down the Potomac. The noise crashed over him, triple amplified. His ears rang. His head felt like plaster.

He had to get up. Hours crawled by.

A maid rapped on the door.

"Not now," Stratton mumbled.

He had to get up. *Move*. Open your eyes.

The room was bright. The clock on the bedstand said eight o'clock.

"Jesus Christ." He had spent a full day in bed.

He made a wobbly journey to the shower. He found a crimson dot on his leg, still tender from the hypodermic injection. He stood under the hot water for twenty minutes, letting his blood wake up.

Sorting out the reality from the nightmare wasn't easy. Just where did Linda Greer fit in now? She had zapped him with something—elephant tranquilizer, it felt like. Why? And where was she?

On her own, that's where. No Langley, no Peking. Wang Bin had become a personal project, but why? And how personal?

Stratton was angry, restless and, above all, baffled. She had let them get away. For whatever reason, that's what she had done. It was one truth that had survived the horrible night.

Stratton toweled off and pulled on a pair of jeans. He called room service and ordered a big stack of pancakes, three eggs and a pitcher of black coffee.

His options were dismal. He could run to the State Department and lay it all out. Someone very polite would call

China, and someone in Peking would reply—very tersely—that the body found in the Ming reservoir *was* positively Deputy Minister Wang Bin; that no clay soldiers were missing from the Xian excavation; that no visa had ever been issued to an American named Harold Broom. That's what the Chinese would say—because they *had* to. They would admit nothing, because they could never permit themselves to be seen as fools.

And that would be it.

A better option would be confiding in old friends at the CIA. But what proof could Stratton offer? Vandalized grave plots? Hardly a red-hot trail.

It all came back to Linda. Was she in league with Broom and Wang Bin? Or was she trying for that solo coup that would edify her career—bringing the old Chinese bastard in from the cold? He remembered their dinner talk in Peking. Yes, that was probably it.

Either way, the lady had guts. Wang Bin was a killer, not easily induced, coerced or charmed. With some defectors it was easy. Bring them in gently. Pay them. Pump them. Pay them some more. A new name, a new passport, off you go.

Linda was wrong if she imagined it would be that simple with the deputy minister. He was the ultimate pragmatist.

Maybe she knew that. Maybe she was way ahead of him. I'm the one who's fresh out of clues, Stratton thought ruefully.

He wolfed down his breakfast and went downstairs. He bought a copy of the *Post* in the lobby and walked out into the sticky heat to think. There was an empty bench on the mall near the Smithsonian, and Stratton sat down. Hearty joggers and lean cyclists flew by him, a reminder that he did not yet have his strength back. The sidewalks swarmed with foreign tourists who seemed to walk twice as fast as everyone else.

Stratton imagined himself back in Tienanmen Square, where the order and propriety that ruled Chinese history seemed also to govern those who came to celebrate it. Here in Washington, among the functional granite monuments to democracy, there was a holiday festiveness; in China, among the wildly extravagant temples, sobriety.

To Stratton's eye, it was not merely a culture gap, but a canyon. Chinese tourists traveled thousands of miles just to stand where the emperor's scholars had once gathered in the

Hall of Supreme Harmony. In Washington, people lined up for blocks to watch the Treasury print money. Talk about awe.

If Americans seemed transparent, the Chinese mind was opaque. For Stratton this had become tragically obvious, first at Man-ling—a fatal grant of trust to a young boy—and now, with humiliating emphasis, at Arlington.

Stratton would never forget Wang Bin's face as Stratton had aimed the gun. Such magnificent defiance. Stratton would have liked him to have begged for his life, but he would have settled for one tear from the steely bastard. A tear for his own brother.

Yet all that had shone in the deputy ministers eyes had been an iron, immutable spirit. Stratton despised it.

He sat on the bench, watching a group of young girls from a parochial school chase a runaway kite, their plaid skirts beating together as they ran. Their laughter trailed off after the kite string.

Stratton opened the *Post*. The front section was clotted with the usual turgid political news. Stratton dismissed it and turned to the local pages to see if there was any mention of the grave robbery. There, on 10-C, a headline midway down the page grabbed his attention: ART BROKER FOUND DEAD IN BURNING AUTO.

The article was an Associated Press report from Grafton, West Virginia:

Two persons were found dead Monday at the scene of a single-car traffic accident on Shelby road, two miles south of Grafton.

Police said the victims were discovered in a burning automobile after the car apparently had run off the highway and crashed. Grafton Police Sgt. Gilbert Beckley said that rescue workers who reached the scene were forced to wait for the fire to subside before approaching the car.

Authorities have identified one of the victims as Harold G. Broom, an art dealer from New York. Police said Broom carried business cards listing him as an associate of the Parthenon Gallery and the Belle Meade Exhibition Center in Manhattan.

The second victim found in the car carried no personal belongings and has not yet been identified, police said.

The accident was reported by a Greyhound bus driver who passed the scene but did not stop.

Tom Stratton stuffed the newspaper into a trash basket, bought himself a lemon ice, and jogged exultantly back to his hotel.

Gil Beckley was not what Stratton expected. He was not a middle-aged hillbilly with hemorrhoids, but an athletic young cop with a Jersey accent and two junior college diplomas on the wall. If Beckley felt it was beneath him to work traffic accidents, he hid the resentment well. In fact, he seemed pleased to meet this angular, quiet man who had arrived with information about the Shelby Road fatalities.

Stratton introduced himself and said, "I read about the accident this morning in the *Post.*"

"That was the *official* version," Beckley said.

"What do you mean?"

"The two people in that car didn't die in any wreck. They were shot. Classic murder-suicide, I'd say."

Stratton was dazed.

"When you called, you said you knew something about the passengers," Beckley prodded. "Can you help us out?"

Mentally Stratton dusted off his story.

"Harold Broom was doing business with a good friend of mine. They'd been traveling together for the last week or so."

"Had you seen them recently?"

"Yes," Stratton said. "Day before yesterday. In Washington. They rented a car."

"So you think the other victim could be your friend?"

"I'm afraid so," Stratton said. "That's why I drove straight over here after I saw the story in the paper."

"We appreciate it," Beckley said. From a bottom drawer in the gray metal desk the policeman withdrew a stiff brown envelope. "How's your stomach, Mr. Stratton?"

Stratton took the envelope. His hands trembled. He scratched at the gummed flap.

He wasn't acting anymore.

"What was your friend's name?" Beckley inquired.

Stratton pretended not to hear. *Be there*, he said silently.

He slipped the photographs from the envelope. They were black-and-whites, the usual eight-by-tens. The top picture captured what was left of Harold Broom after he had been dragged from the smoldering car. His clothes dangled like charred tinsel. His chest and face were scorched; the flesh on the upper torso was scabrous. The face was raw, frozen in a death scream. The eyelids had burned away completely, leaving only a viscous white jelly in the sockets. Broom's outreached arms had constricted into the common rigor mortis of burn victims—elbows sharply bent, fists clenched in front of the face, as if raising a pair of binoculars.

Tom Stratton took a deep breath. He felt clammy.

The next two pictures, taken from different angles, were also of Broom.

"The next one," Beckley said, watching closely. "That's the one you're interested in."

Stratton looked at the photograph and nearly gagged. Through the din of his own heart pounding he barely heard Beckley shouting for someone to bring a glass of water.

The pictures slipped from Stratton's hand and drifted to the floor . . . Broom lying by the road, Broom face-front, Broom from the waist up . . .

And Linda Greer.

Stratton covered his eyes and moaned. His face burned.

Beckley stood at Stratton's side, a hand on his shoulder. "I'm very sorry," the cop said. "Have some water. You'll feel better."

Stratton scooped the photographs from the floor, and, without looking, handed them to Beckley.

"Mr. Stratton, can I ask your friend's name?"

"That wasn't him," Stratton croaked.

"Him?" Beckley was bewildered. "But just now—"

"My friend is a Chinese man. Wang is his name."

"Judging by your reaction to that photo, I thought for sure that the girl was the one—"

"No. And I'm sorry I frightened you."

"Well, it was a pretty goddamn frightening picture," Beckley said. "I'm sorry you had to see it. Still, it's better to know one way or another. Did you recognize the girl?"

"Never saw her before." Stratton drank some water. "You say it was murder?"

"Lover's quarrel, the way I figure it. The girl was a one-nighter, a fiancée, a hooker—we'll nail it down eventually. She got it first, back of the skull, two rounds. Then Broom aced himself, once in the right temple. The gun was a cheap thirty-eight. We found it on the front seat between them."

Beckley reached into the same drawer that held the photographs. He slid a piece of notebook paper across the desk toward Stratton. "We found this in a briefcase that was tossed in some bushes near the car."

The suicide note had been written meticulously in black ink, each letter capitalized:

"DARLING I AM SORRY, I COULD NOT ALLOW YOU TO LEAVE ME. THIS WAY IS BEST."

One glance and Stratton knew who had written it. *I could not allow you to leave me.* Much too clumsy for a fop like Harold Broom.

"What about the fire?" Stratton asked.

"An accident. Here's what I figure: Broom pulls off the highway in a passion. Takes out his gun, plugs the girl, writes his farewell note, then checks himself out. Bang. Leaves the engine running and the goddamn catalytic converter overheats. Catches fire. The whole thing goes up in blazes. That's Detroit for you."

Stratton said, "I'd better go now."

"You knew this Broom character?"

"I met him only once or twice."

"A real asshole, right?"

Stratton shrugged. "I couldn't say." Suddenly he was in the line of Beckley's fire: time to go.

"What about your friend, the Chinaman?"

"I . . . I guess he's all right."

"I'd really like to talk to him," Beckley said, "your friend, the Chinaman. I'd like to keep it nice and friendly, too. Subpoenas are such a pain in the ass."

"I understand," Stratton said. "When I talk to him, I'll be sure to have him call you."

"Right away." Beckley tugged at his chin. "And you've got no idea about the dead girl?"

"No," Stratton replied. "I'm sorry."

I am sorry.

Beckley led him back through a maze of dingy halls in the police station. As he reached the front desk, Beckley realized he was walking alone. He backtracked and found Stratton at the door to the property room. Staring.

"It was in the car," Beckley explained. "Wrapped up in the trunk. Didn't even get singed."

Rigidly Stratton approached the Chinese soldier who stood noble and poised, an unlikely centerpiece amid the flotsam of crime—pistols, blackjacks, bags of grass and pills, helmets, stereo speakers, radios, jewelry, shotguns, crowbars. Each item, Stratton noted, was carefully marked.

The ancient Chinese warrior, too, wore a blue tag around its neck, an incongruous paper medallion.

"What do you think?" Beckley said.

Stratton was overwhelmed. He couldn't take his eyes off the imperial soldier.

"Well, I'll tell you what *I* think," the cop said after a few moments. "I think it's the damnedest-looking lawn jockey I ever saw.

CHAPTER 26

STRATTON SPENT THE NIGHT in Wheeling. He slept turbulently, racked by old dreams and new grief.

First David, and now Linda.

He tried to convince himself that it wasn't his fault. They had argued under the oaks at Arlington: Stratton for vengeance, Linda for patience. Wang Bin was worth more alive than dead, she had said "He's an encyclopedia, Tom. Do you know what he could do for us?"

"Do you know," Stratton had countered, "what he's already done?"

But she had been determined, and Stratton had underestimated her.

Now she was dead, and Wang Bin was dust in the wind, a clever phantom. Stratton was sure he'd already grabbed the money, and with the money came boundless freedom—comfort, respectability, anonymity. That's the way it worked in America. That's what the deputy minister had counted on. In his mind's eye, Stratton pictured the cagey old fellow in his new life—where? San Francisco, maybe, or even New York; an investor, perhaps, or the owner of a small neighborhood business. Maybe something more ambitious: his own museum.

Stratton was desolate in his failure. Without clues, without even a scent of the trail, he had nowhere to go.

Nowhere but home, back to doing what he should have been doing all along. And before that, a detour. A couple of hours was all he needed, a moment really. A chance to say goodbye to the man who had meant so much to him, and whose murder he had been unable to prevent. A taste of better times, something enduring and warm for a lifetime of cold dreams.

Stratton got an early start and reached Pittsville by noon. The moment he passed the city limit sign he pulled his foot from the accelerator, a vestigial reflex from his days as a student. Speed trap or not, the town was still gorgeous.

It was green and cool and hilly, a sleepy old friend. Stratton wished he had never left.

He stopped for lunch at the village sundry, not far from St. Edward's campus. The counter lady, a grand old bird with snowy hair and antique glasses, remembered him instantly and lectured him on his lousy eating habits. Stratton cheered up.

The campus had changed little, and why should it have? The enrollment stayed constant, the endowments generous but not extravagant. Ivy still climbed the red-brick bell tower, and the bells still rang off key. The narrow roads were as pocked as ever, and the college gymnasium—now called an Amphi-dome—still looked like a B-52 hangar.

Stratton discovered he was in no hurry. He was home. He allowed himself to be led by sights and sounds. On the steps of the cafeteria, a shaggy folksinger strummed a twelve-string and sang—Stratton couldn't believe it—Dylan. Stratton dropped a dollar into the kid's guitar case and strolled to the post office to read the campus bulletin board. It was another St. Edward's tradition.

"Roommate wanted: Any sex, any size. Must have money."

"Need Melville term paper within ten days. Will pay big bucks, plus bonus for bibliography. Reply confidential."

"I want my Yamaha handlebars back. $200 firm. No questions."

Stratton shook his head. Nothing had changed.

"You lookin' for work, young man?" came a gruff voice from behind. "'Cause we sure don't need any more liberal agitators on this campus!"

Stratton immediately recognized the voice. "Jeff!"

"*Mr.* Crocker, to you." Crocker beamed and threw an arm around Stratton's shoulders. "How are you, Tom? You look like hell."

"You too."

"Editors are supposed to look like hell. It's in their contract."

"Yeah, well, I've been driving all day and I'm beat."

They walked the campus, making small talk. Crocker had been a reporter for the local newspaper when Stratton had been a student at St. Edward's. Now he was executive editor.

"They even let me teach a journalism class out here."

"God help us," Stratton said with a ghost of a smile. "The *National Star* comes to Pittsville."

They gravitated to the beer cellar in the basement of the cafeteria. It was five o'clock, still early for the campus drinkers, so Stratton and Crocker had no trouble finding a quiet booth.

Halfway through his first beer Crocker said, "I kind of expected to see you at the funeral."

"I couldn't come, Jeff. I was in China."

"With David? When it happened?"

Stratton told him what he could.

"It was such a shock," Crocker said. "The irony. After all those years, to return—only to die."

"He told me he was writing new lectures."

"Yes," Crocker said. "We did a feature story before he left. David always felt there was a thirty-year gap in history, at least for him. By going back he hoped to fill that empty space so he could bring his students up to date. The way he talked, the trip was purely a scholar's survey . . . hell, we all knew better, Tom. You should have seen how excited he was." Crocker polished off the beer. "He was packed two weeks before the plane left. Isn't that the David Wang we knew?"

"Orderly, to the extreme," Stratton said fondly.

"Yup. It was so sad. The service was very lovely."

"I would like to have been here, Jeff. You know that."

"Have you been up there yet?" Crocker motioned with his head. Stratton knew where he meant.

"No, not yet. I'll walk up in a little while. Is the house still open?"

"They decided to lock it up after David died. To protect his library as much as anything." Crocker winked. "The key's in a flowerpot on the porch."

"Thanks."

"On my way back to town I'll tell Gulley you're up there, so he won't get all worked up and send a squad car when he sees the lights."

Stratton said, "I'll only stay a little while."

"Stay as long as you want," Crocker said. "Don't cheat yourself."

Outside, darkness had gathered swiftly under a purple quilt of threatening clouds. Stratton set out for the Arbor with a quick stride, freshened by the cool stirrings of the birch and pine. All around him students lugging books hurried to beat the rain. Past the biology building, which looked and smelled like a morgue, the campus ended and the old trees gave way to a sloping, blue-green valley. All this had once been pasture, part of the old dairy David Wang had purchased after his arrival at St. Edward's. The valley was narrow and sharply defined, and halfway up the far slope Stratton could see the trees, David's trees, a lush wall of maple and pine and oak. At the top of that hill was the old farmhouse. Beyond that, on the downslope past another tall grove, was the bluff where David's coffin lay, near a lone oak. Stratton had no desire to visit the gravesite. An empty place, it mocked him in his nightmares.

The house was something else again—all the hours they had spent together there, the student and his teacher. It was there Stratton had shared his private agony—Man-ling—and tried to explain it over and over until David had gently touched his arm and said, "I understand, Tom. War."

"Murder." Stratton had wept. *"Murder."*

"I understand, Tom."

And from the confession had come a silent bond more powerful than any in Stratton's life. Often in the evening the two of them would sit on the porch, sipping tea, watching the hillside go dark. Stratton learned to talk of other things, and finally the nightmares went away. Because of David, Stratton had left St. Edward's a man reconciled to his past.

Now the wind came in fits, slapping at the leaves of the trees. Stratton jumped a clear brook and bounded up the hill in a rush toward the old clapboard house. He clomped onto the wooden porch at full tilt.

For a few moments he stood there, facing the Arbor, trying to catch his breath. The cool wind raked through his hair and made him shiver.

It was almost nightfall.

Stratton found the flowerpot on a freshly painted window-sill. The house key lay half buried behind a splendid pink geranium.

The key fit easily, but before Stratton could turn it, the door gave way. Crocker was wrong. It had not been locked.

Stratton groped in the darkness, cursing loudly when his knee cracked against the corner of an unseen table. His hand found a hanging lamp and turned the switch.

He stood in the middle of David Wang's library. Ranks of

books marched from floor to ceiling. There was the burgundy
leather chair with the worn and discolored arm rests. There was
the giant Webster's on its movable stand; David would drag it
all over the house, wherever he happened to be reading. And
there in one corner was the newest thing in the room, a
grandfather clock. Never on time, never on key, it had been a
recent gift from the faculty club.

Stratton felt warm and safe in this place.

His eyes climbed to a high spot in one of the bookcases
where David had tenderly arranged several framed photographs of his family. Stratton moved closer and stood on his
toes. One picture in particular intrigued him: two young men at
the waterfront, arms around each other's shoulders. They could
have been twins, they looked so much alike. Both young men
in the sepia photograph smiled for the camera, but those smiles
told Stratton which of them was leaving Shanghai Harbor that
day. David's smile was bright with hope, his brother's strained
with envy.

"Yes, it was a sad farewell."

The voice cut through Stratton like a blast of arctic air. He
had no time to speak, no time to turn around. He heard a grunt,
and then his skull seemed to explode, and he felt himself
falling slower and slower like ashes from a mountaintop.

CHAPTER 27

THE PHOTO ALBUM HAD a royal blue cover and a gold stripe. It was old and worn, with tape for hinges. The album contained faded black-and-white pictures, a half century old, of wicked, life-giving Shanghai. There were photos of New York in the 1930s as well, of a self-conscious young man in stiff white shirt and broad necktie posed before municipal landmarks: Grant's Tomb, the spanking new Empire State Building.

The album had been David Wang's favorite.

He would sit at his desk in the old farmhouse and turn the well-remembered pages. Before a man can understand where he is going he must first come to terms with where he has been. Sometimes David Wang found refuge in the album when he had a visitor. From it he would extract lessons that matched the problem the visitor brought. Once Thomas Stratton, nerves jangled, memories still too fresh, had sat before the cumbersome old farmer's desk and watched David Wang finger the pages to the accompaniment of a gentle, wise man's monotone.

"Ah, Shanghai, what a city it was, Thomas. A cauldron of the very best and the very worst there is to life. Luxury unbounded. But for most, inconceivable misery. Too much misery. It had to change, but alas, it took the Communists to do it. We are all a bit like Shanghai, aren't we? We all change. Every day we are different. And if we are smart, smarter than the Communists, we do not destroy the good. We destroy the bad, edge it out slowly but surely—ruthlessness, cruelty, injustice, rash behavior. We build on what is good, like the body repairing a wound, forcing out the infection, replacing good for bad. Why, I remember as a boy in Shanghai . . ."

Through a cotton wool of pain and confusion Thomas Stratton watched David Wang again at his desk, again with the album in his delicate, thinker's fingers.

But it was not David. Not even the dulling ache in his skull would allow Stratton to believe that. There was no cup of jasmine tea at David's elbow. Instead, a coil of rope, serpentine and menacing, lay on the scarred old desk. There was no crackle from the old fire or soft glow from a desk lamp, only the rattle of an old-fashioned kerosene lantern perched anachronistically in one corner.

David Wang did not sit at his desk. David Wang was dead.

At David's desk, defiling his memory, his goodness, sat his brother. His murderer.

Stratton would have sprung but for the bonds that held him, hand and foot, to the old Harvard chair.

"He was a fool, my brother," Wang Bin said. "An arrogant, intellectual romantic, a superior being who lived in a cage of his own making—too smug to come to terms with reality. No, reality might have been disordered, unpleasant, and that would never do, would it? Of course not. Best to ignore it, then. A fool . . . but you do not agree, Professor Stratton?"

"What are you doing here?" A wounded plea. Stratton barely recognized his own voice.

"I could tell you I came for sentimental reasons. David told me about this place, and what it meant to him. And all you see around you in this room, Professor, are the memories of a childhood we shared. I could tell you I came here to see all this, to taste these old memories . . . but that's not the reason." Wang Bin eyed Stratton. "There is a more practical reason for me to be here."

"Let's hear it."

"Soon enough, Professor." Wang Bin walked slowly around the desk. Knots bit into Stratton's flesh. He would break the chair. It was only wood.

Stratton saw the punch coming out of the corner of an eye; there was nothing he could do. A knobby fist smashed into his cheekbone. Stratton tasted blood.

"My brother," Wang Bin said calmly, "was a fool who could see the truth but chose to ignore it. Even as a child he was a sanctimonious fraud. One year older he was, that is all. Is that a century? Does one year bestow wisdom? Ah, but how David loved to play the elder, he the superior and I the inferior, the ignorant younger brother. My mother and father, they were fooled by him, like everyone else. . . .

"Once I broke a vase, a beautiful Ming vase. It sat there on a polished wooden table, beautiful and ludicrous. And I broke it,

perhaps even intentionally. I smashed it into a million pieces."
Wang Bin paused, with a curious smile. "Like all children, I
was afraid of what my parents would do. So I told my mother
that a deliveryman—an old man who brought fresh crabs to the
house—had carelessly broken the vase with his sack. She
believed me. But that was not good enough for my brother. He
went to Mother and said, 'It was I, your eldest son, who broke
the vase, Mother. Bin is only trying to protect me. I take
responsibility.' Did they beat him? No, of course not. 'What an
honest boy you are,' they said.

"And did David then beat me, or mock me to show me how
much braver he was? No. He never said a word, nothing, as
though by making me wallow in my shame I would drown.
Just as he never said a word to me those days when I would
skip my piano lessons and come back only to find him playing
my exercises, so that downstairs my mother would hear it and
think how dedicated I was, just like my elder brother."

Stratton said, "Why are you here?"

Wang Bin sat down once more at the desk. "We have time
for that, Professor, plenty of time."

Stratton worked the knots at his wrists. "So you were a
jealous little brother," he prodded. "That's your explanation."

"For murder?" Wang Bin seemed amused. "No."

"How could you hate him so much?"

"I am not sure I did. Not at the end." His voice was level,
emotionless. "The day finally came for my big brother to leave
for the United States. How sad was my mother, how proud my
father. All the servants wept, and I wept, too. I wept for the joy
of it, Professor Stratton. He was gone and I would be the elder
son. My parents thought I wept from sadness. How I fooled
them! My father took me aside and said, 'Bin, do not weep.
You must be strong and brave like your brother and in another
year, perhaps two, you will join him to study.' I never would
have gone. To follow him. In anything. *Never.* How little my
father understood of me, or of China.

"When my mother left for the Revolution I joined her
instantly. Here was something my brother could not do, or my
father. To fight a revolution. War is very exciting, Professor
Stratton. Do you remember how the skin tingles, the senses
race? I was barely sixteen—imagine, not yet sixteen!—and I
would call my soldiers and say, 'Comrades, we must take that
bridge. The people's struggle demands it.' And they would say,

'Yes, Comrade,' and they would march with fifty-year-old rifles into artillery and machine-gun fire. They would die unflinching, uncomplaining, with a mindless zeal that someone like you would admire. I loathed their stupidity. And I loathed the Revolution, too. Loved and loathed it.

"It should have been a bright dream, a dream so great my brother could never have known its like. Instead it was a theater of the absurd. 'Yes, Comrade, we will go off and die because the people demand it.' Is it heroic to roll in the mud like a pig when you can be clean, or to march through snow in bare feet when you can ride? It was a peasant's revolution. The peasants won. And ever since, in their bungling, they have disgraced the heritage of the nation with the most splendid history of all.

"The imperial times! The dynasties! That was when China was great. That is when I should have lived." Wang Bin spoke with a trace of sadness. "In the times of the emperor."

"You'd fit right in," Stratton said. "A greedy old man who murdered his brother for profit."

"My brother. My *brother*."

The thumb and forefinger of Stratton's left hand were mobile now, and with them he feverishly worried the knots.

"'Dear elder brother,'" Wang Bin recited in mockery. "'I think of you often after all these years, so many miles away. I should like to see you before I die. It would be wonderful if you could come to China. . . .'

"And so he came, with his cameras and his loud synthetic clothes. 'You must help me, brother,' I said. 'I must leave China for reasons that you would not understand, and I must take with me what is my due.' I showed him my treasures in Xian. He stood beside me and looked at them."

"Clay soldiers, that's all."

Wang Bin stared at Stratton scornfully. Through the heavy drapes a gust of wind rattled the windows and Stratton heard the sudden assault of rain on the glass. He used the sound to mask his movements, tilting the chair just a fraction to give his feet greater purchase against the ropes.

Wang Bin said, "The soldiers are toys for children, a pittance. In Xian I showed my brother the real treasure. Even he was left speechless by its majesty.

"'You must help me,' I said to him. 'With the soldiers we will have enough money to live in splendor wherever we choose. I ask but two things of you: That you allow me to hide you here in China so that I may leave the country on your passport. After two weeks you have only to go to your embassy to say that you lost your passport, and they will give you a new one. Then, once we are together in the United States, you can help me recover the soldiers and sell them. Is that too much to ask of a brother, after all these years? Help me, please. I have lived more than once as a peasant. I cannot live like that again. I will not.'"

"You should've known what his answer would be," Stratton said.

Wang Bin nodded. "He said, 'It is wrong what you are doing, it is a crime. I cannot help you.'" The deputy minister shrugged.

"So you killed him." Stratton's thumb was abraded and hurt painfully. He wished he had longer fingernails. Keep him talking. Above all, keep him talking.

"I did not plan to murder him," Wang Bin said. "I had his room searched, and I had him followed because I was afraid he would rush to his embassy like an old woman. In the end I did kill him, but because I had no choice. In his death was the only means of accomplishing my escape and saving my treasure."

Stratton said, "You're a weak old man, Comrade. Even in death your brother intimidates you. Listen to yourself—the lies, the jealousy, the way you pervert his memory."

One of the knots came loose. The pressure on Stratton's right wrist eased; he twisted it back and forth within the growing circle of rope.

"But that's your stock in trade, isn't it, *Comrade* Deputy Minister? The perversion of history. That's why we're here."

"Ah, yes." Wang Bin smiled a winter's smile. "My artifacts."

"And your coffins!"

"They make excellent shipping crates." Wang Bin folded his hands but looked impatient. "Don't tell me you mourn the tourists, Professor. I did not kill them all. The first, a fat capitalist, died quite naturally. Death by duck, your embassy called it. A clever name for a common occurrence, I learned. And it gave me the idea. His was the first coffin."

The rope rubbed raw against Stratton's wrist. Feeling flooded back into his fingers. Another minute . . .

"You couldn't have done it all alone."

"Certainly not. I had many trusted associates—a doctor for the lethal poisons, welders for the caskets, diggers, of course. Fortunately they understood that I was directing a secret project for the Party. That lie was necessary, you see, to assure their complete loyalty and their perpetual silence."

"And your buddy, Harold Broom. Was he, too, working for the glory of the Party?"

"Broom was a worm, a drunken cheat. I chose him only because David would not cooperate. Broom cheated me about money, and then he conspired with the Greer woman."

"Poor Harold," Stratton sneered. And poor Linda.

Another twist. Just one more. Make the fist small. Slide the rope over . . . there! Stratton's right hand was free. He clawed at the knot on his left wrist, blessing the rain pummeling the house.

"The Greer woman was another worm, wasn't she?" Stratton said harshly. "Well, she was the only one who could have saved you, Comrade."

Wang Bin looked quizzically at Stratton. "It is not my salvation that brings us here, but your death. You must die as Miss Greer had to die. The difference is that you are troublesome and she was dangerous—more dangerous than you because she was smarter. She did not come as you have, thrashing about, making great noise and great threats. She did not care about smuggling or murder. Or morality, Professor. She had only one goal: information. I respected that. She was not like the professor of stupidity who seeks revenge for a pompous friend, or perhaps merely wants to cleanse himself of past sins. . . ."

Wang Bin allowed the phrase to dangle, watching Stratton.

"Did you think that I did not know about the pregnant peasant woman who was slashed from her throat to her belly? It had to be you. You were the only invader who escaped from Man-ling."

"I don't know what you're talking about."

"Oh yes, you know. Your face says so. You would have lived longer, Stratton, if you had been less impulsive and more clever. Miss Greer was very clever; she must have been a good spy. The way she dealt with you, for example, quickly and noiselessly, outside the cemetery. Then she rode with us, Broom and I, bought us dinner, talked . . . and made her proposal. It was very civilized. 'I know everything,' she said, 'about your brother and the soldiers. I know everything and none of it matters. If you come with me and talk to us—tell us what you know—you may keep the money and remain in the United States under our protection.'"

Wang Bin paused for effect, like one of the professional storytellers who nightly enthrall the old men at dank teahouses in provincial China. Stratton was picking up speed; his left hand was nearly free.

When Wang Bin resumed, he had become another person, a canny old grandfather. "For Harold Broom, who would have sold his mother, it was as though Miss Greer spoke from the heavens. He choked on his chicken dinner. 'Me too?' he asked. 'No prosecution?'

"Miss Greer smiled. She had a lovely smile, Stratton. Did you notice that? She smiled at Mr. Broom and said, 'Of course. You, too.' And I said, 'Miss Greer, this is a very fair offer. I can be of great assistance to your government. But please tell me so an old man will know your thoughts: What will happen if I refuse?' Miss Greer looked very sad. 'We would have to arrest you and deport you to China,' she said. 'But I am sure that will not happen. . . .'"

The rope came free. Stratton bunched it in his left hand so that it didn't fall to the floor. He calculated the distance from chair to desk. It would have been easy, except for his feet, still bound to the chair. If he launched himself pogo-style he might—just might—reach far enough to grab an arm, the shirt, the neck—anything would do.

Wang Bin said, "Of course I gave Miss Greer my consent. 'I realize when I have been defeated,' I said. 'Your terms are very generous and I accept them. Let us leave now.'

"Broom could not contain his glee. Miss Greer seemed surprised—it had been so easy. And after that, who could deny a confused and defeated old man the right to sit alone in the back seat with his thoughts? Miss Greer, you see, was not as clever as she thought. She never looked for a gun—and the price of that mistake was death. The world will think she died as Broom's lover, mistress to an international crime."

Wang Bin glowed in self-satisfaction: another victory, among so many.

Now. It had to be now. Stratton tensed to spring.

Too late.

Wang Bin must have had the gun on his lap the whole time. There was no other way he could have leveled it so quickly.

It was a fat, black .45, the kind the United States government issues its agents. Linda Greer's gun.

"Stratton, you have been maneuvering your hands as I spoke," Wang Bin said quietly. "If you move again, I shall shoot. I can do it, believe me. I spent many more years in the army than you did."

Stratton sagged, full of self-disgust.

"It's hard for me to believe you could actually be David's brother, or Kangmei's father," he said. "You have dishonored your country, your ancestors, your family, all in the name of greed."

"Ah, Kangmei, my lovely daughter. She excited you, yes? You were not the first, I assure you. It was probably she who made possible your escape. I should have foreseen such a thing, but it is too late. China's system will deal with her—for that, the system is efficient."

"This country's got a system, too," Stratton said. "You'll get caught, Bin. The spooks—Linda's friends—will snatch you up and turn you inside out. You'll tell them everything, too. You won't be able to help it—drugs, sensory deprivation, shock. When they're finished, you'll be as dead and dusty as your goddamn clay soldiers."

"I don't think so, Professor."

"Believe me." Stratton fought to keep his voice steady. "I'll make you a better offer than Linda Greer did. Go now. Run. Get out of here. I'll give you twenty-four hours before I come looking, and then it'll just be me. Alone. No police."

Wang Bin's response was icy, bemused. "I think not, Stratton. No one is looking for me now, and no one will. I drowned in Peking, you see. Drowned before I could see my ministry dishonored by two thieves—imperialist American running dogs who looted the treasures of the people of China. Harold Broom. And Linda Greer. When she is identified, and the emperor's soldier is found in the car, her superiors will understand where her true loyalties lay: she was a thief. I was very careful, Stratton. I provided all the pieces to the puzzle: the soldier, the suicide note and the list."

"What list?"

"The list of Mr. Broom's buyers, of course. Wrapped up with the soldier, in the trunk of the car. You look surprised."

"No," Stratton said. But he was. Sgt. Gil Beckley hadn't mentioned the list—he was an even better cop than Stratton had thought.

"I had no need for the customers anymore, Professor. The money is quite safe, and so am I. All clues point to Mr. Broom and Miss Greer. There will be no pursuit. But you must accept that on faith, Stratton. I have already anticipated your own quiet removal."

"People will look for me . . . ." But Stratton saw that it was useless.

Wang Bin had won.

Thomas Stratton would be the last sacrifice of an ancient funeral rite.

With the speed and deftness of a snake—a cobra—Wang Bin's hand flicked the coil of rope from the desk. A noose settled over Stratton's head.

Wang Bin hauled Stratton, wheezing, until he was suspended almost horizontally between the desk and the heavy chair which held his feet. He squirmed and grunted, lamely pawing at the rope on his neck.

"Something else I learned in the army," Wang Bin said. "Careful, Stratton. The harder you struggle, the worse it will be."

Stratton felt the rope slacken and instantly he was on the floor, heaving. His shirt was soaked with cold sweat.

"Your original question, Professor Stratton: Why am I here? It's very simple. I am here to borrow some tools." Wang Bin stood up. One hand held the gun. With the other hand he fitted a shapeless, faded hat—David's gardening hat—onto his head. "There is a shovel out on the porch. You will carry it."

Wang Bin wrapped Stratton's tether around his right fist and pulled hard.

"Now we shall go for a walk, Mr. Stratton. There is something you must do for me before you die."

CHAPTER 28

THE PUPPET DANGLED waist-deep in a grave.

His shovel bit through sodden red clay made heavy and unstable by rainwater that sluiced into the pit. The puppet dug by the dancing light of two hurricane lamps, abetted by stalks of lightning that made him think of deranged Chinese characters.

The rain had stopped, but it would come again. Such was the promise of distant thunder, alien battalions marching, and of the brusque summer wind that chilled without cooling.

The puppet dug awkwardly, his head erect, the position enforced by the rope that arched from his neck over a limb of a lonely oak, and into the darkness below.

In that darkness stood Wang Bin, a furtive scout.

"Kuai-kuaide!" he barked above the wind. "Faster!"

Wang Bin jerked the rope, yanking the puppet's head, forcing a fresh sob through lips that begged for air.

Thomas Stratton was dying:

He was dying with cruelty and calculated humiliation that no Western mind could fashion.

He could dig, and die when he finished; a shot from Linda Greer's revolver.

He could refuse to dig and die now at the end of a rope swinging as lifeless as yesterday's shirt.

But he could not die with any dignity, any pride. They had been stripped from him by the murderer who supervised his agony.

Professor of stupidity.

Wang Bin had been right. Stu-pid, stu-pid, stu-pid, muttered the wind through the Arbor.

The solution had been there all the time. In the grave of David Wang. It had been there from the beginning, and Stratton had not realized it.

The puppet did not dig to satisfy Wang Bin's sadism, nor merely to create his own eternal shroud.

He dug because there was something to recover from David's grave. Not an empty coffin, as Stratton had assumed, or even another carved soldier.

It was to his brother's coffin that Wang Bin had consigned his real treasure.

What was it?

Stratton was too dazed even to speculate. He dug mindlessly, an ashen marionette.

"Slack," he gagged. "More slack . . . I can't breathe."

The rope eased a grudging fraction, and in the next aching instant Stratton's shovel struck the lid of the coffin. The clunk was unmistakable, and it brought Wang Bin bobbing forward to perch at the lip of the grave.

"Careful!" he commanded excitedly. "*Xiao xin,* fool!"

Gradually Stratton uncovered the coffin lid, the cheap Chinese metal streaked with moisture and freckled with incipient rust. Like a teacher bestowing reluctant favor on a backward child, Wang Bin paid out rope to allow Stratton more movement.

Shovel plunging, the puppet dug his way around the coffin from corner to corner.

"*Huang di,*" Wang Bin said, a reverent whisper.

"What is it?" gasped Stratton.

"Do not stop now, Professor. You are about to have the history lesson of your life."

Wang Bin positioned himself at the foot of the grave. The barrel of the pistol poked from his shadow, an ominous telescope on Stratton's midsection.

"Pull it out now," the deputy minister said. "Be careful."

Stratton staggered to the gentle slope of soil at the peak of the grave. He squatted in the mud, wrapped both blistered hands around the head of the coffin and pulled it toward him. The metal was slick, and Stratton's purchase poor.

The coffin edged a few inches from its bed and then slid back as Stratton's legs flew out from under him. The rope stopped his fall, but left him choking and scrambling in a tortuous pushup pose.

Wang Bin played out the rope and Stratton collapsed, prying with nerveless fingers to loosen the noose.

"Pull, you must pull again," came the thin, ice-pick voice of his captor. "Pull, donkey. Pull."

Stratton levered himself to a sitting position, encouraged by a fresh jerk on the rope. "I can't," he cried. "I need air."

Wang Bin fired once. The bullet slapped into the mud between Stratton's knees.

The puppet lurched back into the grave. Moments later he had dragged the coffin out of the pit onto the muddy slope, bracing it there with a heavy rock.

Wang Bin inched forward along the side of the open grave. "Now break the welds, Professor. Use the point of the shovel." The rope hung loosely from his left hand now. The time for donkeys was nearly over.

Stratton found the welds soft and accommodating; a child could have fractured them. The lid of the coffin sprang open. Unbidden, Stratton stripped away a protective layer of gray quilts. Then he slumped against the grave wall to stare.

Russian dolls, he thought dully, a game of Russian dolls— one inside the other.

"What is it?" Stratton murmured again.

The gleam of Wang Bin's smile was visible in the darkness: "It is beauty, Professor—or can you no longer recognize it? It is beauty. It is history. It is mine."

Inside the coffin that was never meant for David Wang lay another coffin, cushioned by green quilts and chocked with fresh-cut wood.

The small coffin was exquisite, a masterpiece of latticework gold studded with gems—diamonds, rubies, pearls—that sparkled even in the sallow lantern light. It was like nothing Stratton had ever seen. Beauty and majesty unsurpassed.

"I know what it is," Stratton marveled. So this was the deputy minister's private excavation at Xian. No wonder David had raged. A crime against humanity, he had called it.

Indeed, it was more than that.

"Open it." The eyes of the old man flashed in triumph. The voice was placid, confident. "Open it, Stratton. There are latches on the side.

Stratton opened it.

He looked, then spun away and retched into the grave.

"*Huang di*," Wang Bin said. "Son of Heaven. Ruler of the Middle Kingdom. Beloved ancestor."

It was the Emperor Qin.

He lay as serenly as when his vassals had placed him at the heart of his colossal tomb, protected by his army of ceramic soldiers. Twenty-two hundred years ago.

The ultimate artifact.

Thomas Stratton had never imagined anything so macabre. It was hideous, a loathsome caricature of life, a rotted monster that did not belong on this verdant hillside, David's place.

No one would ever know what secrets the emperor's alchemists had employed to prepare him for eternal reign. But they had failed. They had not cheated time, but perverted it. A mummy can have dignity, like a man making his own grave. Wang Bin's emperor had none. It was a green-tinged parody of empty sockets, spore-covered bones, shreds of dusty silk and a rictus grin.

For this abomination men had died. David had died. Stratton would die.

Drenched, fatigued, bleary, Stratton looked up at Wang Bin. "Why?" he asked feebly.

"Think, Professor. As a student of history, as an observer of mankind." He held the rope and the gun where Stratton could see them. "You know what it is, Professor. It is the most cherished archaeological treasure in all China. Its value is both symbolic and very real. It is—truly—priceless. My government—" Wang Bin caught himself, smiled self-consciously. "Excuse me, my *former* government will do anything to recover this artifact. It will do anything, in fact, to conceal the circumstances of the theft. You see, Stratton, in China the scandal would be more of a calamity than the actual crime. There is no limit to what my former colleagues might do to prevent such a thing."

"So you're a blackmailer, too," Stratton said derisively.

Wang Bin stiffened. "I am not familiar with that term," he replied, testing the rope with a sharp twitch. "However, I do intend to seek what is due to me after a lifetime of devotion."

"The soldiers weren't enough?"

"*Think*, Stratton. There are seven thousand celestial soldiers. There is only one imperial casket. There is only one . . ." His voice trailed off in the night. His eyes fell to the grave, gazing at the withered creature within.

Stratton watched the gun and waited.

"By now they know," Wang Bin said smugly. "The comrades know of my achievement. They know what they must do, for I left precise instructions. The men who would have purged me are the same men who will beseech me for this treasure. They will pay enormously for my future comfort, and for my silence. And, in return, I will give them back their precious little corpse."

"And then you disappear?"

Wang Bin nodded. "I disappear from history. My name will never again be mentioned in Peking. Those who worked with me . . . I cannot say what will become of them. The comrades who pursued me, however, will certainly suffer. They were too slow and much too stupid. Their defeat and humiliation is my vindication, Stratton. That much even you can understand."

Stratton understood. He understood why the celestial soldiers were not enough. He understood the genius of the crime, the genius of the vengeance.

And he knew why Wang Bin—so small and unimposing—frightened him so.

"Close the coffin now," the deputy minister ordered. "Remove it from the grave."

"I can't."

The rope cracked. Stratton was on his toes, then peddling in the air, gulping for breath. Then he was on his knees, on all fours. Dizzy. Dying.

David, help me.

"Now," said the brother. "Remove the emperor's coffin!"

"No."

For this Thomas Stratton would not die.

With all his strength he hurled a wet handful of dirt in Wang Bin's face and dove across the grave with a scream.

Sometimes you have to take a shot. It was something you were taught but never spoke of. Sometimes the only remote chance is to give the enemy one shot and hope to survive it. Bobby Ho had remembered, there on the bloody stage at Manling.

Diving low, Stratton survived because Wang Bin made a mistake. Logically, he should have jerked on the rope with all his weight; that would have snapped Stratton's neck.

But Wang Bin chose the gun instead. He fired reflexively, and missed by a hair's breadth.

The bullet scored the top of Stratton's shoulder and exploded in the grave behind them. When Stratton hit Wang Bin, the almond eyes were riveted in horror—not at his assailant, but at the coffins.

Then they fought along the rim of the pit. They fought like the maniacs they were, with hands and feet and teeth: Stratton younger, heavier, but exhausted; Wang Bin possessed of unquenchable fury.

Stratton finally saw it—a slow-motion frame—as they teetered on the lip, Wang Bin's hands like talons on his neck.

The bullet meant for Stratton had found another target: the emperor's skull. After twenty-two centuries his warriors had failed him. A traitor's gunshot had reduced the legend to an anonymous pile of powdered bone.

Not for that.

I will not die for that.

With power he had never known, Tom Stratton ripped free of Wang Bin's clinch. With the heel of his right hand he delivered a killing blow beneath the old man's chin, a blow that would paralyze the nervous system in the microsecond before it broke the neck.

Stratton hurled Wang Bin into the grave and fell back in the mud.

It was the rain that roused him—fresh rain, thunder and the wind that scoured his wounds, pierced his lethargy. Stratton was sick again. Then, as recognition returned, he cautiously crawled to the edge of the grave.

Wang Bin had joined his emperor forever.

He had crashed on his back into the coffin, smashing beneath him the delicate, lacework-gold bier. The impact had jarred the coffin off the rock and sent it sliding down the slope back into the muddy tomb.

With a grunt, Stratton reached down and slammed the lid of David's casket, sealing the two sleepers. Then, determinedly, ignoring throbbing limbs and a bloody shoulder, Stratton set to work.

He had been digging for ten minutes when he heard the sounds. Stratton wiped the water from his eyes and paused to listen: branches chattering in the wind. What else could it be?

Stratton had covered the entire coffin with a foot of wet red earth when he heard it again.

Faint raps. Then a clawing, a muffled disturbance: the scuttle of rats in a barn.

It came from the grave.

Wang Bin was alive.

His body quivering, the rain cascading off his back, Stratton bent for a long and horrible moment over the shovel.

Rap. Rap.

"No!" Stratton screamed. "No! No, you!"

He shoveled relentlessly then, with black fear and desolate conviction. Dig. Lift. Throw. Dig. But don't think. Lift. Never think. Throw.

Stratton had no memory of finishing. There was but an hour until dawn when he levered the headstone back into its silent place, tucked a shapeless old gardening hat in his back pocket, and left the rain to wash away his traces:

†

David Wang

1915–1983

Teacher and Friend

Rest in Peace

EPILOGUE

IN LATE SEPTEMBER, Thomas Stratton took his students to the Boston Museum to see a traveling exhibition of terracotta soldiers from the Qin Dynasty. They were impressed.

In October, he read a story in the Boston *Globe* that amused him:

China Won't Disturb
Tomb of First Emperor

By James X. McCarthy
Special to the Globe

PEKING—Chinese officials have a message for the Emperor Qin Shi Huangdi, dead these 2,200 years.

Rest in Peace, Emperor.

The emperor is remembered by history as the man who first unified China. In his spare time he built the Great Wall and buried alive Confucian scholars who dared to suggest that he might be mortal.

Since his death (natural causes) in 210 B.C., the emperor has lain under a gigantic man-made mountain near the central Chinese city of Xian. The area around the tomb has become one of the world's great archaeological digs, yielding more than 7,000 life-sized, priceless terracotta soldiers and horses who guarded the tomb as an imperial guard of honor.

Scholars had hoped that the Chinese, who are anxious to capitalize on the find as a tourist attraction, would soon begin excavations of the tomb itself.

Sorry, it won't happen any time this century, says scientist Gao Yibo.

"We are reluctant to open the tomb itself," he said in an interview. "To dig faster does not mean to dig better. We must work slowly to evaluate what we already have, and to preserve a legacy for archaeologists of the future."

Painstaking evaluation and reconstruction of the existing finds, which lie in three giant pits about two-thirds of a mile from the emperor's tomb itself, will take at least until the end of this century, said Gao.

"We leave the emperor himself to our children. He will be safe in the ground until we are ready for him," said Gao, who this month became the new deputy minister in charge of all of China's archaeological discoveries and the museums that display them.

Continued on page 16

In November, Stratton won permission from a bemused college administration, which had regarded him as a popular underachiever, to teach a course in Asian history, literature and philosophy. Stratton's detailed prospectus outlined what he called the Wang Syllabus.

In December, two visitors came. Stratton was expecting them.

"I'm Tony Medici, this is Jerry Flanagan. We're from the Smithsonian," said the dark one, a rangy man with sharp, veteran's eyes who wore a button-down shirt. The young one had red hair and a scowl he probably practiced in the mirror.

"I'm Mother Goose. Sit down."

"That'll save a lot of pointless bullshit." Medici grinned.

"We understand you have some information about Chinese artifacts . . ."

"Three big ones, to be exact," said Flanagan.

"That's what I said in my letter."

"Yeah, I saw it. We'd like those items back."

"How badly do you want them?"

"Hey, if you even *know* we want them you're in deep trouble. National security. We can put your ass away for a long time.

Stratton ignored the redhead. Medici was the pro.

"How bad?" he asked again.

"Well, it is a matter of some concern. We've searched, of course. Even got a hint that maybe one of our . . . uh, that a government employee might have been mixed up in it. You might even know the lady."

Stratton gave him nothing.

"How bad?"

"All the way up to the White House, since you ask. You got 'em?"

"I know where they are."

"How much?" Flanagan snapped.

"They're not for sale."

"What then?"

"A swap."

"For what?"

Stratton told him.

Medici blew air between his teeth. "I don't know if we want the merchandise that much."

"It's up to you."

"I mean, that kind of thing . . . it's out of style, isn't it, Stratton? These days we don't just sneak in . . ."

"You do it or I do it."

"I don't believe this," said Flanagan.

"Shut up, Jerry." Then to Stratton: "I'll have to check."

"There's a pay phone down the hall."

Stratton went back to marking papers. The redhead fidgeted.

"You an art teacher?"

"Something like that."

"Never did much for me in college."

"I know."

"When Tony comes back we'll probably drag you out of here in handcuffs. I'd like that, *Professor*."

Medici was back in twenty minutes.

"You've got a deal," he said without preface, measuring Stratton with curiosity.

"What!"

"Shut up, Jerry. There are some conditions, though."

Medici consulted a notebook. "First, we get *our* friends' merchandise back. Then we go lookin' for yours. It'll take some time."

"I know."

"There's something else." Medici read slowly from the notebook. "You must promise not to undertake, organize or direct any incursion into the People's Republic of China, or attempt in any way to enter the People's Republic under your own or any assumed identity, for any purpose."

"Tony, who *is* this guy?" Flanagan whined. "What's going on?"

"Anything else?" Stratton asked.

Medici mumbled. Stratton barely caught the words.

"They said to say please."

Flanagan coughed.

Stratton said, "Tell them I agree."

He handed the agents two sheets of paper. The name of Sgt. Gil Beckley was written on the first.

"Who's this?" Flanagan said, frowning.

"A cop in West Virginia. Be nice to him. A piece of your merchandise is locked up in his property room. He's also got a list that you'll find very interesting."

Broom's roster of stolen warriors and their buyers. It had been found in the trunk of the car with the last Chinese soldier, exactly as Wang Bin had planned. Stratton had phoned Gil Beckley to make sure; the next day, Stratton had written his letter to Washington.

"What kind of list?" Flanagan demanded.

"The best kind. Short and simple. It'll help you find what you're looking for." Not just the imperial artifacts, Stratton thought, but Linda Greer, too. She deserved much more than a pauper's grave.

The second paper Stratton handed to the agents was as good as a map. Medici studied it briefly.

"Okay, brother, you got it. We'll be in touch."

Stratton walked them to the door. Flanagan left, shaking his head. Medici paused.

"I was in Nam," he said. "Fourth Division Lurps. We heard stories . . . well, I'm proud to know you."

Stratton said good-bye. He walked back to his desk and opened the middle drawer. The envelope was stained, dog-eared. It carried a Hong Kong Stamp.

He did not open it. He did not need to. He knew what was inside. Six words that spelled two lifetimes.

"Thom-as, I cannot live without you."

All Pan Books are available at your local bookshop or newsagent, or can be ordered direct from the publisher. Indicate the number of copies required and fill in the form below.

Send to: Macmillan General Books C.S.
                Book Service By Post
                PO Box 29, Douglas I-O-M
                IM99 1BQ

or phone: 01624 675137, quoting title, author and credit card number.

or fax: 01624 670923, quoting title, author, and credit card number.

or Internet: http://www.bookpost.co.uk

Please enclose a remittance* to the value of the cover price plus 75 pence per book for post and packing. Overseas customers please allow £1.00 per copy for post and packing.

*Payment may be made in sterling by UK personal cheque, Eurocheque, postal order, sterling draft or international money order, made payable to Book Service By Post.

Alternatively by Access/Visa/MasterCard

Card No. | | | | | | | | | | | | | | | | | |

Expiry Date | | | | | | | | | | | | | | | | | |

Signature   _____

Applicable only in the UK and BFPO addresses.

While every effort is made to keep prices low, it is sometimes necessary to increase prices at short notice. Pan Books reserve the right to show on covers and charge new retail prices which may differ from those advertised in the text or elsewhere.

NAME AND ADDRESS IN BLOCK CAPITAL LETTERS PLEASE

Name _____

Address _____

_____

_____

_____

8/95

Please allow 28 days for delivery.
Please tick box if you do not wish to receive any additional information. ☐